IMAGES
of America

CASTLE SHANNON

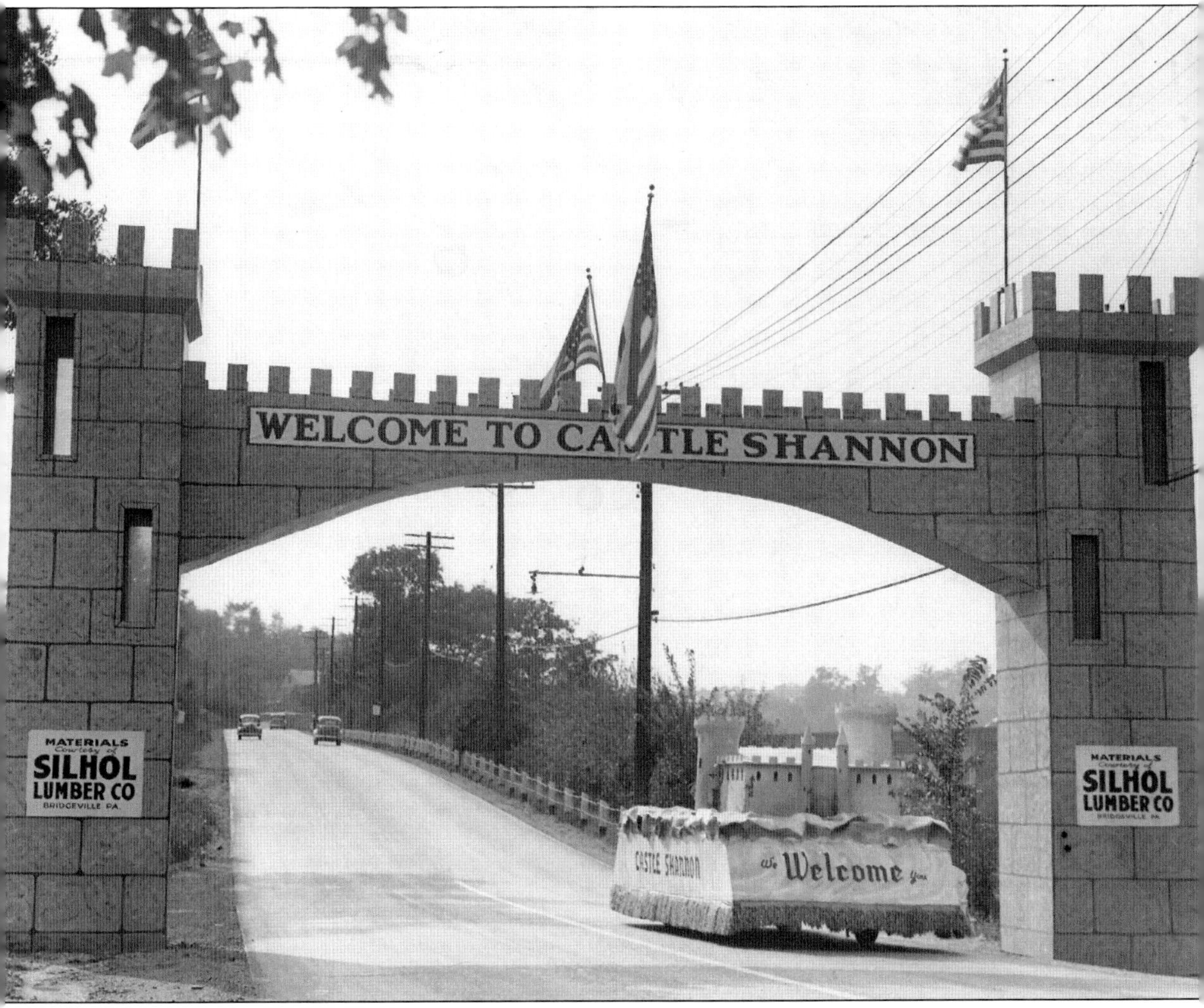

Castle Shannon did its part to help celebrate Allegheny County's sesquicentennial in 1938. From September 2 to 24, all communities in the county were asked to spruce up their neighborhoods with appropriate markings. Castle Shannon staged its celebration on September 9. The castle bridge and tower were built by Silhol Lumber, then located in Castle Shannon. The event coincided with the Allegheny County Fair held in nearby South Park. This castle gate was on Library Road near Hamilton School. (Photograph courtesy of Paul Dudjak.)

On the Cover: Castle Shannon police chief Andy Orr (third from left, dark glasses) is seen with members of his force in this photograph taken in 1960. (Photograph courtesy of Castle Shannon Borough.)

IMAGES
of America

CASTLE SHANNON

Sam Sciullo Jr. on behalf of the
Castle Shannon Revitalization Corporation

ARCADIA
PUBLISHING

ISBN 978-0-7385-9286-2

Published by Arcadia Publishing
Charleston, South Carolina

Printed in the United States of America

Library of Congress Control Number: 2012933988

For all general information, please contact Arcadia Publishing:
Telephone 843-853-2070
Fax 843-853-0044
E-mail sales@arcadiapublishing.com
For customer service and orders:
Toll-Free 1-888-313-2665

Visit us on the Internet at www.arcadiapublishing.com

Contents

Acknowledgments

Without the help and cooperation of the Castle Shannon Revitalization Corporation, plus the contributions of others who share an interest in all things Castle Shannon, this book would not have been possible. Special thanks go to borough councilman and Revitalization Corporation member Michael Warhold, who opened many doors and helped secure a number of important photographs.

Jean O'Malley, another council member and wife of the late Castle Shannon mayor Tom O'Malley, was also helpful and gracious with her time and mementos. Castle Shannon fire chief Bill Reffner opened his offices and files so that information and photographs could be discovered. Fireman Kevin Brannon, whose surname is synonymous with the Castle Shannon Volunteer Fire Department, also went out of his way to help make this project become a reality. So, too, did Cathy Jakubowski, principal of St. Anne School, and Rev. Larry Kemp, pastor of Emmanuel Evangelical Lutheran Church. Harry Munson was extremely generous with his time and effort in meeting certain publishing guidelines.

The biggest nod of gratitude must go to retired Castle Shannon letter carrier Paul Dudjak, whose interest and passion for Castle Shannon history are boundless. As Castle Shannon's unofficial historian, he provided the greatest portion of the facts and information that constitute this book. Always available and willing to talk about Castle Shannon, Paul Dudjak worked diligently and overtime to ensure that important deadlines were met.

A special note of thanks goes to photographer Charles LeClaire, whose work includes many of the more recent images of Castle Shannon. Ric Evans, son of the late Castle Shannon mayor and councilman George "Jasper" Evans, was generous in supplying many of the pertinent photographs that appear in these pages. Paul Fey, a Castle Shannon resident, produced a valuable cache of Castle Shannon sights and scenes from the early years of the community. Additional photographs were provided by Shirley M. (Limbers) Fey-Miller, Mary A. (Bach) Schenot, Sue M. (Schenot) Limbers, Carmelita S. (Limbers) Ingold-Kramer, Paul H. Fey Jr., Paige D. Miller, Camden L. Miller, Michael D. Fey, James M. Fey, Richard C. Miller, Dana R. (Ingold) Mack, and Earl F. Limbers.

INTRODUCTION

"What part of Pittsburgh are you from?" is a question many people from this area are asked if they're away from the city and talking to a stranger who happens to be from back home. "Castle Shannon," comes the response. "Oh, the Grove," the first person says. Or maybe, "Yes, the fireman's carnival. I go to it every year."

In the beginning, back in the late 1700s, people did not come to the area now known as Castle Shannon to dance, play bingo, or ride the Ferris wheel. Those earliest settlers were looking to build a way of life, and the region's fertile land meant farming and timber. The area's hilly terrain also proved to be abundant with coal, which would later lead to Castle Shannon becoming one of Western Pennsylvania's leading coal-mining centers. Eight mines were operating early in the 20th century. None remain open today, but with a significant boost from the Pittsburgh & Castle Shannon railroad line, which made it convenient for transporting people, supplies, and natural resources, the borough, which was formally established in 1919, has forged its identity.

Castle Shannon evolved from geographic parts of Mt. Lebanon, Bethel Township, and Baldwin Township. Indeed, for many years, youngsters from Castle Shannon had their pick of high schools they could attend, and it was not until 1965, when the Castle Shannon schools merged with those in Dormont and Green Tree to form the new Keystone Oaks School District, that preteen adolescents had their scholastic agendas preordained.

Other important components formed the foundation for Castle Shannon. In 1919, the borough's first government was formed. Three years later, the Castle Shannon Volunteer Fire Department, now one of Pennsylvania's most respected firefighting units, had its start. The borough even had a newspaper, *The News*, which was published from 1904 to 1908. In 1928, South Pittsburgh Water Company installed water lines and fire hydrants in Castle Shannon. By 1935, Castle Shannon even had an organization and meeting place for teachers and parents of students from the town's elementary schools—the Parents-Teachers Organization.

Another Castle Shannon staple, the Memorial Day parade, had its start in the early 1960s, and youth baseball and softball leagues for boys and girls became more prominent in that decade.

Today, there are a number of high vistas from which to view Castle Shannon. The business centers along Willow Avenue, Route 88, and Castle Shannon and Mt. Lebanon Boulevards are surrounded by hills and streets that include the many residential areas of the borough. The St. Anne Cemetery provides a stunning panorama of virtually every part of Castle Shannon. The parking lot of the new municipal center is also a fine place to see Castle Shannon in its entirety.

It started with a railroad line that attracted citizens to Castle Shannon. Schools, churches, houses, and businesses continued to grow and expand from the tracks. Welcome to Castle Shannon.

One

Early Years

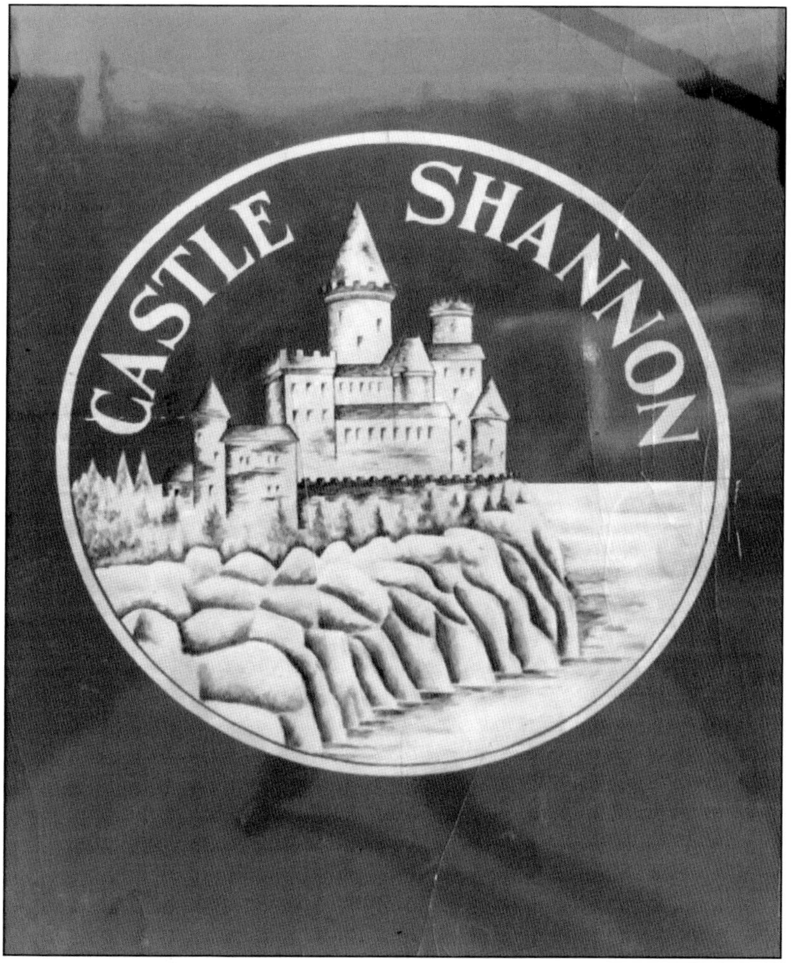

The emblem of Castle Shannon has undergone a number of slight variations throughout the borough's history, but the castle perched atop the bluff has been a mainstay of the image. Original families arrived in the territory in 1786 looking for timber and fertile farmland. One large farm was owned by David Strawbridge, who called his property Castle Shanahan. It eventually evolved into its common name, Castle Shannon. This logo appears on Castle Shannon's fire trucks. (Photograph courtesy of Castle Shannon Volunteer Fire Department.)

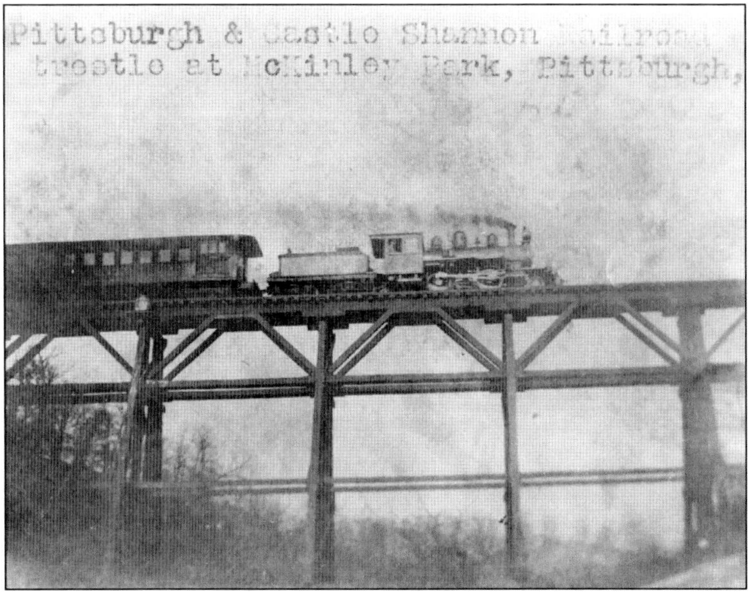

A Pittsburgh & Castle Shannon Railroad engine tender and passenger car are shown. The bridge, then known as the High Trestle, is the current Bausman Street heading up to McKinley Park. Train conductors would stop on the bridge to collect fares so passengers would be unable to make a quick exit without paying their fares. (Photograph courtesy of Castle Shannon Volunteer Fire Department.)

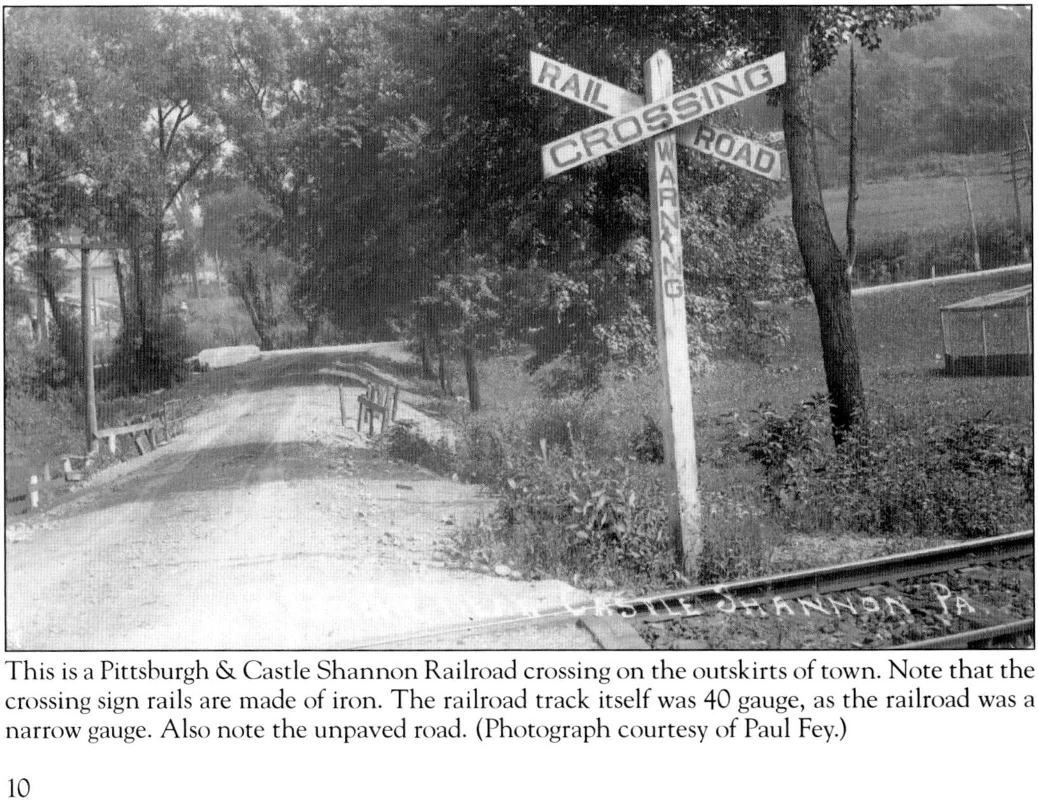

This is a Pittsburgh & Castle Shannon Railroad crossing on the outskirts of town. Note that the crossing sign rails are made of iron. The railroad track itself was 40 gauge, as the railroad was a narrow gauge. Also note the unpaved road. (Photograph courtesy of Paul Fey.)

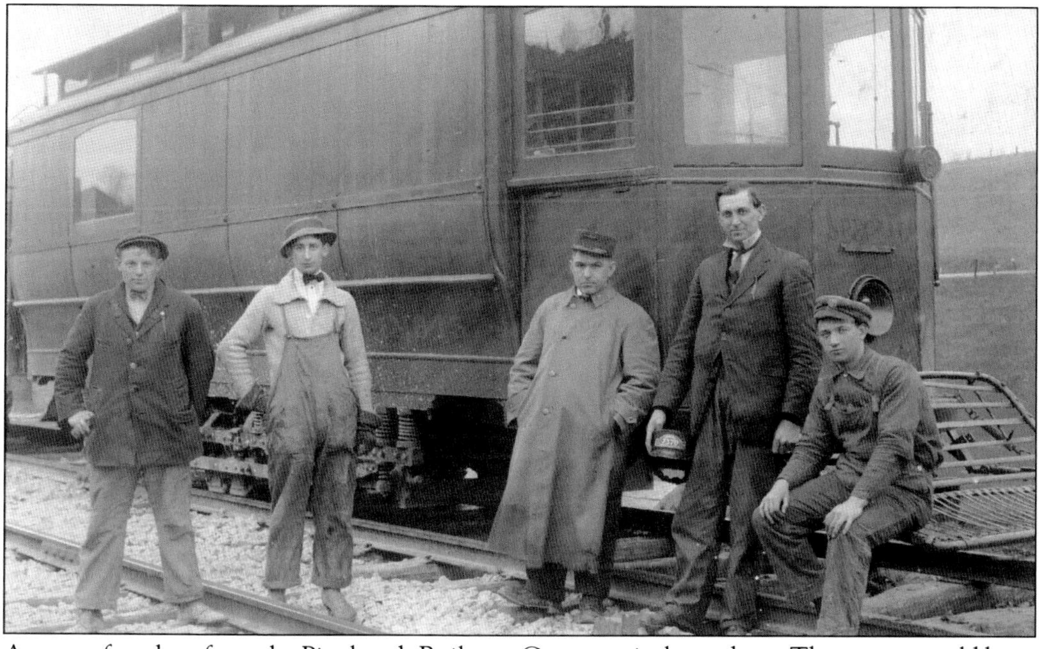

A team of workers from the Pittsburgh Railways Company is shown here. These men would have done work on the trolley tracks. The Pittsburgh Railroad instituted the trolley line for which Castle Shannon became noted. This line ran from the city of Pittsburgh south to Washington and Charleroi, Pennsylvania. (Photograph courtesy of Paul Fey.)

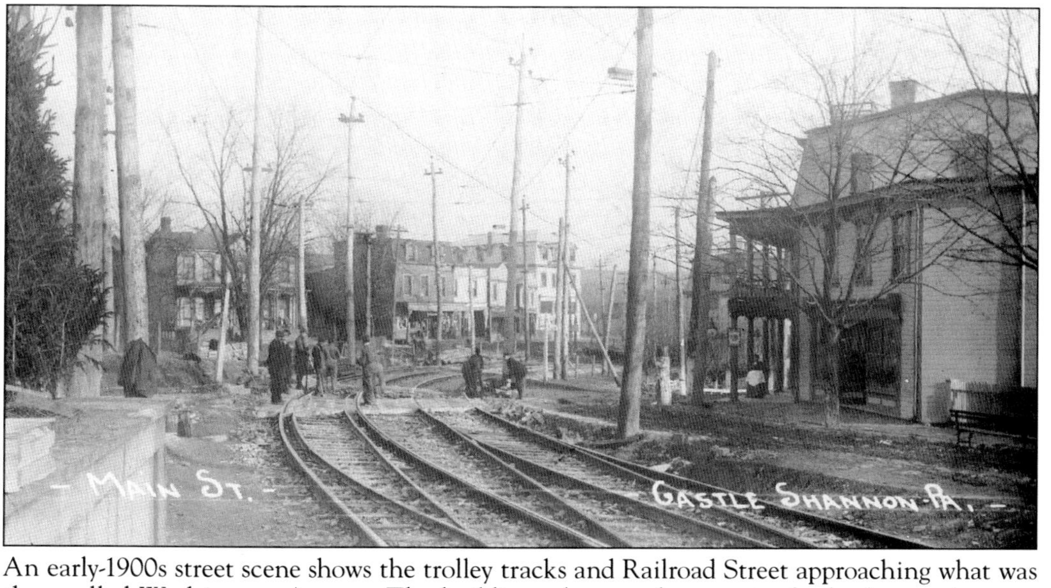

An early-1900s street scene shows the trolley tracks and Railroad Street approaching what was then called Washington Avenue. The buildings that can be seen in the background are on Willow Avenue between Park Way, which later became Park Avenue, and Poplar Avenue, still prominent in Castle Shannon more than a century later. The structure to the extreme right is a store. The Castle Shannon Hotel, prominent for its pillars and balcony, is adjacent to the store. (Photograph courtesy of Paul Fey.)

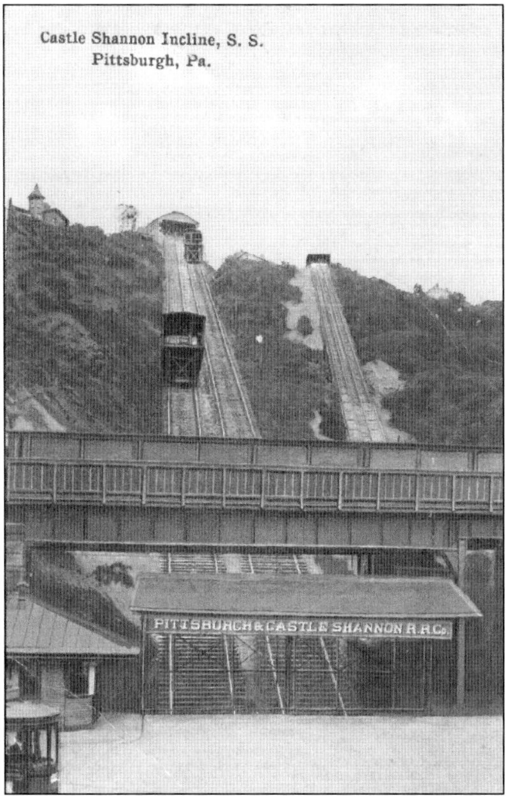

This is a front-side view on the North Slope of the Castle Shannon Incline. The incline ran from East Carson Street near Arlington Avenue on Pittsburgh's South Side, to Bailey Avenue on Mount Washington. The incline was designed by engineer Samuel Diescher and was built in 1890. Eventually demolished in 1964, it had exceptionally large cars and carried not only people, but horses and buggies as well. (Photograph courtesy of Paul Fey.)

The Pittsburgh Terminal Railroad and Coal Company opened the Castle Shannon Mine in 1902. Pictured here are some of the men who worked inside that mine. The mine enabled Castle Shannon to become a hub for coal mining in Western Pennsylvania. A total of eight mines were operative in 1904. This one was located behind the present-day site of a Burger King restaurant on Route 88, behind the trolley tracks. (Photograph courtesy of Ric Evans.)

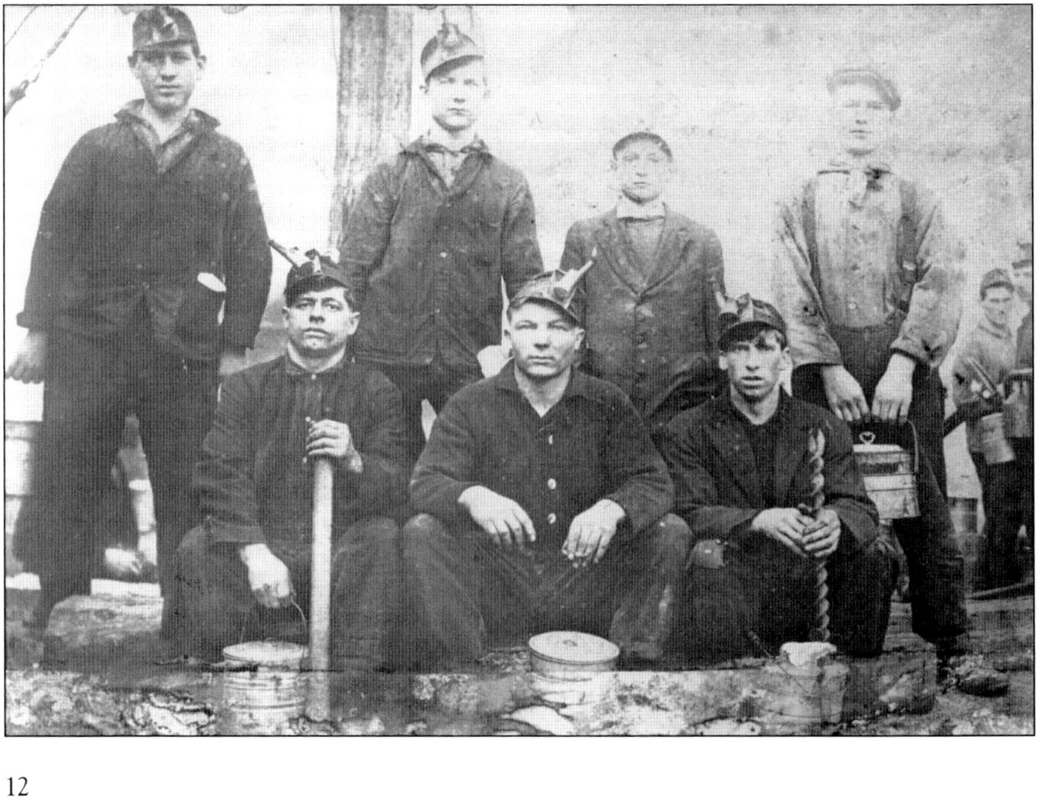

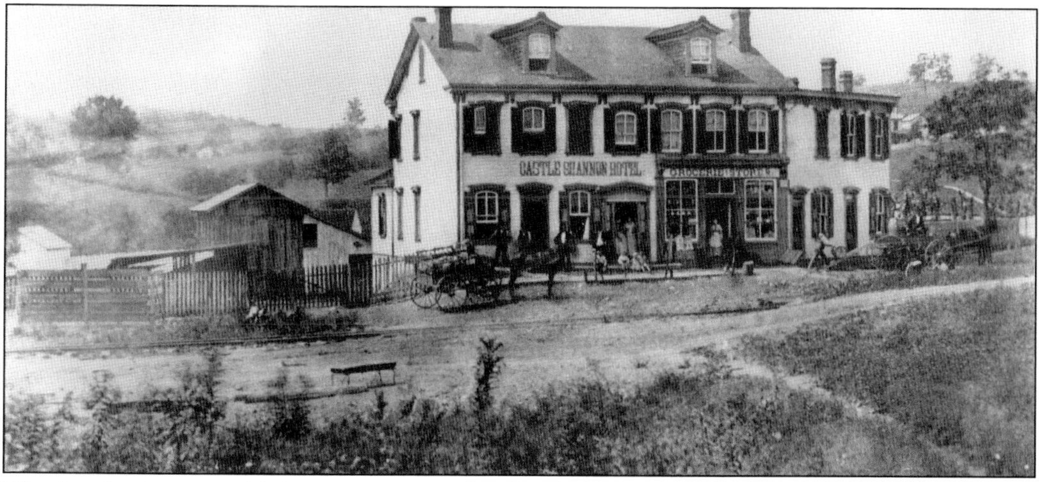

The first business establishment in town, the Castle Shannon Hotel, was built in 1874 by Phil Goeddel, who was a postmaster in the late 1800s. Its most prominent owner and manager was Mary Ann Schenot, who operated the facility from 1903 until the 1930s. Schenot also was a prime benefactor of the Castle Shannon Volunteer Fire Department, and proceeds from the hotel helped the fire department get its start in Castle Shannon. (Photograph courtesy of Ric Evans.)

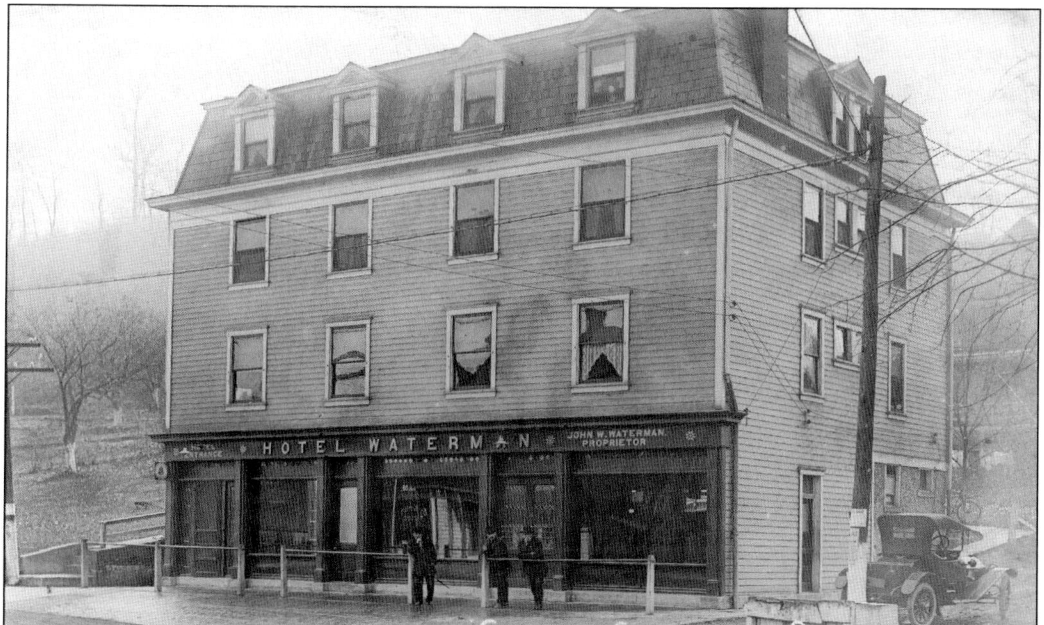

Situated at the intersection of Washington Avenue and Library Road, the Hotel Waterman was a popular spot for farmers and travelers going between Pittsburgh and Washington County. Proprietor John W. Waterman (1872–1935) opened the four-story frame hotel in 1907 on a plot of the old McCully farm. The bar, restaurant, and kitchen were located on the first floor, while the 16 rooms to rent were on the upper levels. The front of the hotel had a hitching post and watering trough for horses. Waterman died from injuries suffered in a fall in 1935. His wife, Anna, ran the hotel before selling it in 1945. (Photograph courtesy of Paul Fey.)

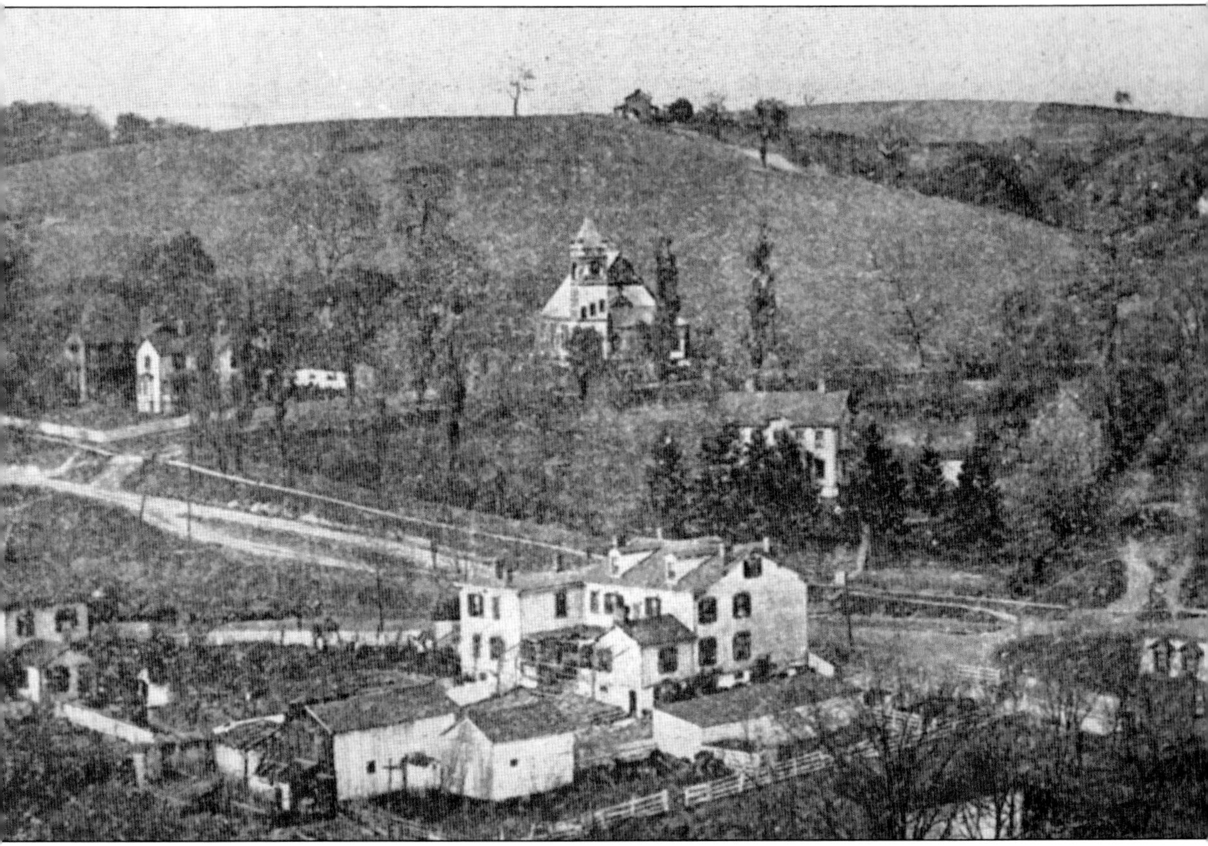

This panoramic photograph was taken around 1900, before trains and trolleys entered the town, and before Castle Shannon had become Castle Shannon. Note the concentration of buildings in the lower right; it is now part of Willow Avenue and constitutes what was the first commercial section of the community. The street going up and off the page to the right eventually became Poplar Street. The familiar bank building, scene of the 1917 robbery, had not been built. The

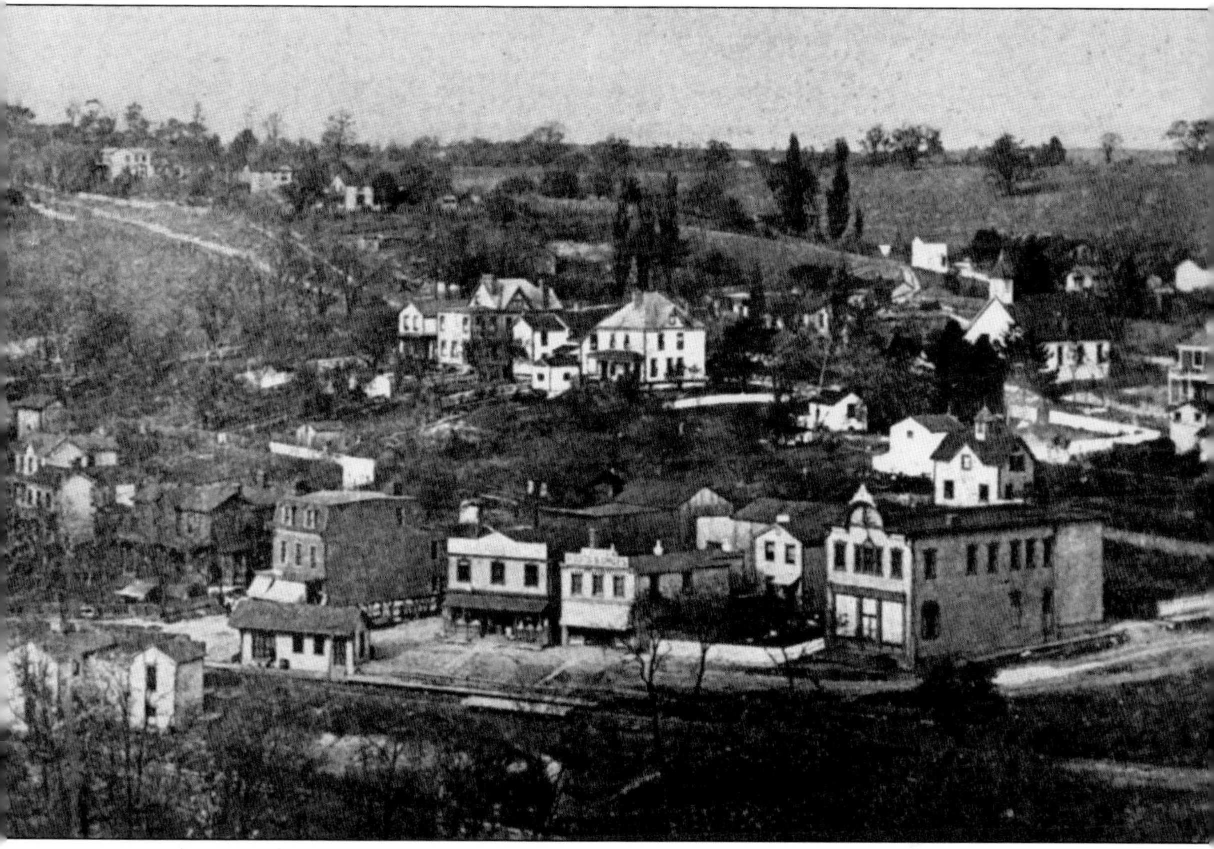

structure that was the Castle Shannon Hotel can be seen dominating the area in the lower left portion of the photograph. A white fence surrounds the property. The first cluster of houses was built in the area near the Lutheran church and where Myrtle School and Castle Shannon Community Library were later erected. (Photograph courtesy of Bob Barson.)

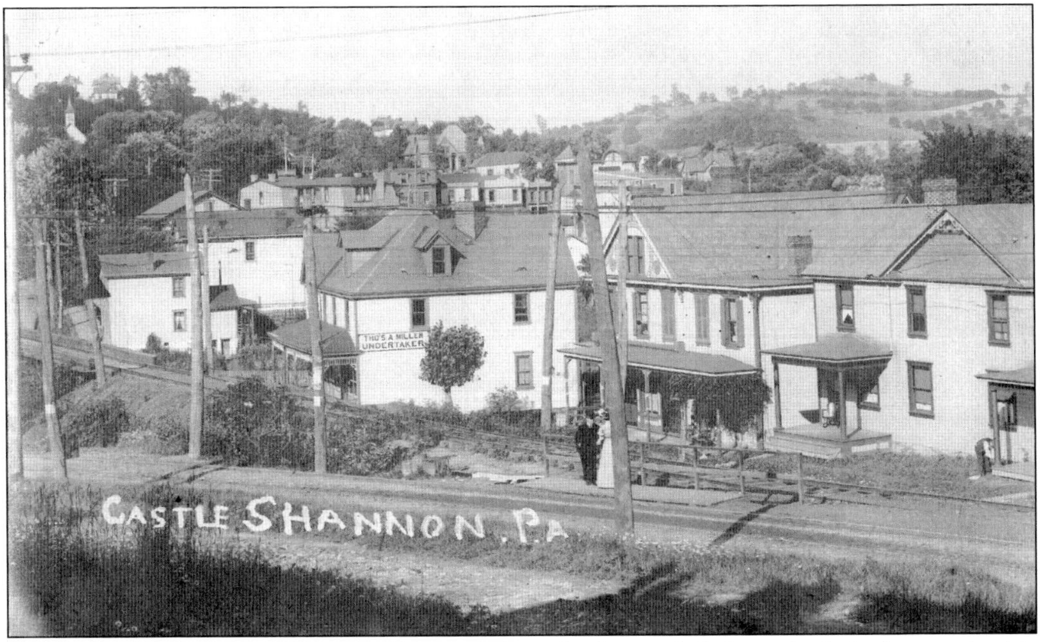

Thomas A. Miller, undertaker, plied his craft from the house slightly to the left of center in this photograph from Railroad Street. The tracks heading to the right are of the Pittsburgh Railways Company. The tracks in the opposite direction continue through Mt. Lebanon, Dormont, and Beechview. These rails are on the old right-of-way of the Pittsburgh Southern Railroad. (Photograph courtesy of Paul Fey.)

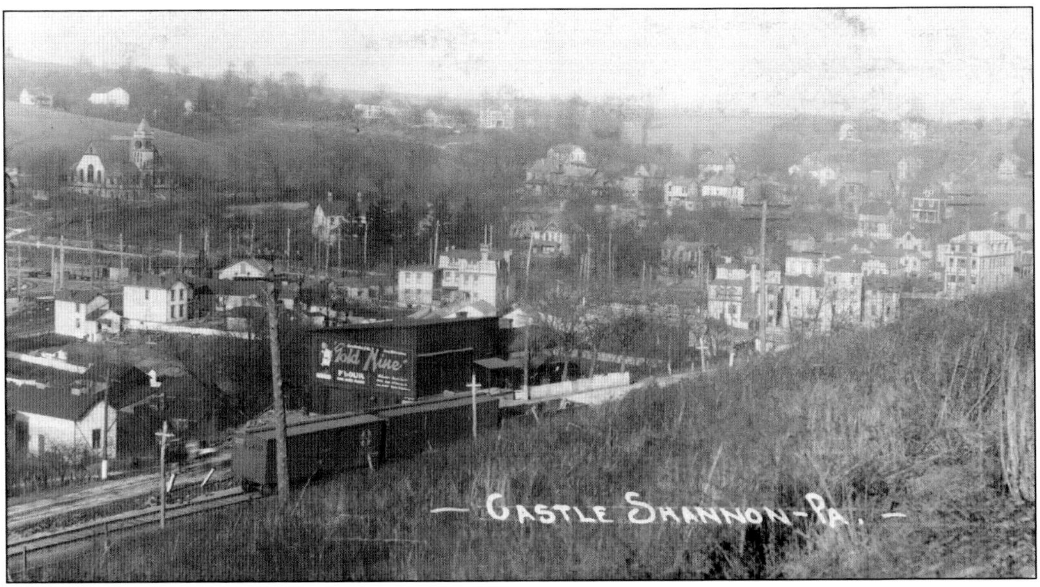

This panorama taken from the Thompson Terrace, looking northeast, shows Library Road and Washington Avenue in the heart of Castle Shannon. Boxcars of the West Side Belt Railroad can be seen in the foreground, as can the "Gold Mine" inscription painted on the side of the structure alongside the railroad tracks. This view of Castle Shannon dates from between 1913 and 1915. (Photograph courtesy of Paul Fey.)

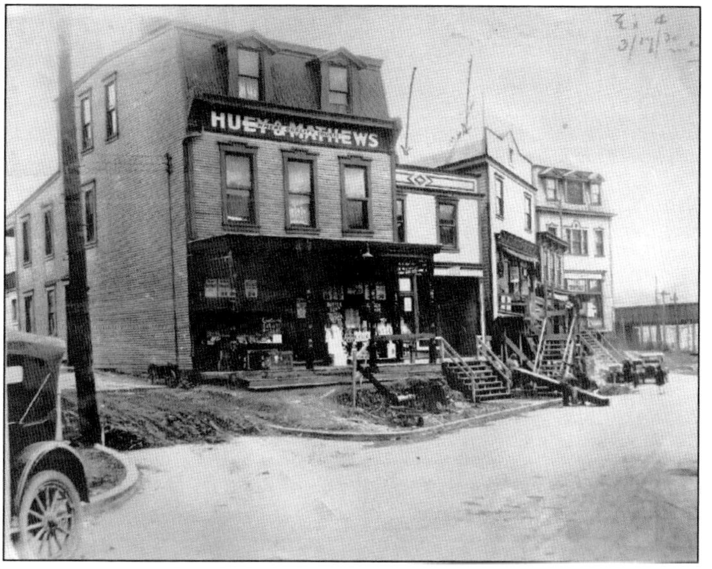

During the late 1920s and early 1930s, Willow and Poplar Avenues were lowered. On this block of Willow Avenue, the second floors of the buildings were originally first floors. The new additions became the first floors. Huey and Matthews grocery store was originally Beltzhoovers's General Store. The site is now a vacant lot. The middle building is an A&P store, while the Odd Fellows Hall is the structure to the extreme right. (Photograph courtesy of Paul Fey.)

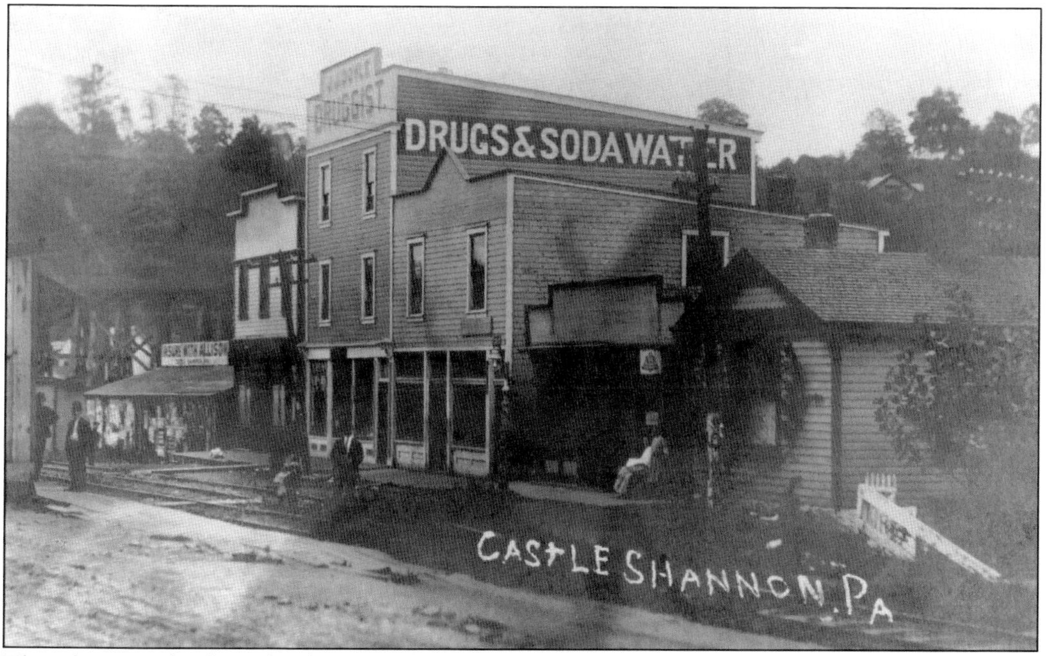

This photograph of Castle Shannon's business district displays the Deer, Baumgarten, Doyle, and Klein Buildings. The area was between Washington Avenue and the Pittsburgh & Castle Shannon Railroad tracks. Peter Deer was a conductor on the Pittsburgh & Castle Shannon Railroad. Joseph Jessee Doyle owned a drugstore, and Charles Baumgarten owned a barbershop. Mrs. Peter Klein rented her building to A. Lewis Clothing Store and Allison Insurance. (Photograph courtesy of Paul Dudjak.)

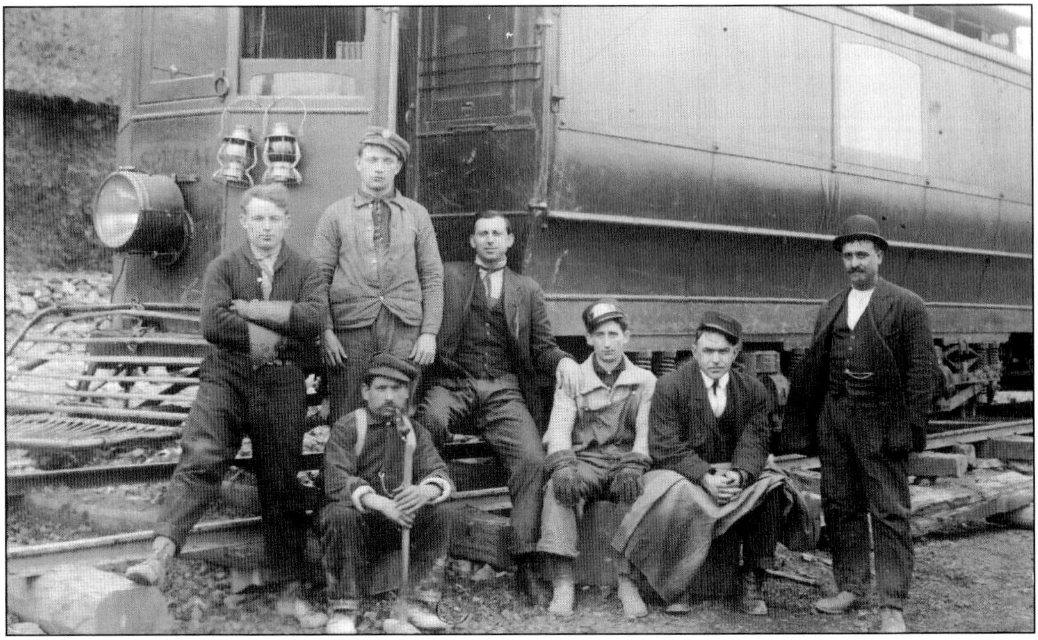

This photograph shows another group of workers from the Pittsburgh Railways Company. Note the various clothing styles. The railroad line did much to spur the growth of Castle Shannon. For two years, free transportation and lumber movement were provided to anyone who was building a home in the new settlement. Coal was moved along these lines 24 hours a day in the early 1900s. (Photograph courtesy of Paul Fey.)

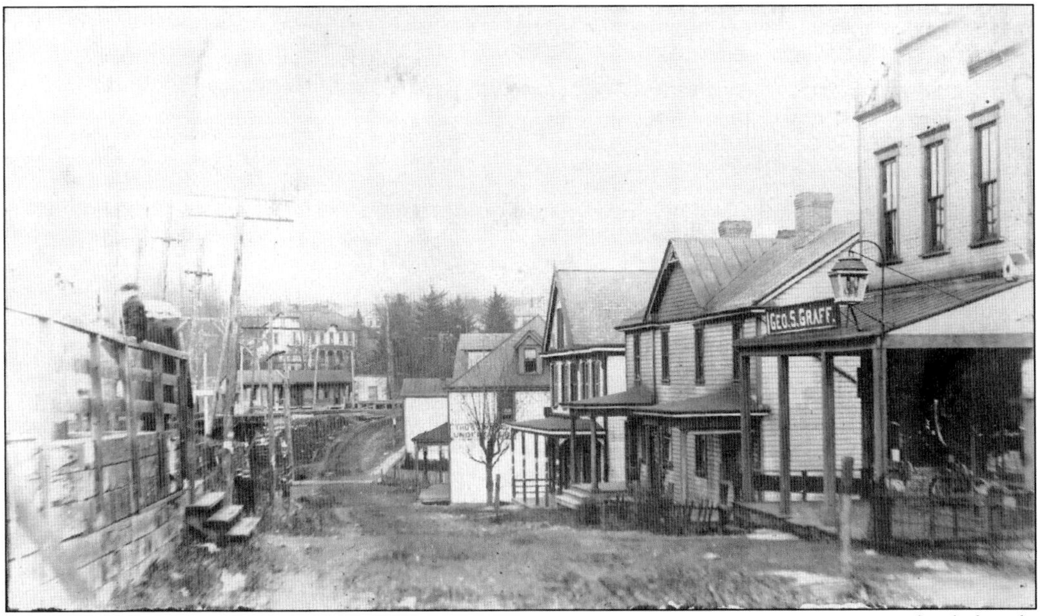

This photograph shows Railroad Street looking toward Washington Avenue. On the left side of the dirt road, a wooden wall was constructed to support the roadbed of the trolley tracks. George S. Graff (1862–1912), who settled in Castle Shannon in 1883, owned the two-story frame commercial building. He dealt in gas and coal stoves, hot-air furnaces, tin, and general hardware. He also did roof repairing and painting. (Photograph courtesy of Paul Fey.)

From 1913 to 1917, members of the Castle Shannon Golf Club competed against a team from the Mt. Lebanon Country Club for this cup, the South Hills Trophy. The competition was held over two days, with nine holes played on the Castle Shannon links, and the other nine at Mt. Lebanon Country Club, off Bower Hill Road. The Nassau scoring system was used. Castle Shannon won the cup in 1913, 1914, and 1915. Both clubs disbanded, in sorts, in 1917, and helped start what is now St. Clair Country Club. (Photograph by Maria Sciullo.)

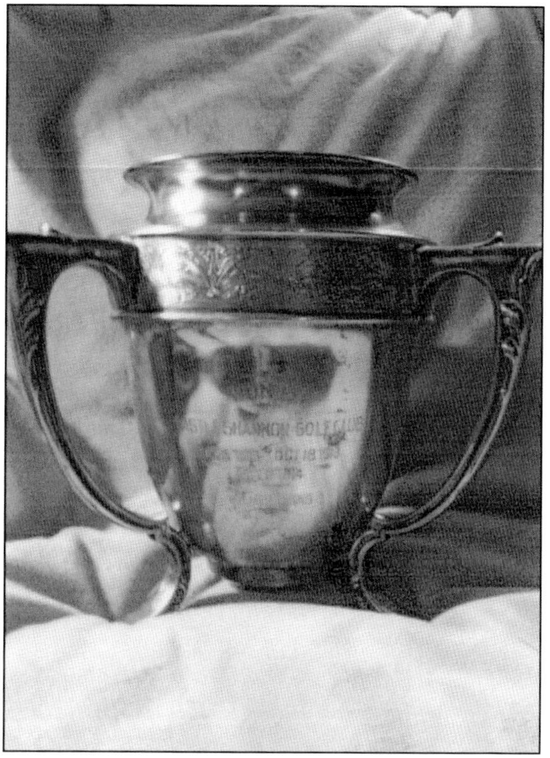

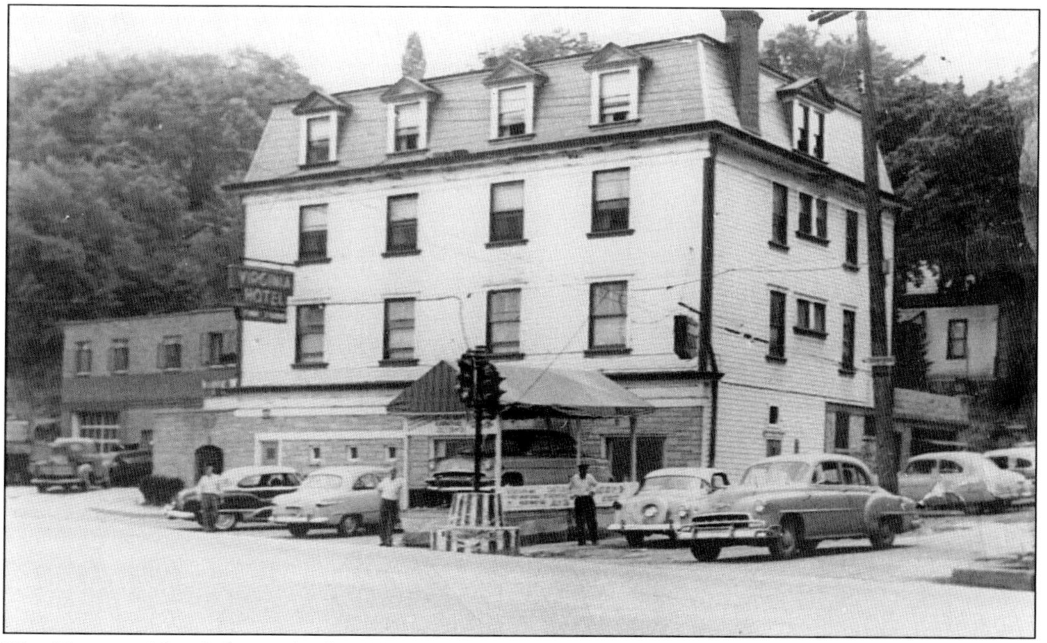

The Virginia Hotel, formerly the Waterman Hotel, was located at the corner of Library Road and Castle Shannon Boulevard. Virginia Manaigo bought the hotel from Anna Waterman in 1945. The establishment became a popular drinking spot for locals. The hotel closed in 1965 and was eventually torn down. Dugan's Gas Station was later built on the site. (Photograph courtesy of George "Jasper" Evans and Ric Evans.)

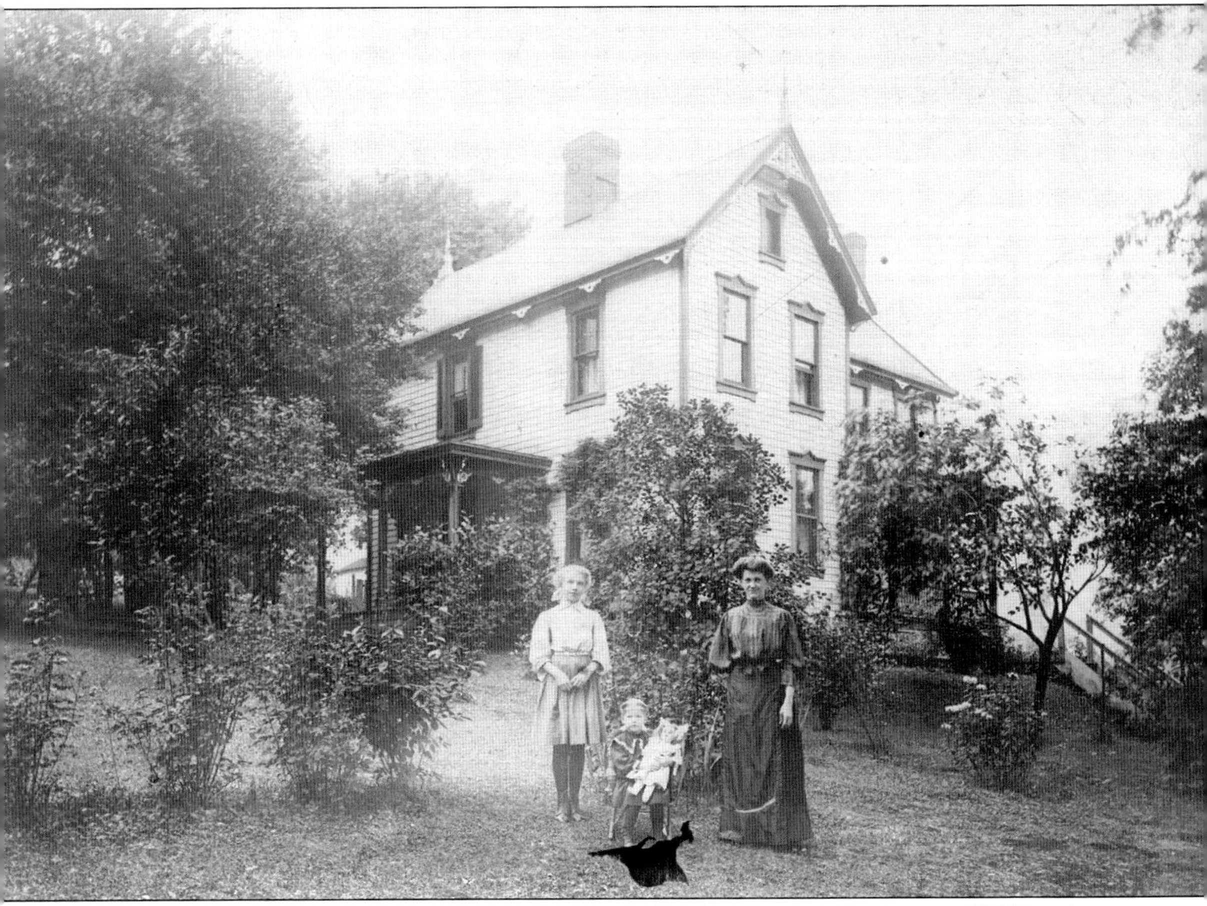

This 1880 photograph shows a family newly installed in their home at the corner of Willow Avenue and Bockstoce Street. This was one of the first houses built in the area of Castle Shannon due south of what later became the location of Castle Shannon Borough Building and baseball field. Note the dress of the woman at far right. The little girl is holding a doll. (Photograph courtesy of Castle Shannon Borough.)

Two

In the Community

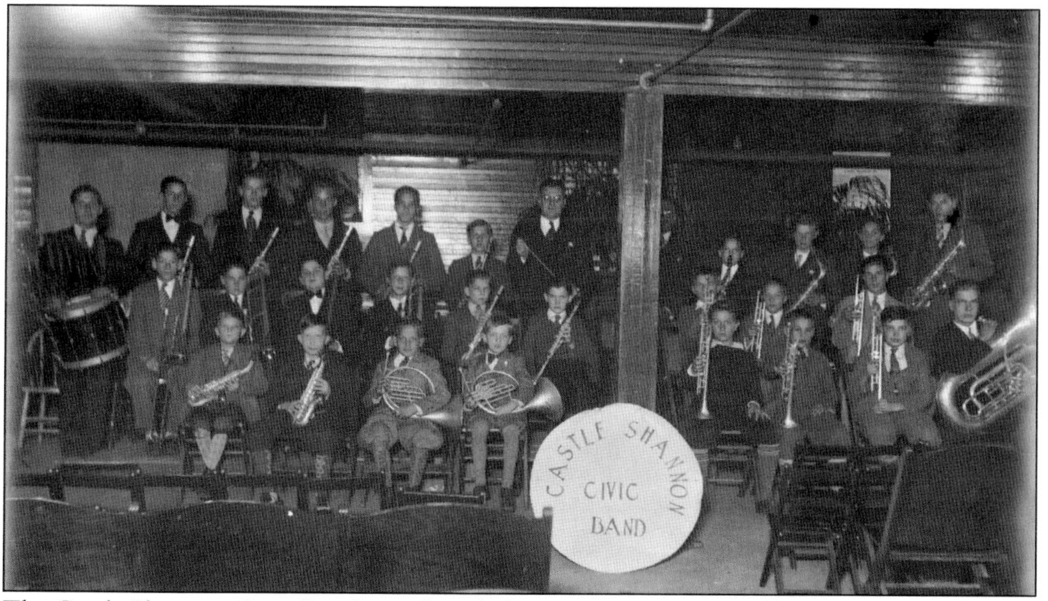

The Castle Shannon Civic Band, now largely forgotten, was an ensemble composed of residents of all ages that played at community events during the 1930s and 1940s. This was a concert band. It was not until Leo Yagello organized his Castle Shannon Junior High band that the borough had a marching band to represent it in city parades such as on Memorial Day and St. Patrick's Day. (Photograph by George "Jasper" Evans, courtesy of Ric Evans.)

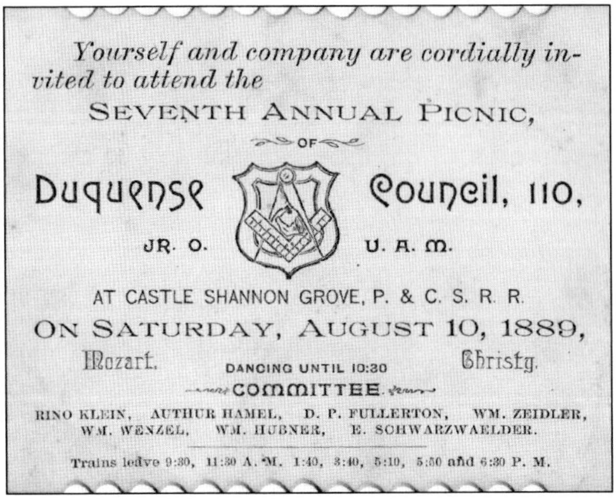

Yourself and company are cordially invited to attend the

SEVENTH ANNUAL PICNIC,

OF

Duquense Council, 110,

JR. O. U. A. M.

AT CASTLE SHANNON GROVE, P. & C. S. R. R.

ON SATURDAY, AUGUST 10, 1889,

Mozart. DANCING UNTIL 10:30 Christy.

COMMITTEE.

RINO KLEIN, AUTHUR HAMEL, D. P. FULLERTON, WM. ZEIDLER, WM. WENZEL, WM. HUBNER, E. SCHWARZWAELDER.

Trains leave 9:30, 11:30 A. M. 1:40, 3:40, 5:10, 5:50 and 6:30 P. M.

The presence of the Pittsburgh & Castle Shannon Railroad would often attract picnics and groups to Linden Grove. Shown here is an invitation from the Duquesne, Pennsylvania, Council for an event staged August 10, 1889. The Grove was popular for many people around the Pittsburgh area due to its relatively close location and easy access, first by rail and later by trolley cars. Riders on streetcars headed to Castle Shannon might find themselves seated alongside well-dressed patrons en route to the Grove for an evening of dancing. (Photograph courtesy of Paul Fey.)

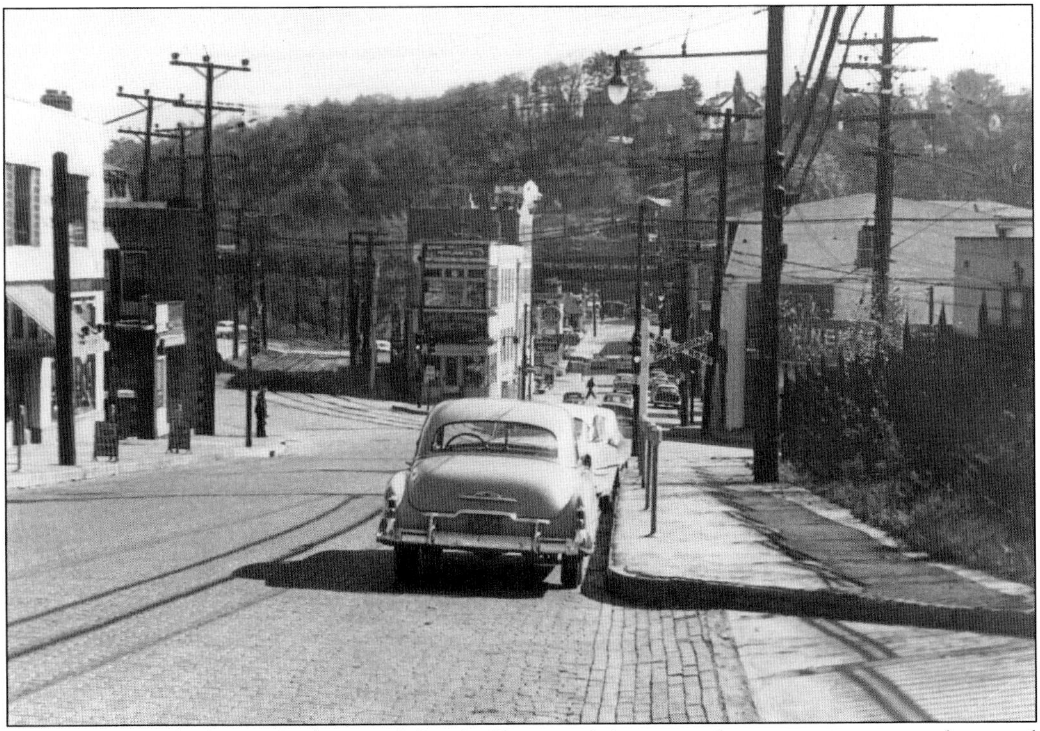

This photograph shows the heart of Castle Shannon's business district as it appeared around 1960. This is the view down Castle Shannon Boulevard toward the intersection with Route 88, another primary hub for Castle Shannon businesses. At the extreme left is Vitte's Hardware Store, and in the center is the old Castle Shannon Electric. In subsequent years, businesses in building have sold everything from movie posters to different types of memorabilia, and it has housed a beauty salon. Notice the old-style car and the familiar brick road of Castle Shannon Boulevard. (Photograph courtesy of Paul Dudjak.)

The Castle Shannon Volunteer Fire Department has traditionally observed the start of the holiday season by putting up a Christmas tree in a prominent part of town, where it is easily visible to motorists and pedestrians. A customary spot for the tree has been the intersection of Mt. Lebanon and Castle Shannon Boulevards, just before the Port Authority of Allegheny County mass transit parking lot and trolley stop. (Photograph by George "Jasper" Evans, courtesy of Ric Evans.)

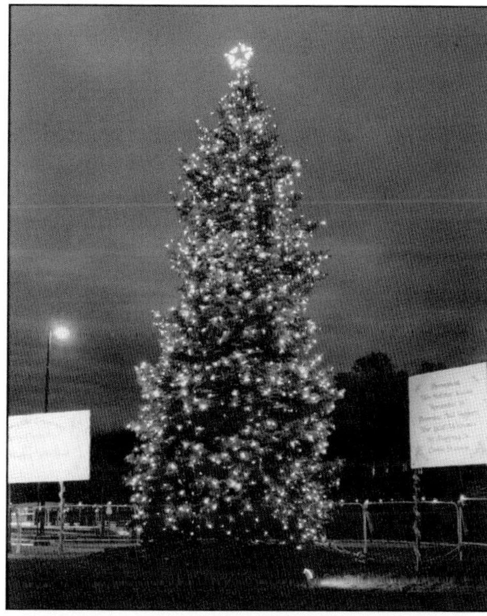

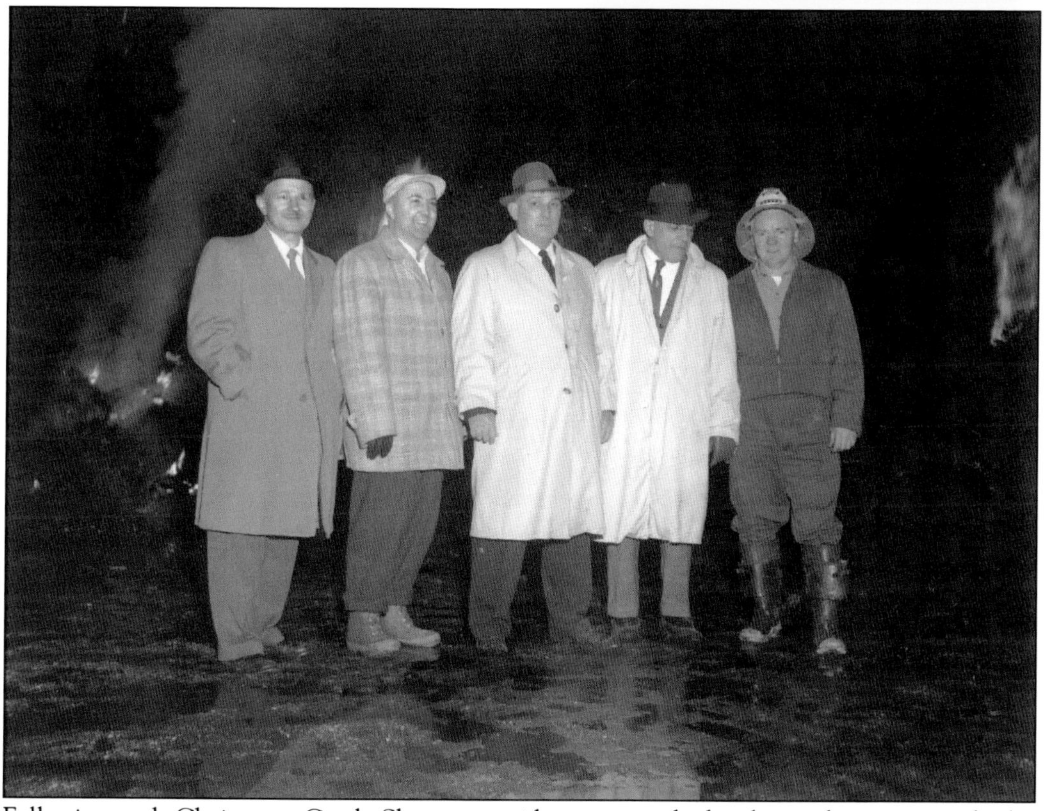

Following each Christmas, Castle Shannon residents were asked to bring their trees to the lot adjacent to Hamilton School for a community tree burning. Presiding at the 1958 event are, from left to right, Castle Shannon Junior High School band director Leo Yagello, Rotary Club member and attorney Sam Sciullo, Mayor Ed Obringer, Councilman Carl Rizzo, and fireman Alex Brown. (Photograph by George "Jasper" Evans, courtesy of Ric Evans.)

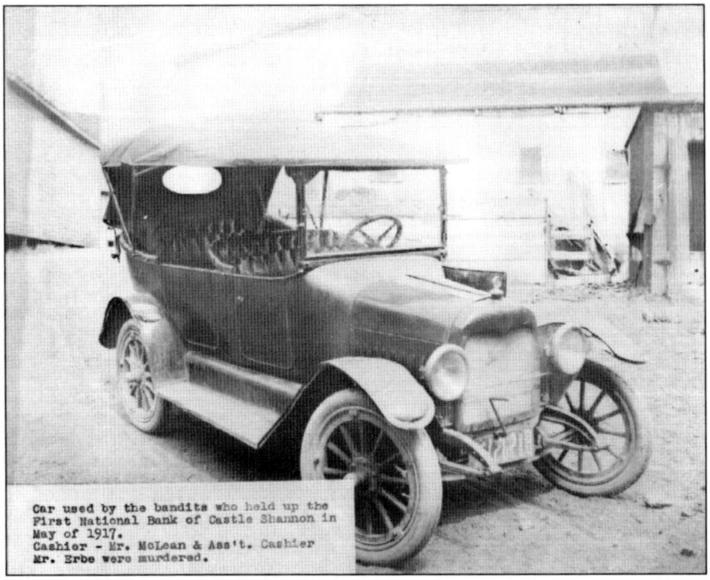

This is the car used by perpetrators of the May 14, 1917, robbery of the First National Bank in Castle Shannon. More than $18,000 was taken in the crime. Approximately $10,500 was immediately recovered from one of the bandits, who was shot during the attempted escape. The balance of the money was never recovered or discovered. (Photograph courtesy of Ric Evans.)

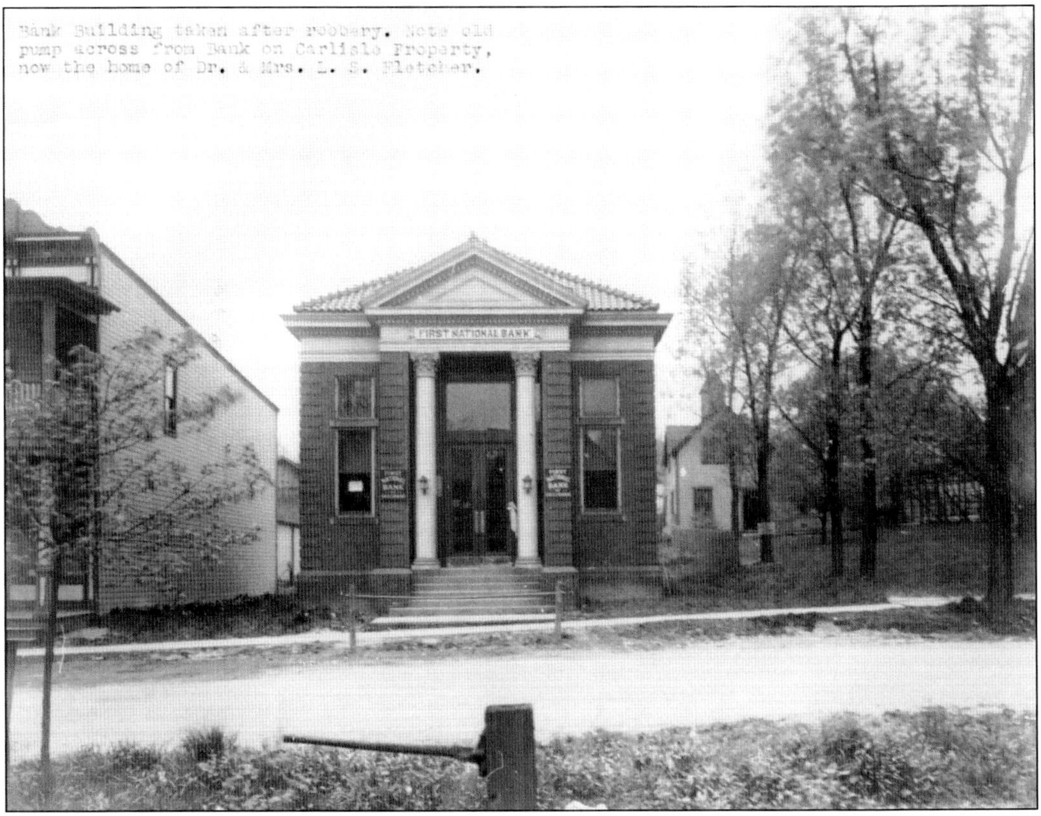

Built in 1904 as the Castle Shannon Savings and Trust Company, this building was incorporated into the First National Bank from 1909 until 1956, when it became Fidelity Trust for three years. Contemporary Castle Shannon residents remember the edifice, in its final years as a bank, as Pittsburgh National Bank. In its early years, the bank had a hitching post for horses out front. (Photograph by George "Jasper" Evans, courtesy of Ric Evans.)

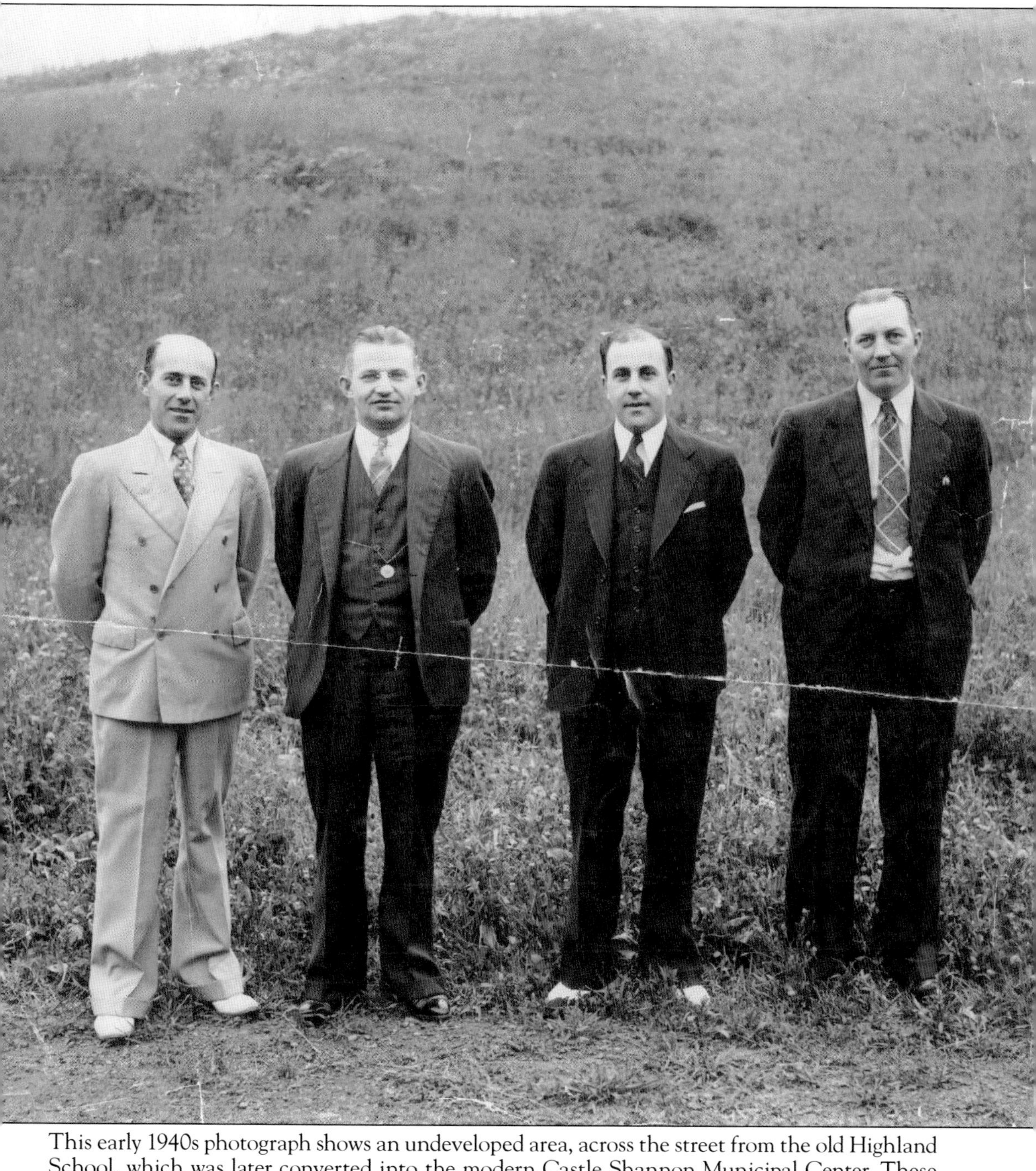

This early 1940s photograph shows an undeveloped area, across the street from the old Highland School, which was later converted into the modern Castle Shannon Municipal Center. These four men constituted the Castle Shannon Volunteer Fire Department's carnival committee during parts of the 1930s and 1940s. They are, from left to right, Frank Rizzo, Charles Brannon, Tony Rizzo, and an unidentified man. The Rizzos were brothers. Brannon was an early member of the fire department who began a family tradition: a total of nine Brannons would join the department over the years. (Photograph courtesy of Castle Shannon Volunteer Fire Department.)

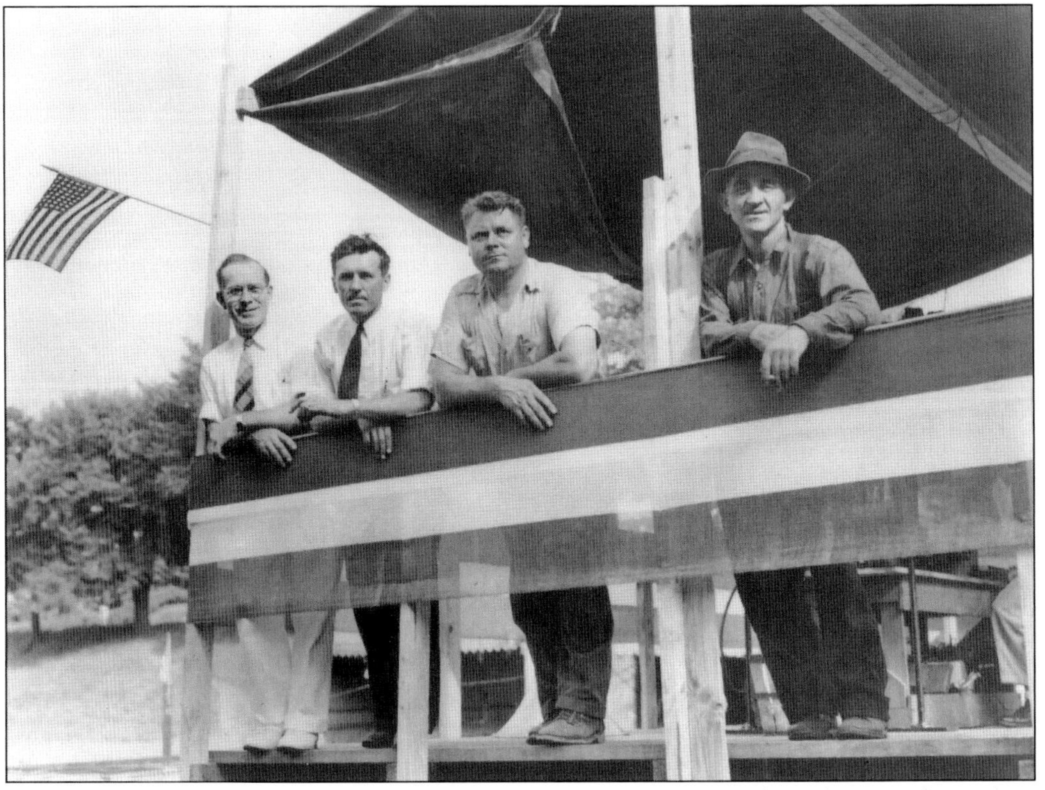

From left to right, Frank Karkalla, George Hamrock, Steve Bittner, and Frank Lang admire their handiwork, having built the speaker stand for the annual Castle Shannon Firemen's Carnival. This photograph was taken in 1932, when the carnival was held at a field near Grove Road where soccer games also were played. Some carnivals were staged underneath the railroad trestle on Castle Shannon Boulevard near the area that later became a gas station and, after that, Family Video Store. (Photograph courtesy of Paul Dudjak.)

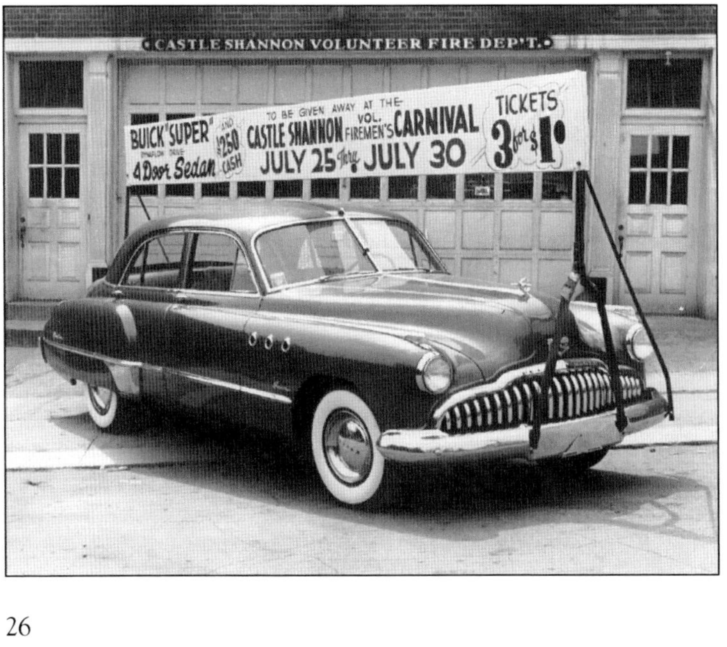

Each year, the Castle Shannon Volunteer Fire Department raffles off at least one car on the final night of the event. In some years, there were as many as three cars. More recently, only one car has been offered. This Buick Super sits proudly in front of the old firehouse on Park Avenue. (Photograph courtesy of Castle Shannon Volunteer Fire Department.)

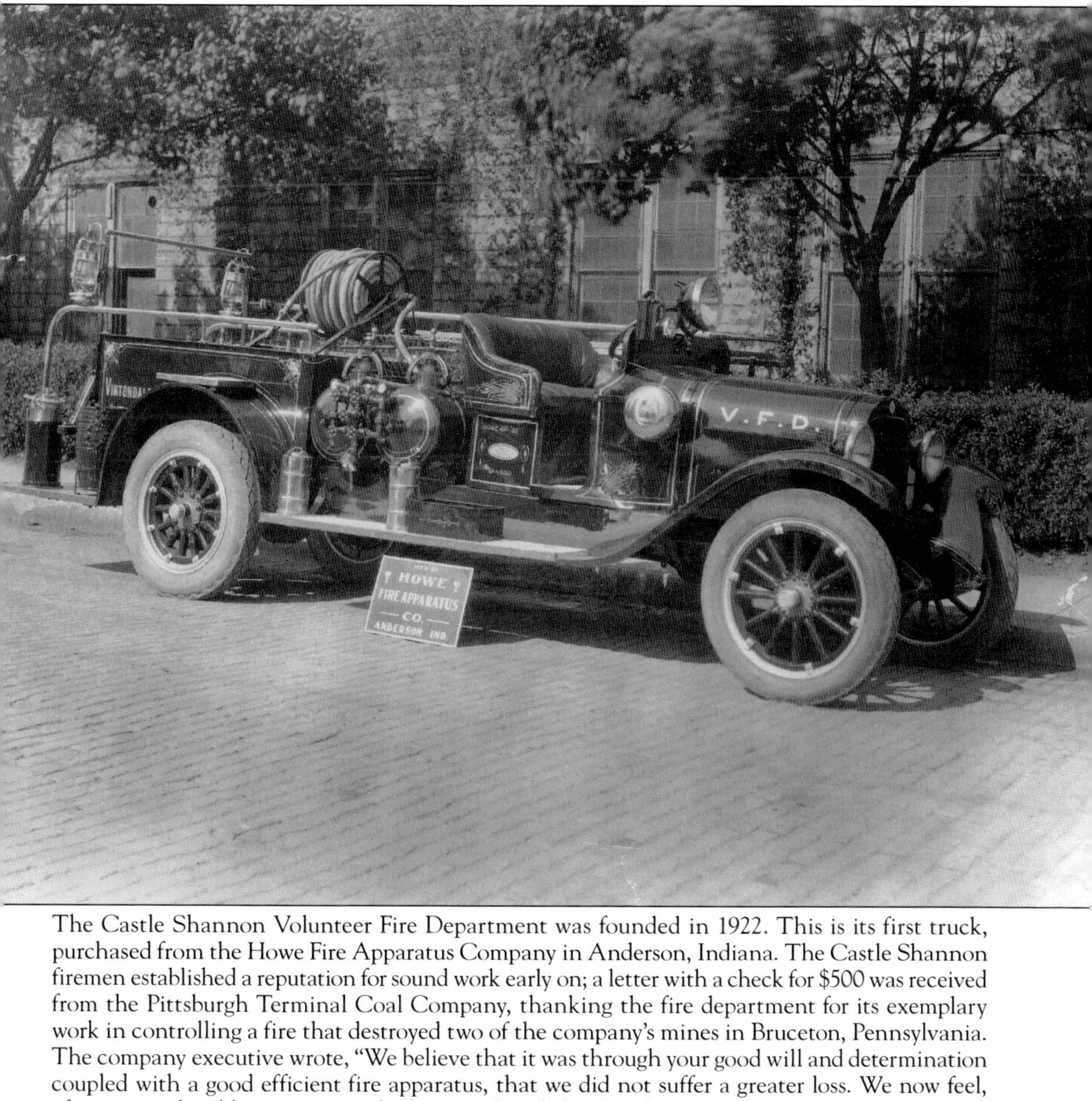

The Castle Shannon Volunteer Fire Department was founded in 1922. This is its first truck, purchased from the Howe Fire Apparatus Company in Anderson, Indiana. The Castle Shannon firemen established a reputation for sound work early on; a letter with a check for $500 was received from the Pittsburgh Terminal Coal Company, thanking the fire department for its exemplary work in controlling a fire that destroyed two of the company's mines in Bruceton, Pennsylvania. The company executive wrote, "We believe that it was through your good will and determination coupled with a good efficient fire apparatus, that we did not suffer a greater loss. We now feel, after seeing the able manner in which you reduced this fire that your training and apparatus are a worthy benefit to the community, and we hereby donate to the Volunteer Fire Department of Castle Shannon, Five Hundred Dollars ($500), to be used in defraying the expenses in organizing your fire department." (Photograph courtesy of Paul Fey.)

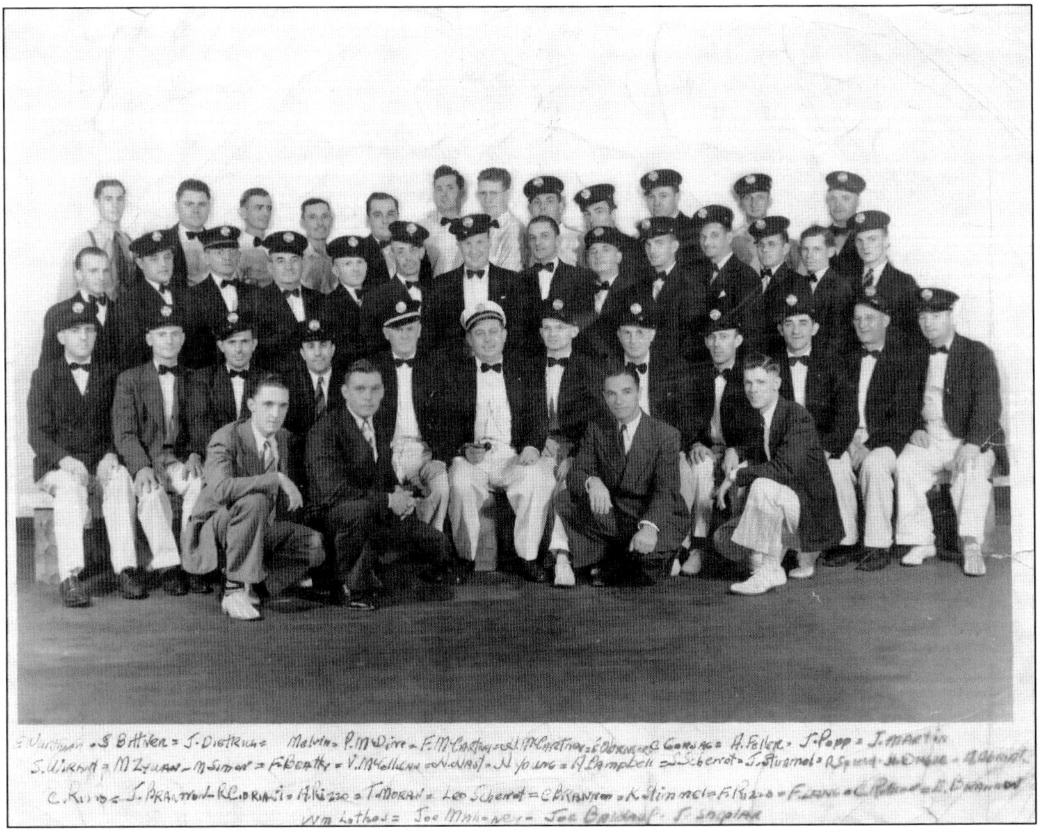

No, this is not a photograph from the milkman's convention. This is the Castle Shannon Volunteer Fire Department, nattily attired in this 1940s-era image. In the fourth row, sixth and seventh from the left, are brothers Frank and Hugh McCartney. Until the end of his life, Frank would set up shop outside Castle Shannon grocery stores, selling carnival raffle tickets. (Photograph courtesy of Castle Shannon Volunteer Fire Department.)

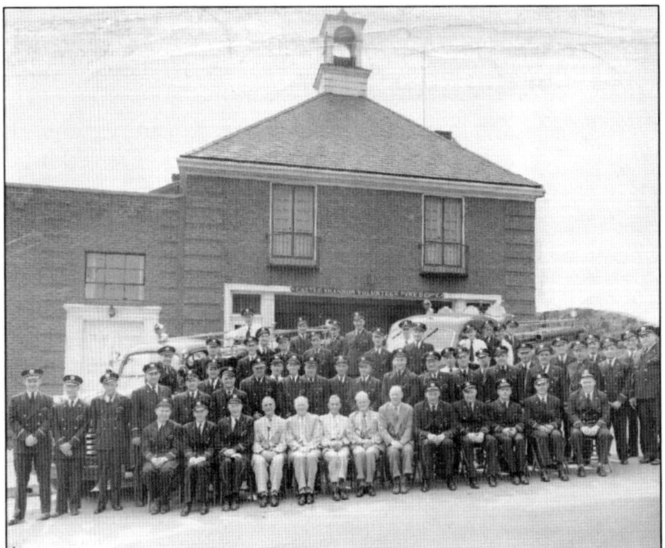

The Castle Shannon Volunteer Fire Department poses for this photograph in 1949 outside the firehouse on Park Avenue. The men not in uniform are political and community leaders who were asked to pose for the picture. In the first row, fourth from left, is Jim Campbell, longtime tax collector for the borough. The fireman third from left (next to Campbell) is Red Young, who also served Castle Shannon as a policeman. Campbell's son, Jim, was later Castle Shannon's chief of police. (Photograph courtesy of the Castle Shannon Fire Department.)

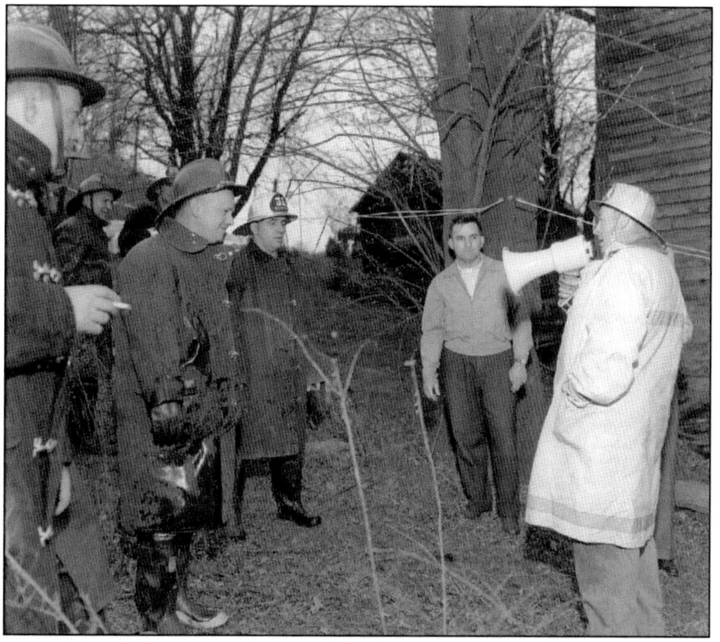

Castle Shannon Volunteer Fire Department chief Al Feller addresses his unit during an exercise in the borough. Feller, who died in 1981 at the age of 79, was the town's fire chief for 22 years. The fireman directly in front of and facing Feller is Alex Brown, who was Feller's successor as fire chief. Note the fireman at the extreme left with a cigarette in his hand. (Photograph by George "Jasper" Evans, courtesy of Castle Shannon Volunteer Fire Department.)

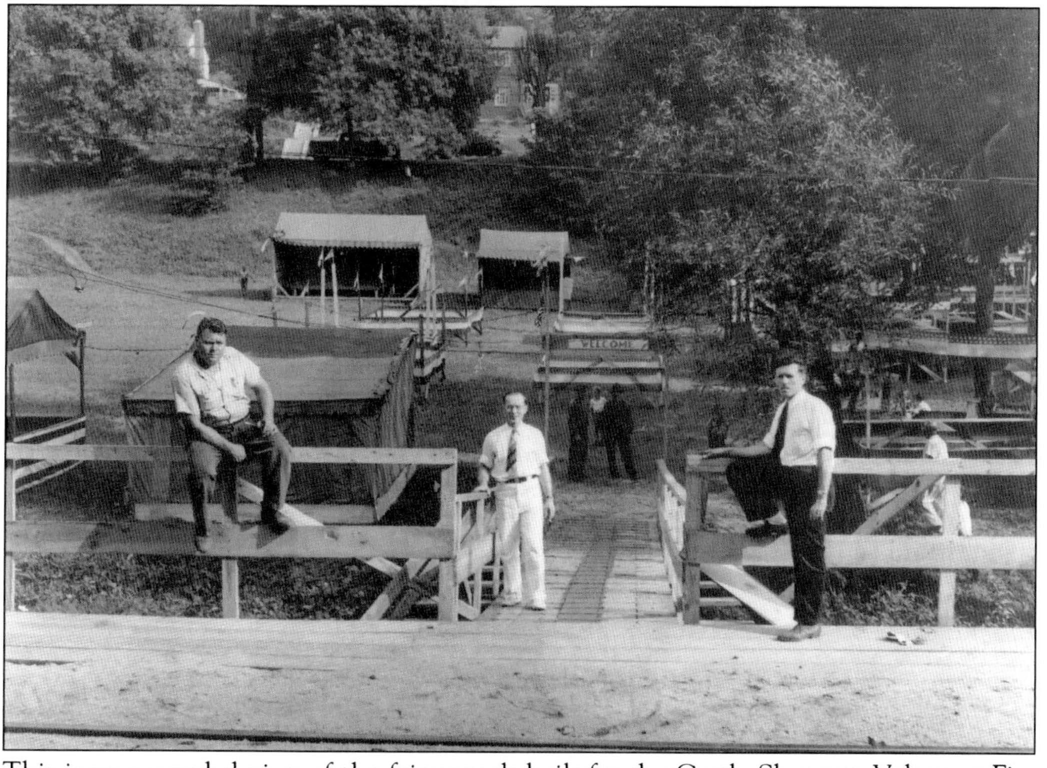

This is an expanded view of the fairgrounds built for the Castle Shannon Volunteer Fire Department's 1932 summer carnival. Posing near the entrance to the grounds are, from left to right, Steve Bittner, Frank Karkalla, and George Hamrock. The tents in the background are very similar to the ones used today. This was 30 years before the firemen built Memorial Hall next to Hamilton School. (Photograph courtesy of Paul Dudjak.)

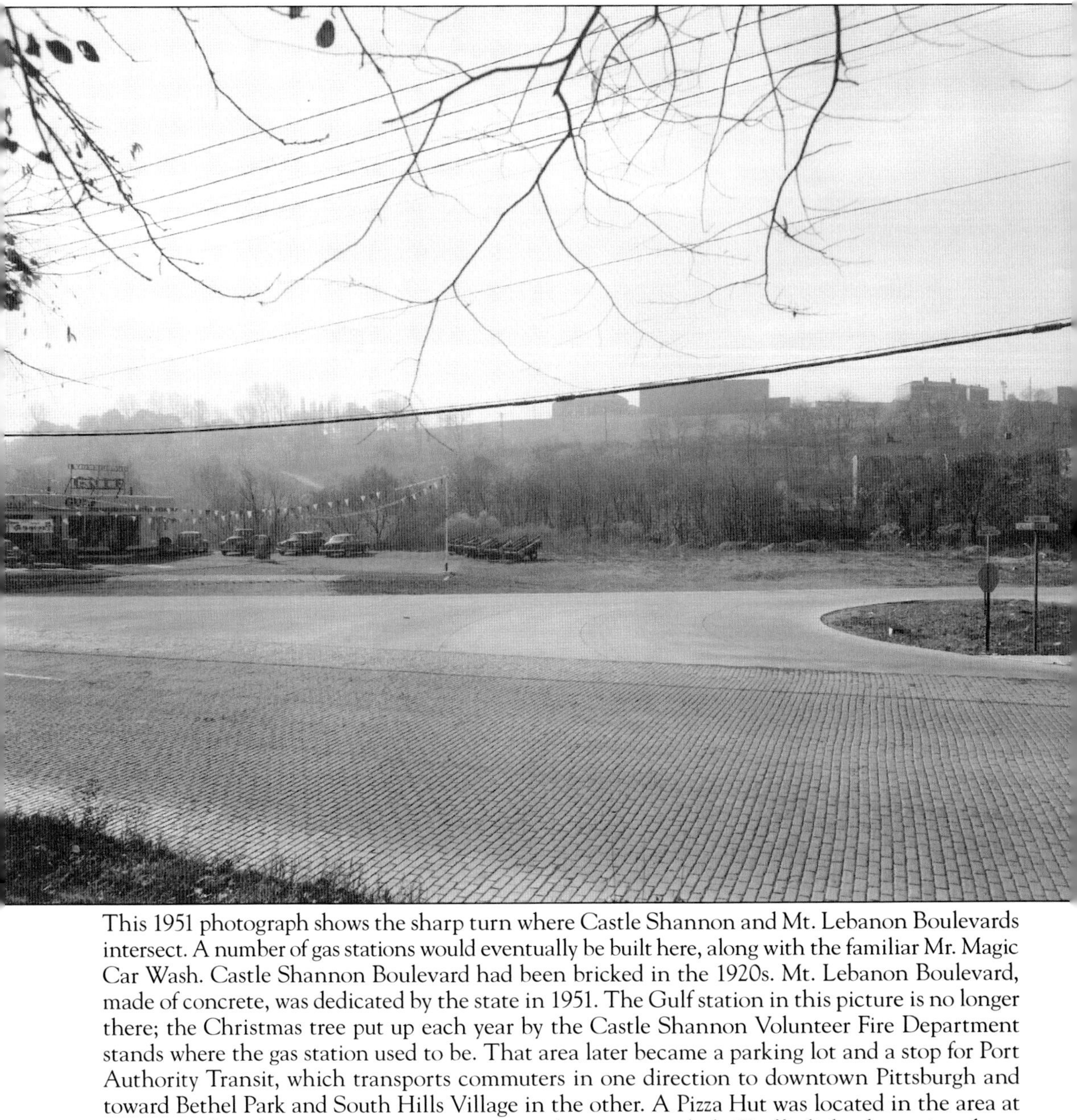

This 1951 photograph shows the sharp turn where Castle Shannon and Mt. Lebanon Boulevards intersect. A number of gas stations would eventually be built here, along with the familiar Mr. Magic Car Wash. Castle Shannon Boulevard had been bricked in the 1920s. Mt. Lebanon Boulevard, made of concrete, was dedicated by the state in 1951. The Gulf station in this picture is no longer there; the Christmas tree put up each year by the Castle Shannon Volunteer Fire Department stands where the gas station used to be. That area later became a parking lot and a stop for Port Authority Transit, which transports commuters in one direction to downtown Pittsburgh and toward Bethel Park and South Hills Village in the other. A Pizza Hut was located in the area at extreme right, where a stop sign once instructed motorists to halt. Traffic lights have since been installed. The property and building were vacant as of 2012. (Photograph by Ed Walsh Studio.)

This late-1940s "practice" fire brought down the old Fetterman homestead on Route 88, directly across the street from Hamilton School. It was common for the Castle Shannon Volunteer Fire Department to burn down old houses and buildings rather than subject them to the wrecker's ball. Note the grade-school students in the foreground. (Photograph courtesy of Castle Shannon Volunteer Fire Department.)

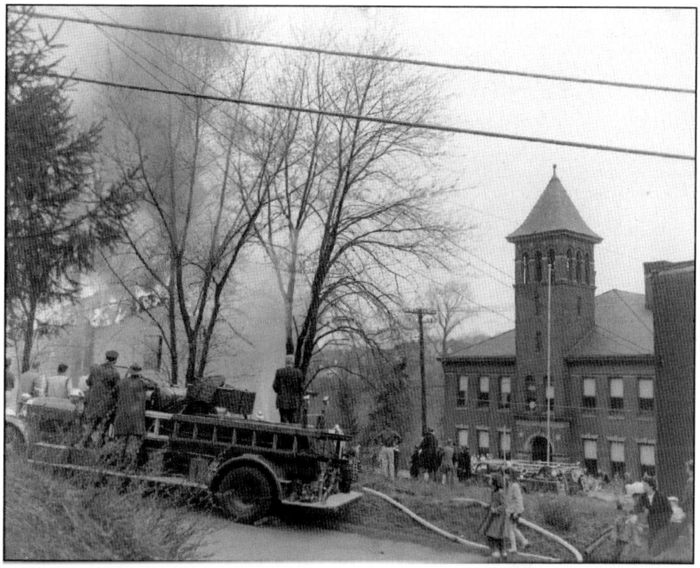

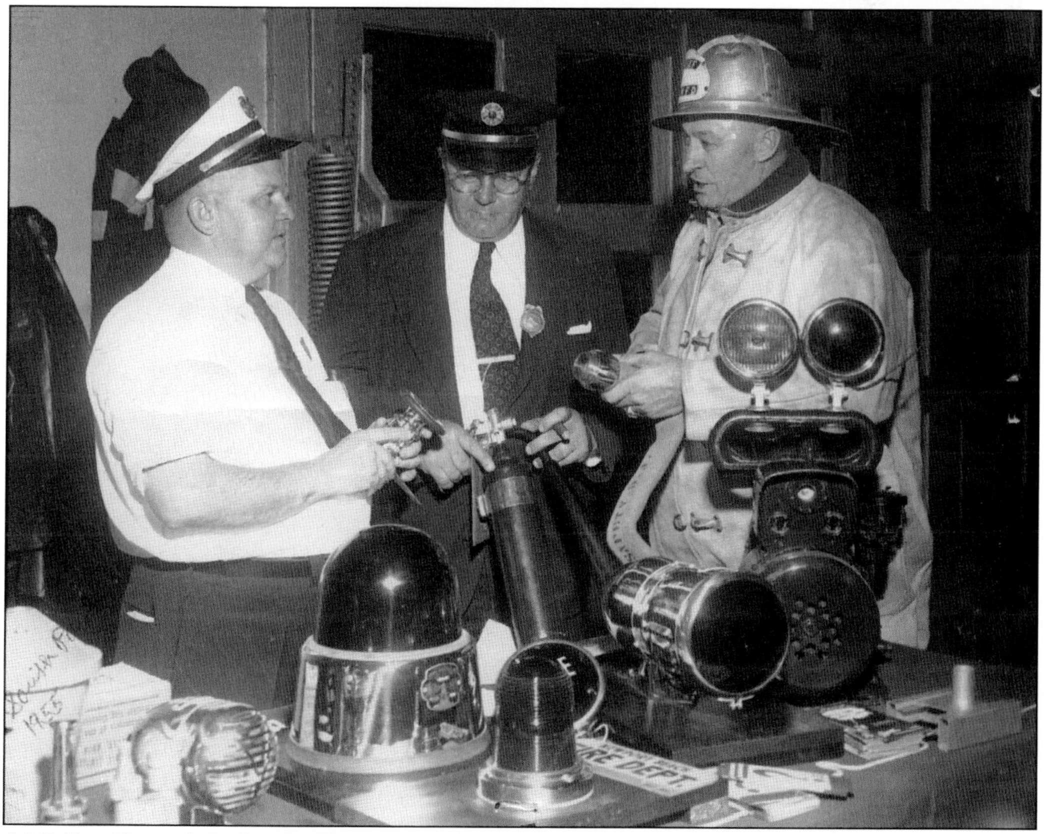

Al Feller (far right), Castle Shannon Volunteer Fire Department chief, shows and examines various fire apparatus during an exposition at South Park in 1955. Feller was a president of the Firemen's Association of Allegheny County and was an honorary member of Elmer Zeiler's Post 512 of the Castle Shannon Veterans of Foreign Wars. (Photograph courtesy of Castle Shannon Volunteer Fire Department.)

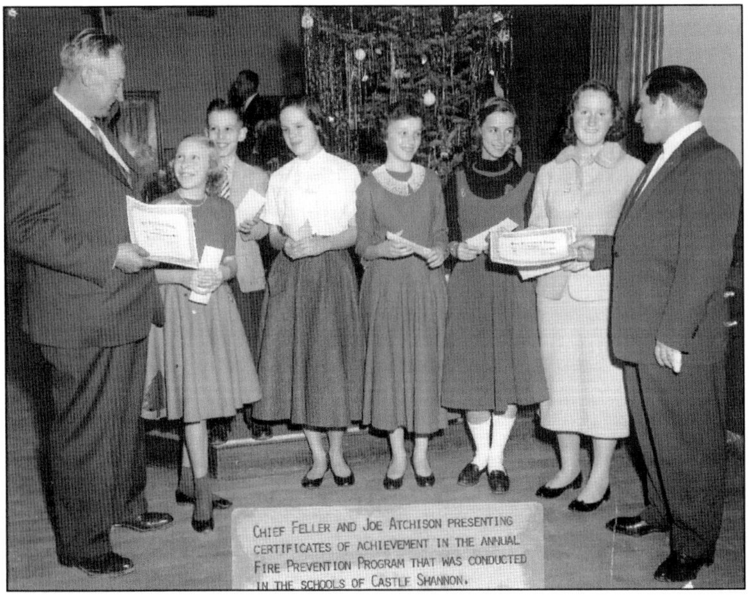

Castle Shannon Volunteer Fire Department chief Al Feller (far left) and fireman Joe Atchison (far right) present certificates of achievement to winners of the Fire Prevention Essay Contest. The ceremony, held during the holiday season, took place in the firehouse on Park Avenue. The contestants were students from Castle Shannon schools. (Photograph by Vic Polk Studio.)

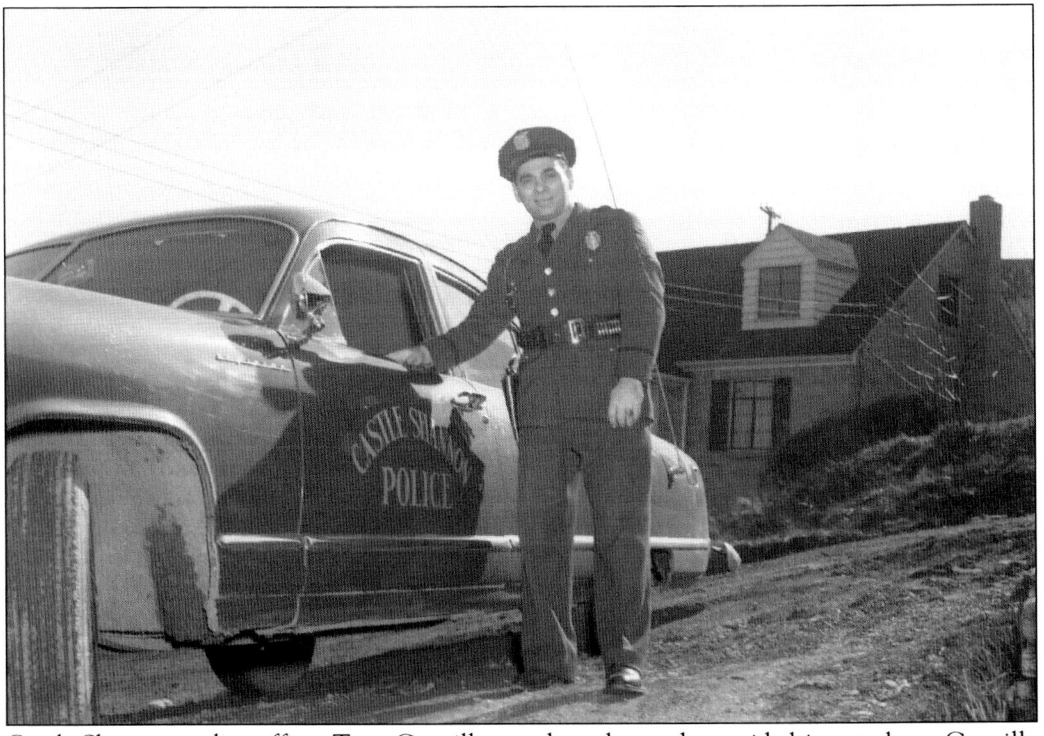

Castle Shannon police officer Tony Cancilla stands at the ready outside his patrol car. Cancilla also was a member of the Castle Shannon Fire Department, and his wife was a member of the Castle Shannon School Board. (Photograph by George "Jasper" Evans, courtesy of Ric Evans.)

The father of the Rizzo brothers was a lamplighter in Castle Shannon who taught his sons the trade. The three brothers—Carl (left), Tony (center), and Frank—were members of the Castle Shannon Volunteer Fire Department. Carl was a town councilman, while Frank was Castle Shannon's secretary for many years. Frank was a Democrat; Carl was a Republican. (Photograph by George "Jasper" Evans, courtesy of Ric Evans.)

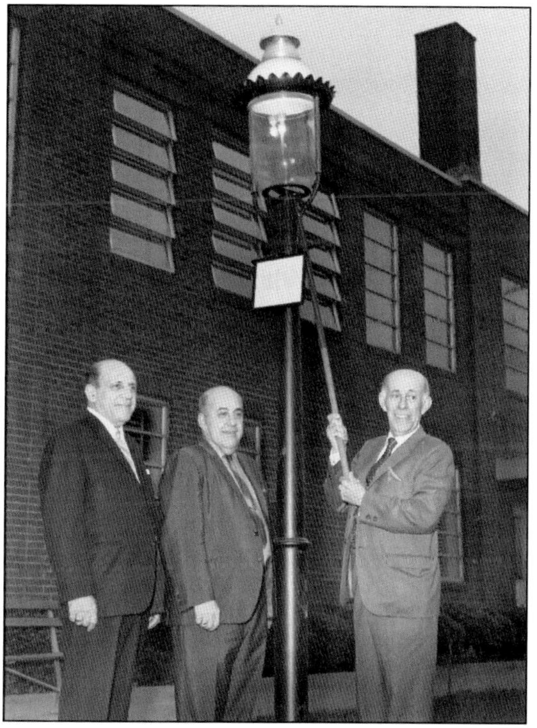

This early-1950s photograph shows the site of St. Anne School, which was dedicated in 1953. The little trolley stop along the tracks in foreground is no longer there. It was moved across the road on the same side. Route 88 is just above the trolley tracks. Note new houses that were built on McCully, Clara, and Blossom Hill Roads. Older houses on Steger Street were already established residences. (Photograph courtesy of St. Anne School.)

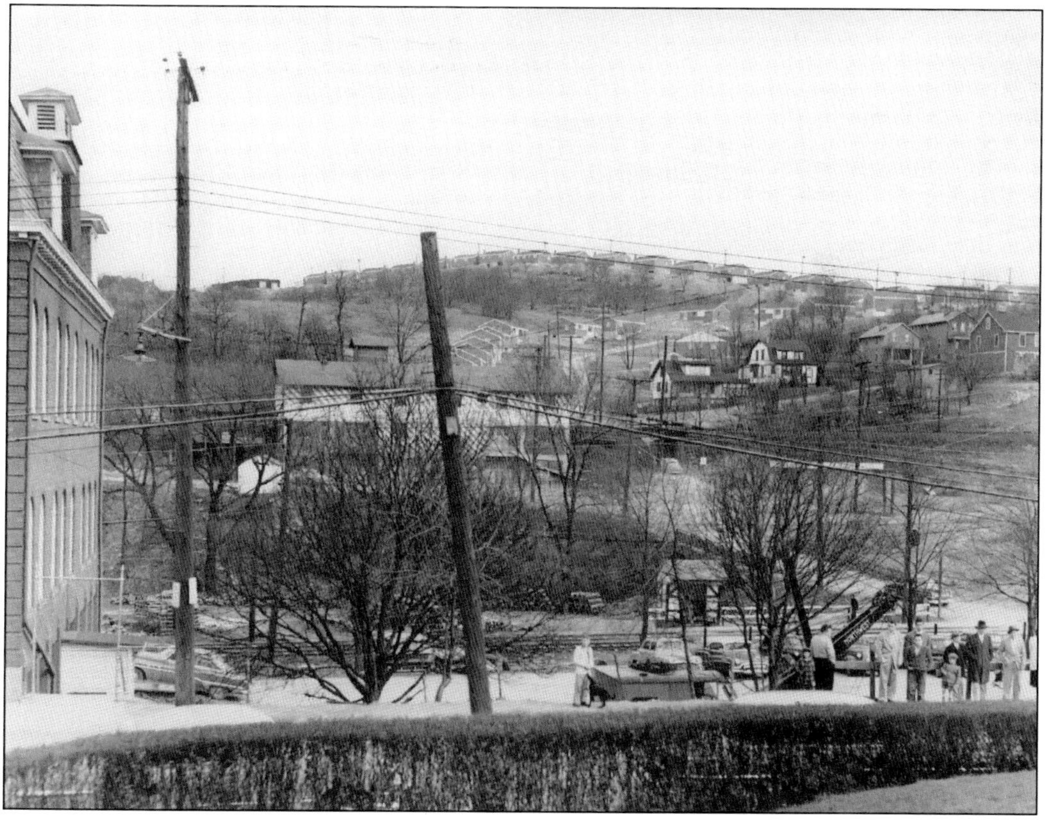

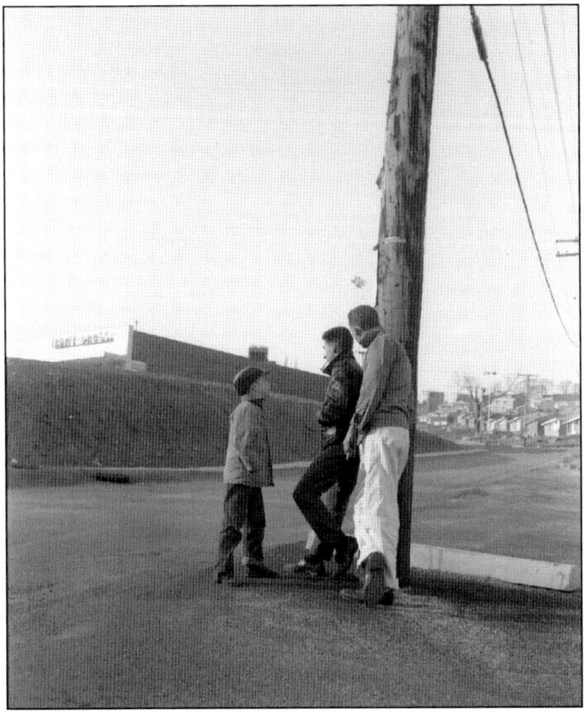

No, Castle Shannon was not a casting site for *Rebel Without a Cause*. Instead, this 1960s photograph shows local youth in the area across the street from Sleepy Hollow Shopping Center. A Giant Eagle grocery store was the anchor of the Sleepy Hollow Shopping Center for many years before it closed in the latter part of the 21st century's first decade. A line of residential duplexes takes up much of that area now. (Photograph by George "Jasper" Evans, courtesy of Ric Evans.)

The Castle Shannon Band would sometimes perform in the St. Patrick's Day parade in downtown Pittsburgh. The ensemble was later disbanded when Castle Shannon became part of the Keystone Oaks School District. (Photograph by George "Jasper" Evans, courtesy of Ric Evans.)

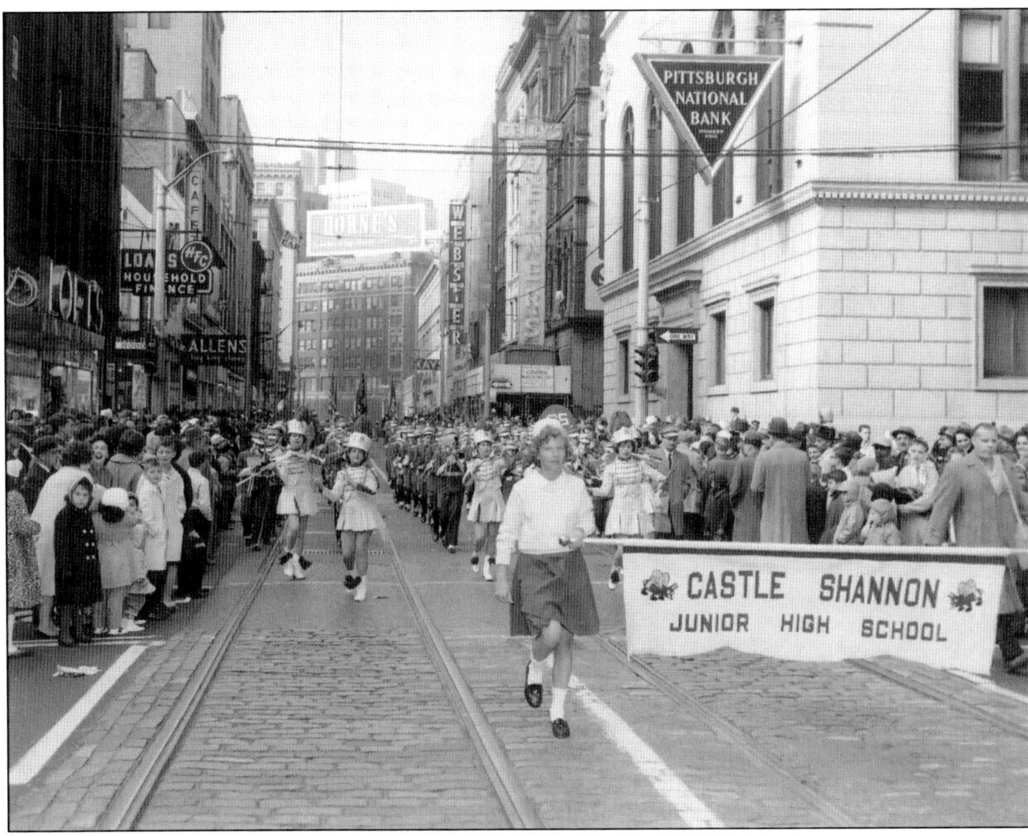

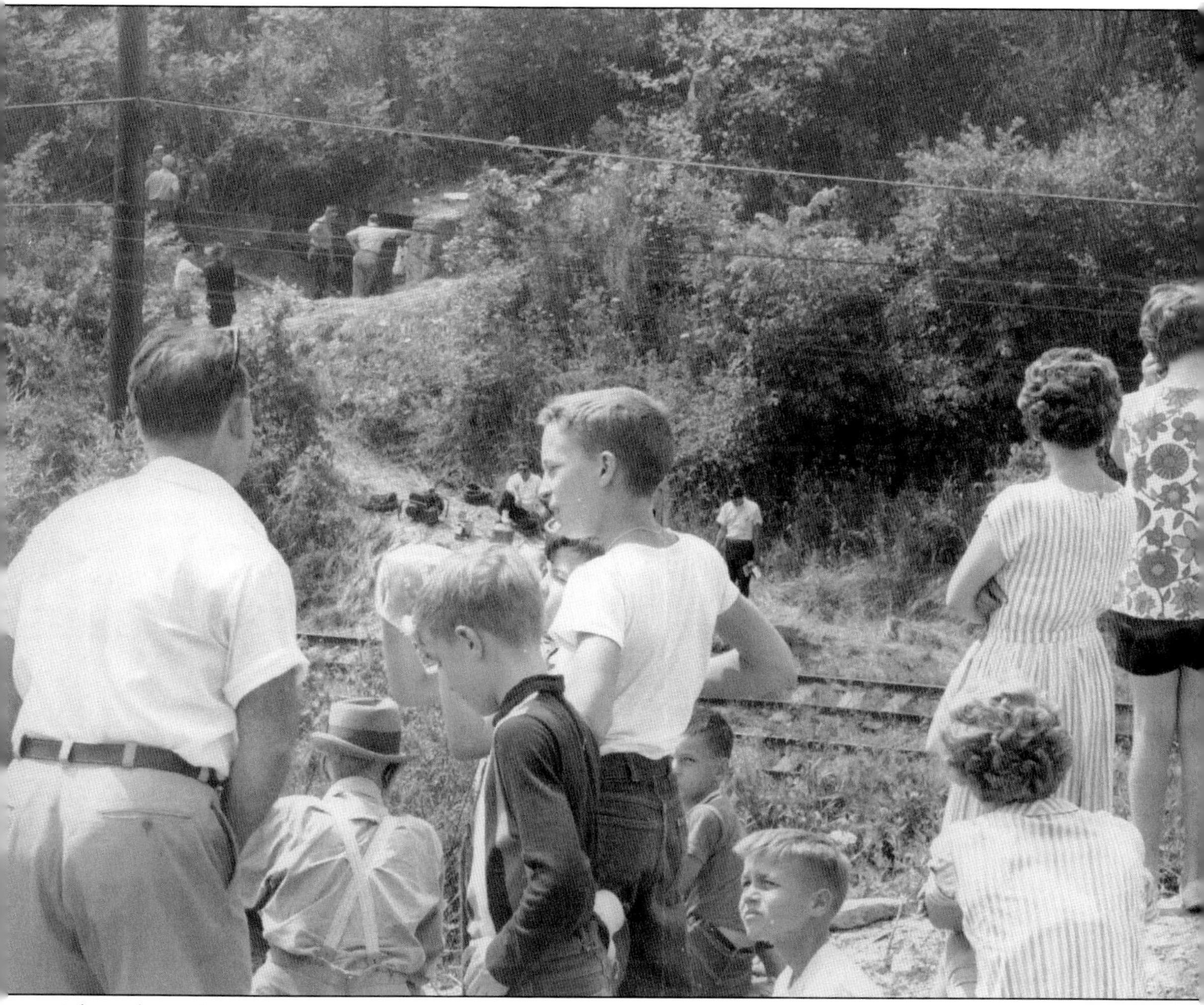

Three boys from Baldwin Township and Mount Washington put Castle Shannon front and center on state and national news on July 12 and 13, 1963. A fourth boy who was with them decided not to explore the closed mine located behind what is now the site of a Burger King on Route 88, and it was his fear that may have saved the other kids' lives. When his buddies failed to return to the opening, he notified the authorities, and an overnight rescue search was undertaken. The three adventurers were found, safe, in shafts located underneath the Linden Grove area. The entrance to the mine can be seen in the upper left portion of the photograph. Concerned and curious townspeople mill about at a safe distance. Note the trolley tracks. Trolleys heading to the left would be traveling to Castle Shannon's business center; those traveling in the other direction would be heading toward downtown Pittsburgh. (Photograph courtesy of Castle Shannon Volunteer Fire Department.)

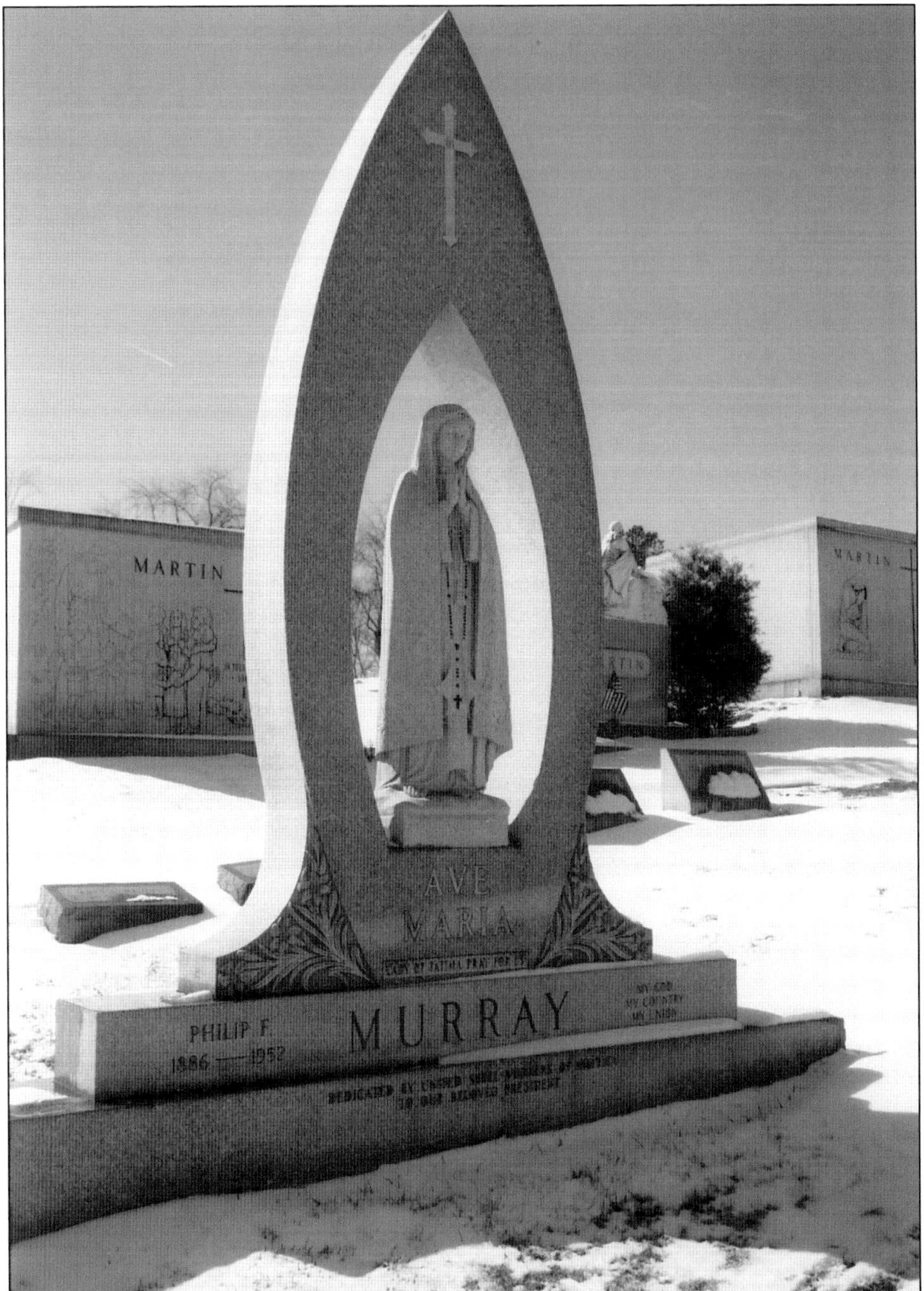

Philip Murray was buried in St. Anne Cemetery on November 13, 1952, following a funeral mass at St. Paul Cathedral in Oakland. An immigrant from Scotland, Murray rose through the ranks of both the United Steelworkers of America and the United Mine Workers of America. In 1991, Murray was inducted into the Labor Hall of Fame. "Unions are created to make living conditions just a little better than they were before they were created, and the union that does not manifest that kind of interest in human beings cannot endure," Murray said. (Photograph by Charles LeClaire.)

The St. Anne Church bell tower was dedicated in memory of Philip Murray, labor leader. It was built by the United Steelworkers of America Union, and was dedicated on November 9, 1963. Pennsylvania governor David L. Lawrence attended the ceremony, as did David McDonald, president of the United Steelworkers. When the church itself was built, two wraparound stairways, attached to each side of the bell tower, allowed pedestrians to walk up to the church. The stairways were later removed. (Photograph by Charles LeClaire.)

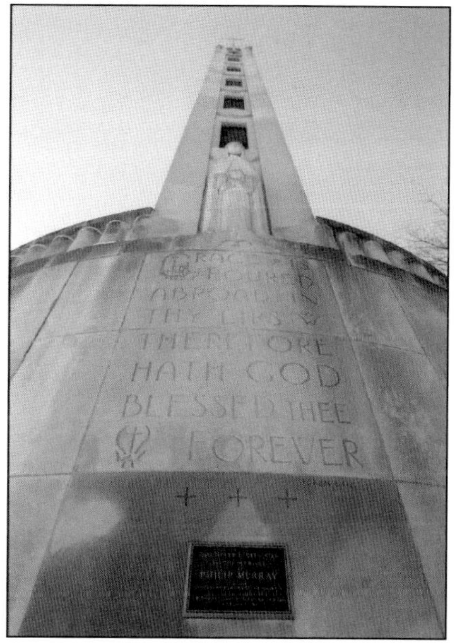

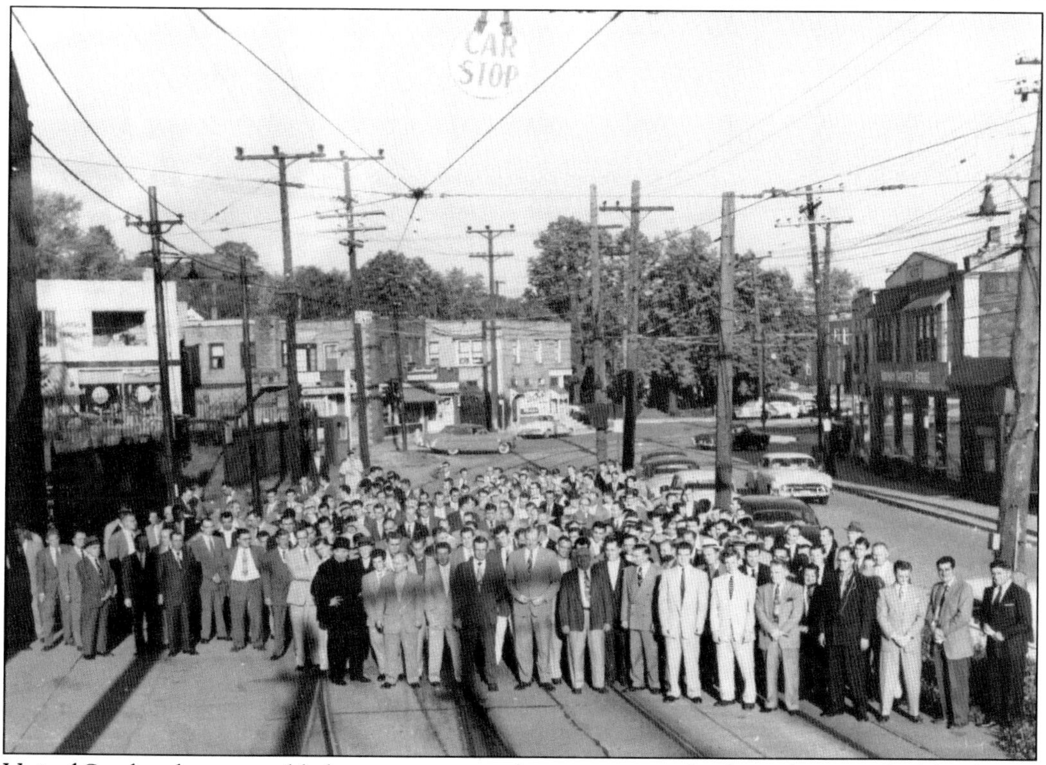

United Steelworkers assembled en masse to pay their respects at the funeral service for labor leader Philip Murray. These workers pose for a picture in the business center of Castle Shannon across Willow Avenue. Murray was born May 25, 1886, at 77 Baird's Row in Blantyre, Scotland. Blantyre was a coal-mining town, much like Castle Shannon. The first miners' union was organized there in 1817. Murray and his father arrived in Irwin, Pennsylvania, in 1902. (Photograph by George "Jasper" Evans, courtesy of Ric Evans.)

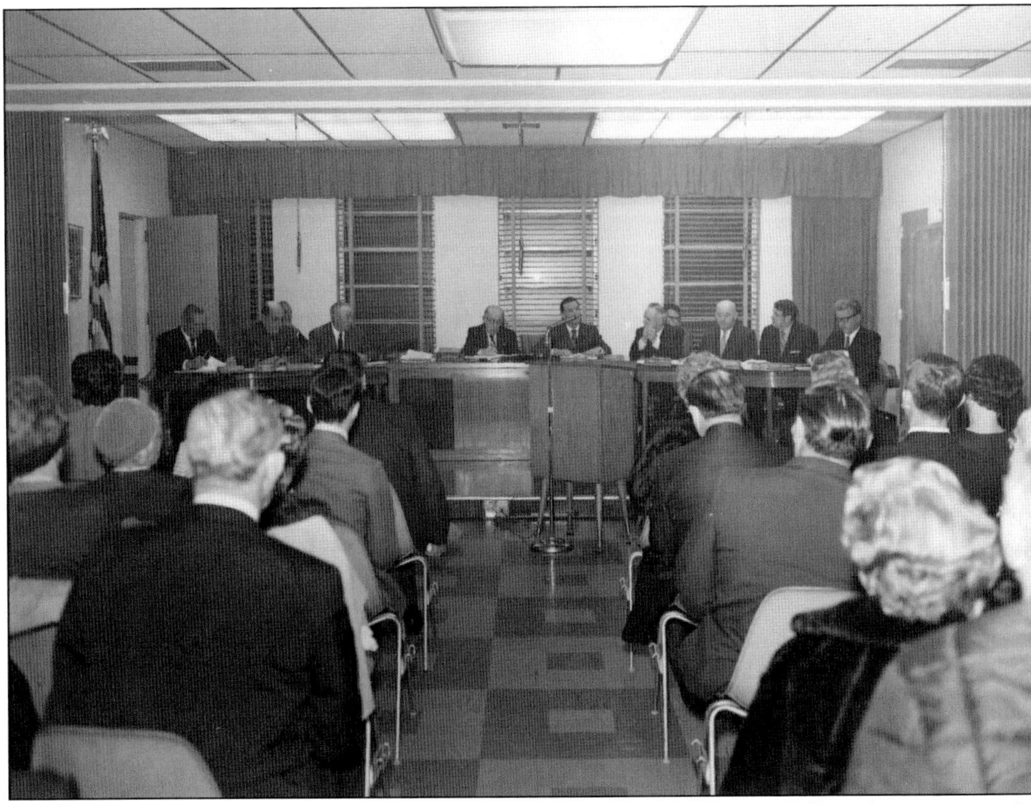

The old Castle Shannon Borough Building along the trolley tracks at Willow Avenue served a number of purposes for Castle Shannon during its existence. Not only did it house the borough's police department and a few jail cells, but the upstairs contained the town's public library until a permanent facility was built in 1966. The old borough building also was where Castle Shannon conducted its monthly council meetings and an occasional public presentation. (Photograph by George "Jasper" Evans, courtesy of Ric Evans.)

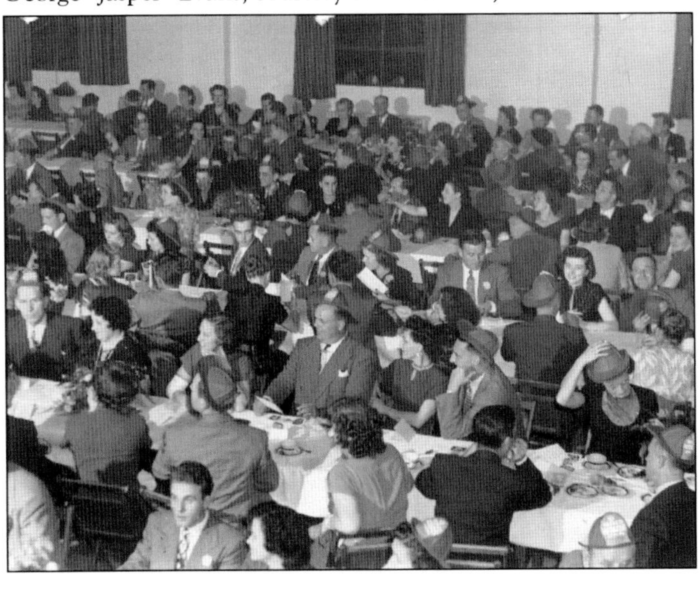

Revelers are seen enjoying themselves at one of the Castle Shannon Volunteer Fire Department banquets traditionally held each fall at the fire hall. Party favors from this 1950s-era dinner were fire hats, as modeled by more than a few of the diners. The fire department also staged an annual Christmas party for children of the firemen in the same venue. (Photograph courtesy of the Castle Shannon Volunteer Fire Department.)

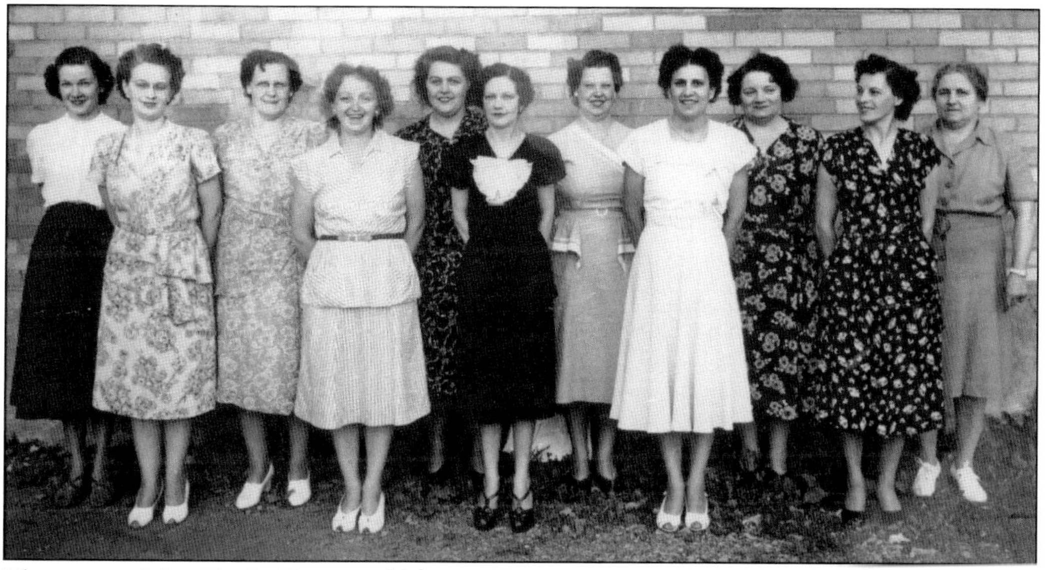

The wives of the Castle Shannon Volunteer Fire Department organized the Ladies Auxiliary shortly after the department was established. The women would assist in fundraising efforts. Only 11 ladies constitute the group in this early photograph. Fourth from right is Betty Campbell, sister of firemen Carl, Frank, and Tony Rizzo. (Photograph courtesy of Castle Shannon Volunteer Fire Department.)

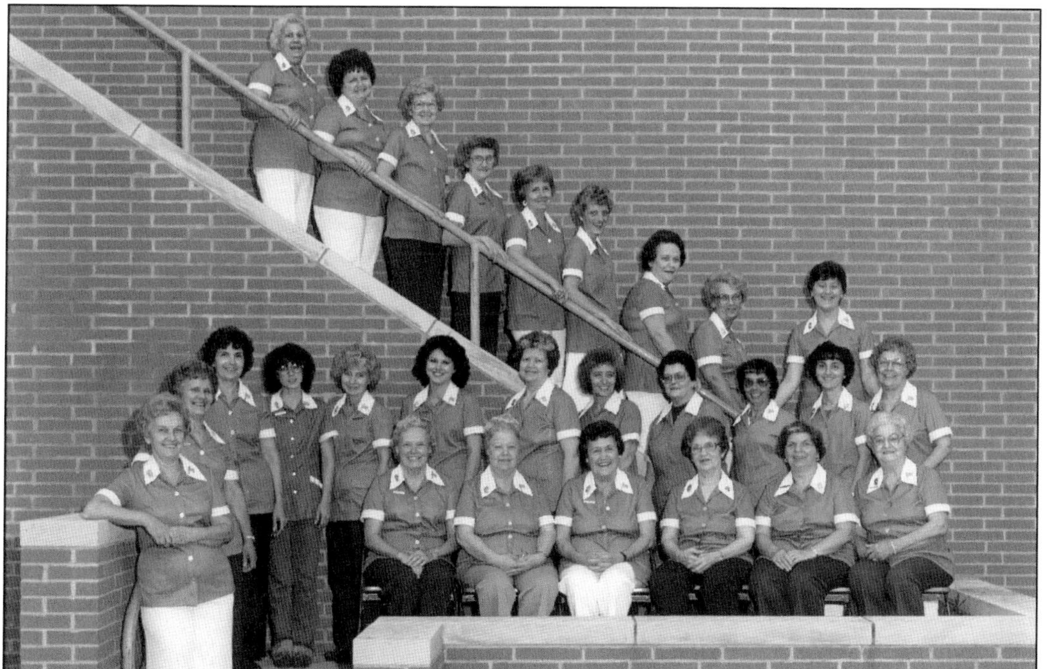

In July 1982, members of the Ladies Auxiliary pose for this photograph at the new fire hall adjacent to the old Hamilton School. Betty Campbell is at the top of the stairway. In the second row, fourth from right, is Aileen O'Brien, whose husband, Jim O'Brien, was fire chief at the time. (Photograph by George "Jasper" Evans, courtesy of Lucille Ashley.)

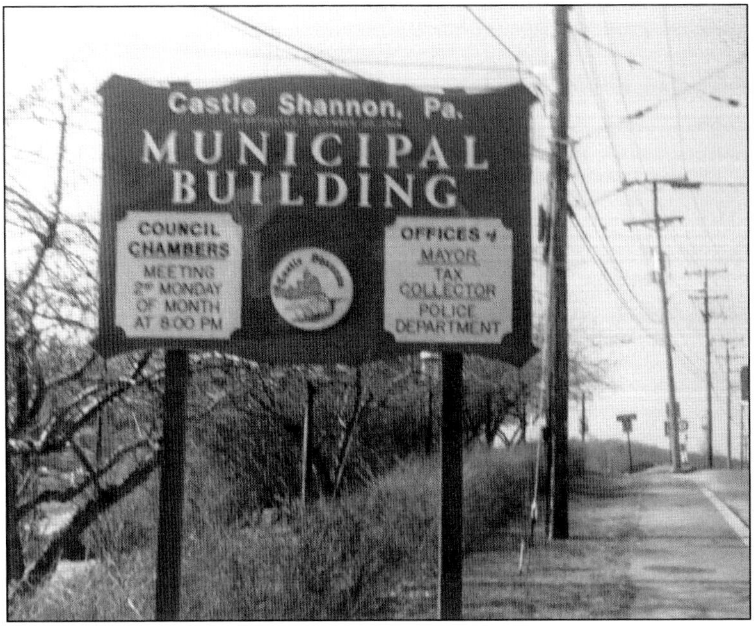

The sign adjacent to Castle Shannon's former borough building was located on Castle Shannon Boulevard, opposite Vitte's Hardware. The familiar Castle Shannon logo appears in the center of the sign. There was a Port Authority trolley stop directly in front of the borough building, and the borough's public baseball field and tennis and basketball courts were located near the property. (Photograph courtesy of Mary Scabilloni.)

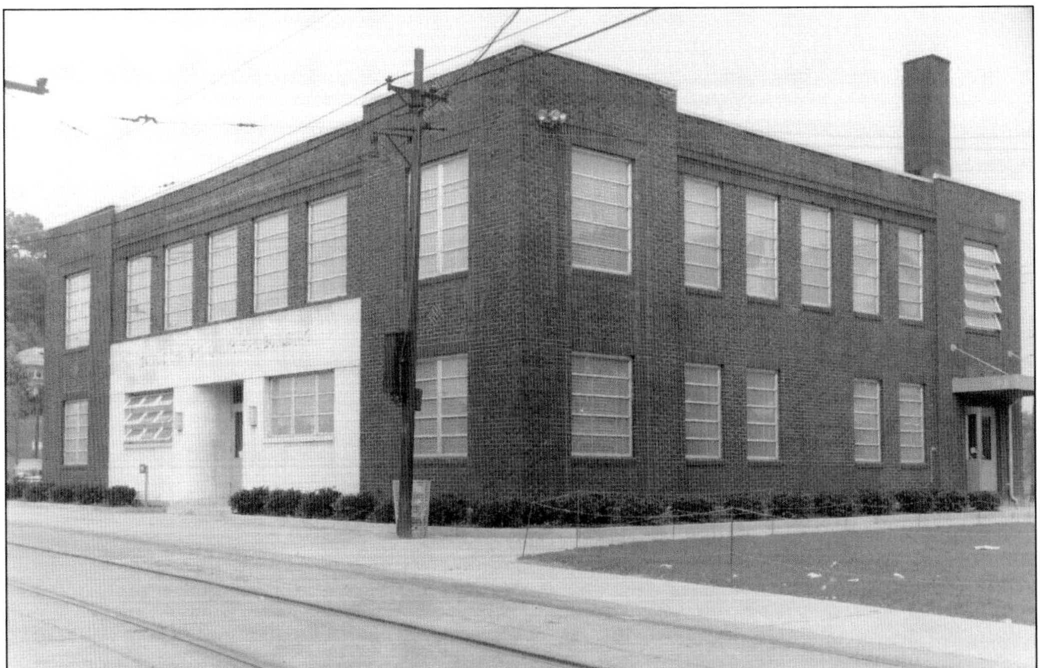

This is the Castle Shannon Borough Building familiar to most local residents over the age of 20. It was centrally located in the business district on Willow Avenue and was easily accessible by rail, conveniently located along several trolley routes. It housed the offices of the mayor and tax collector, as well as Castle Shannon's police department. (Photograph by George "Jasper" Evans, courtesy of Ric Evans.)

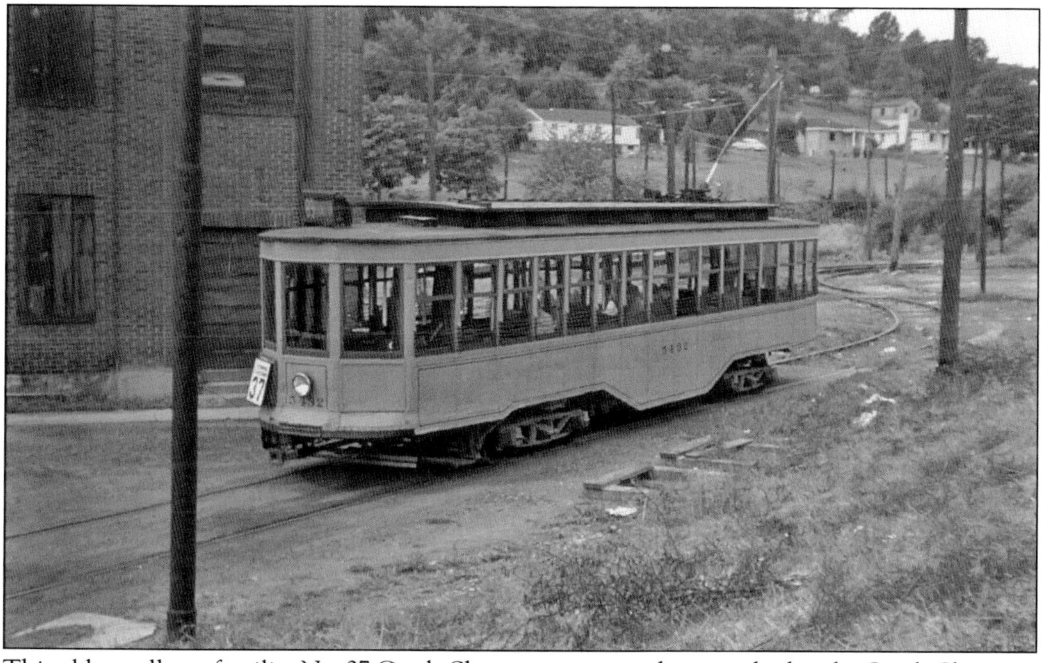

This older trolley, a familiar No. 37 Castle Shannon car, was photographed at the Castle Shannon Loop on September 9, 1956. It was officially known as Pittsburgh Railways 5432. The trolley car is going past the old Pittsburgh Railways Building. (Photograph by William D. Volkmer, courtesy of John F. Bromley.)

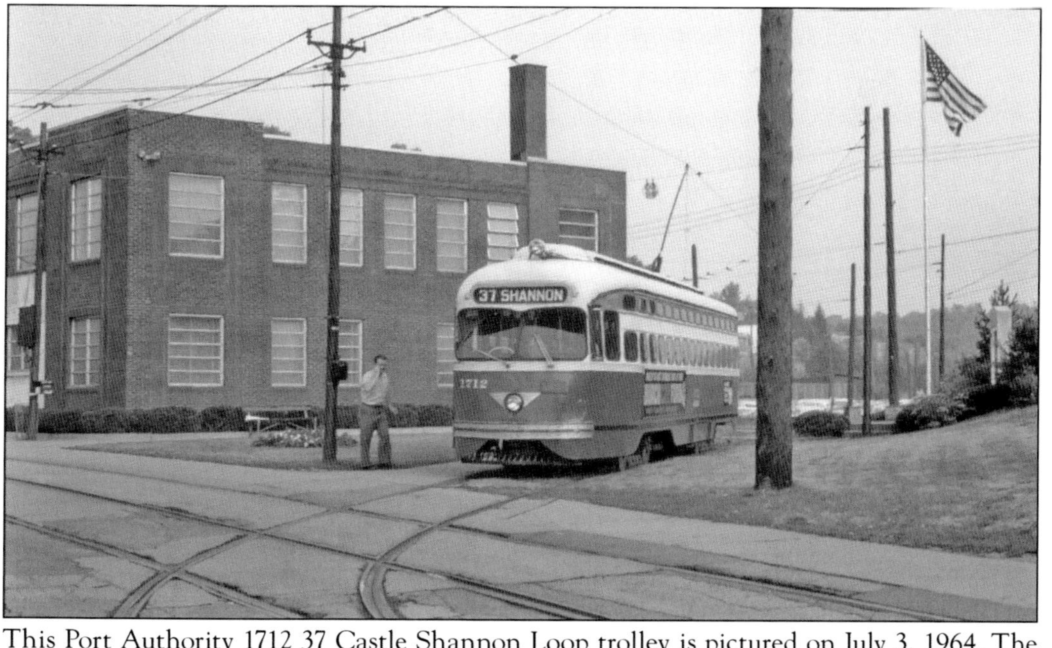

This Port Authority 1712 37 Castle Shannon Loop trolley is pictured on July 3, 1964. The trolley is going past the Castle Shannon Borough Building at a point where there was a trolley turnaround. The photograph illustrates the significance and prominence of trolley cars in Castle Shannon. To the right of the flag is a war memorial that has since been relocated to a nearby area. (Photograph by John F. Bromley.)

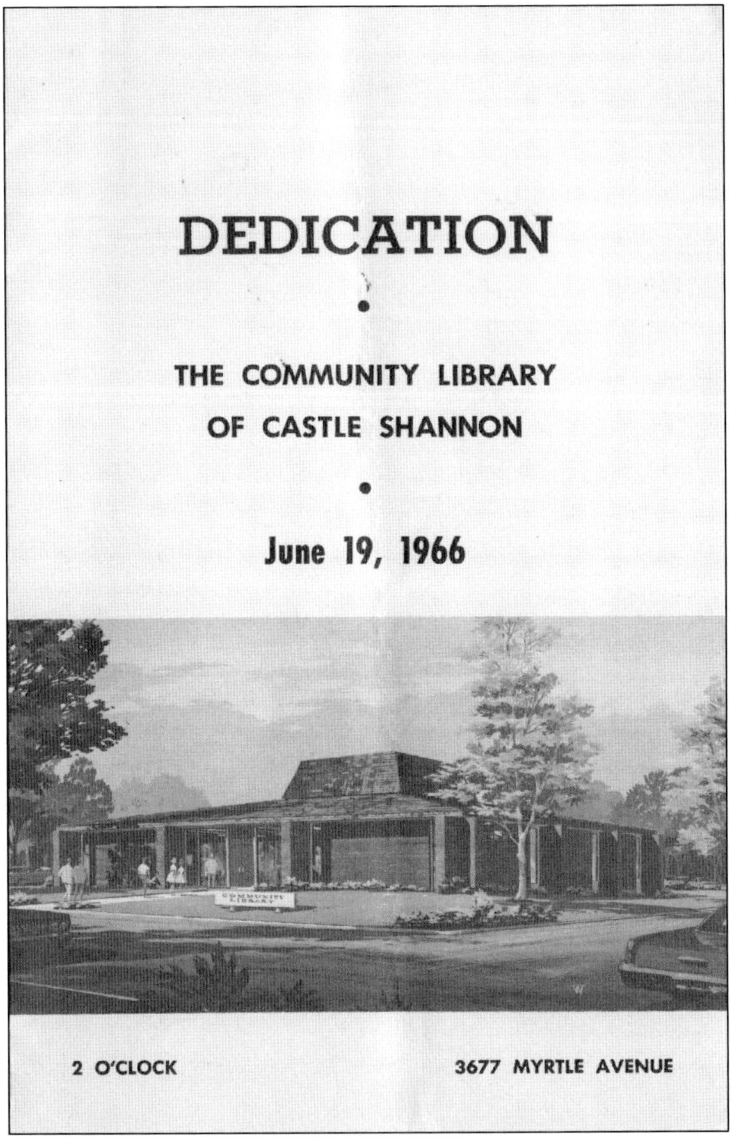

DEDICATION

•

THE COMMUNITY LIBRARY

OF CASTLE SHANNON

•

June 19, 1966

2 O'CLOCK 3677 MYRTLE AVENUE

This is the official program from the dedication for the Community Library of Castle Shannon on June 19, 1966. The dedication ceremony was split between two venues—Keystone Oaks Junior High School (later Myrtle Elementary) and the library itself. Making the introductions at the junior high school portion of the ceremony was Castle Shannon attorney Walter Riehl. The Reverend Eugene Harkins of St. Anne Parish delivered the invocation, and Tom O'Malley, president of Castle Shannon Borough Council, made the opening remarks. At the library, the Reverend L. Reynolds Mahard of the Castle Shannon Presbyterian Church said a prayer. The American flag was raised by American Legion Post No. 490, and the national anthem was played by the Keystone Oaks Junior High School Band under the direction of Leo Yagello. Architects of the building were Allan B. Mitchell and Associates. The chief fundraiser from Castle Shannon was Hazel Bost, who was a driving force in the project; a garden at the library would later bear her name. Before the new library was built, Castle Shannon residents had to take a stairway to an upper level of the borough building to read and borrow books. (Photograph courtesy of Castle Shannon Borough.)

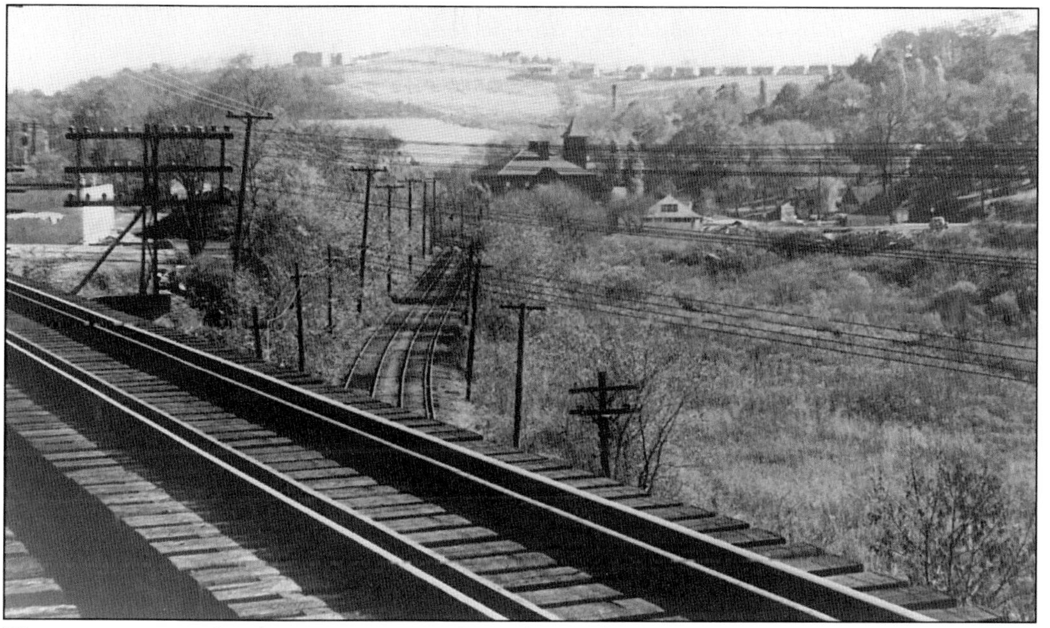

The importance of rail transportation through Castle Shannon is on display in this 1950s photograph. The Pittsburgh & West Virginia Railway trestle passes over the Pittsburgh Railways trolley track, which is headed in the direction of Pittsburgh. Hamilton School can be seen in the center of the picture. High above, in the upper left, is Highland Elementary School. Note how undeveloped the neighborhood was in those days. It has since grown exponentially. (Photograph courtesy of Paul Dudjak.)

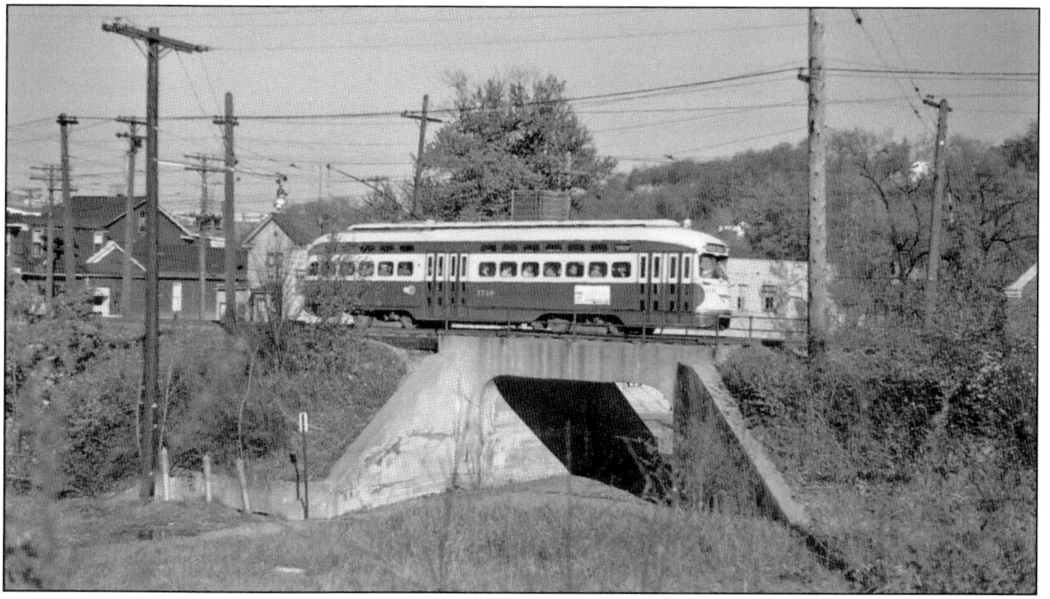

A Pittsburgh Railways trolley 1719 passes over a tunnel near the borough building on Willow Avenue on May 1, 1959. The road, which led to an upper level of Willow Avenue that ran parallel to the business section of Willow Avenue, was later eliminated, and the tunnel was destroyed when major reconstruction was done in the area of the old borough building and the Ice Castle skating rink was installed. (Photograph courtesy of John F. Bromley.)

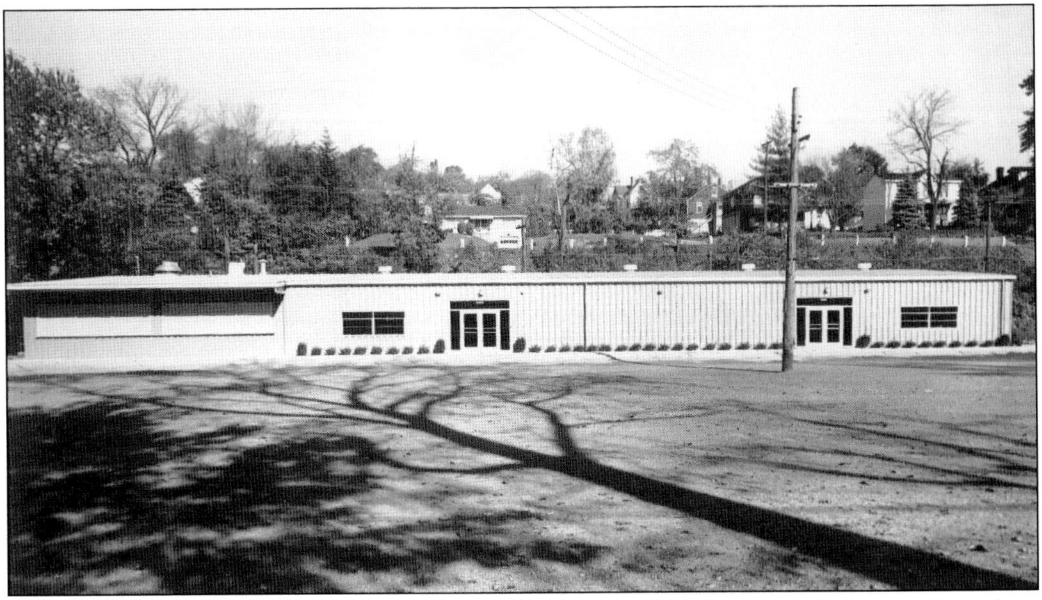

Since the Castle Shannon Volunteer Fire Department owned the land adjacent to Hamilton School, it made sense for the organization to put something on it. Memorial Hall was opened for business in 1962. The hall has been used for countless wedding receptions, plus weekly bingo games, along with firemen's meetings. The considerable grounds next to the hall gave the fire department a flat, large, practical space to hold its annual summer carnival. This photograph is from October 13, 1962. (Photograph Castle Shannon Volunteer Fire Department.)

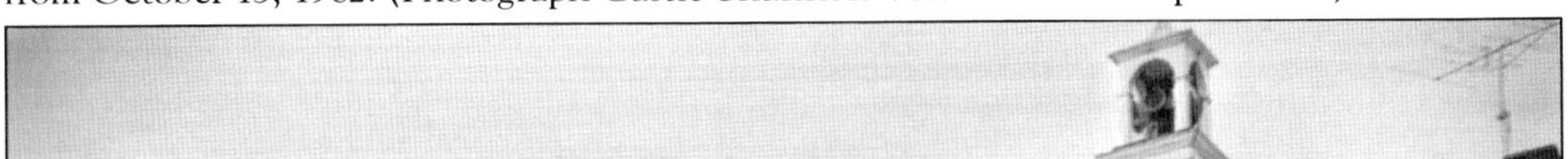

A picture postcard shows the old Castle Shannon Volunteer Fire Department headquarters on Park Avenue. The postcard reads: "75 active members—all uniformed—25 retired members. For the ultimate in efficient, economical fire protection, It's the volunteers, who give this community service without pay, day in day out regardless of the weather." (Photograph courtesy of Paul Fey.)

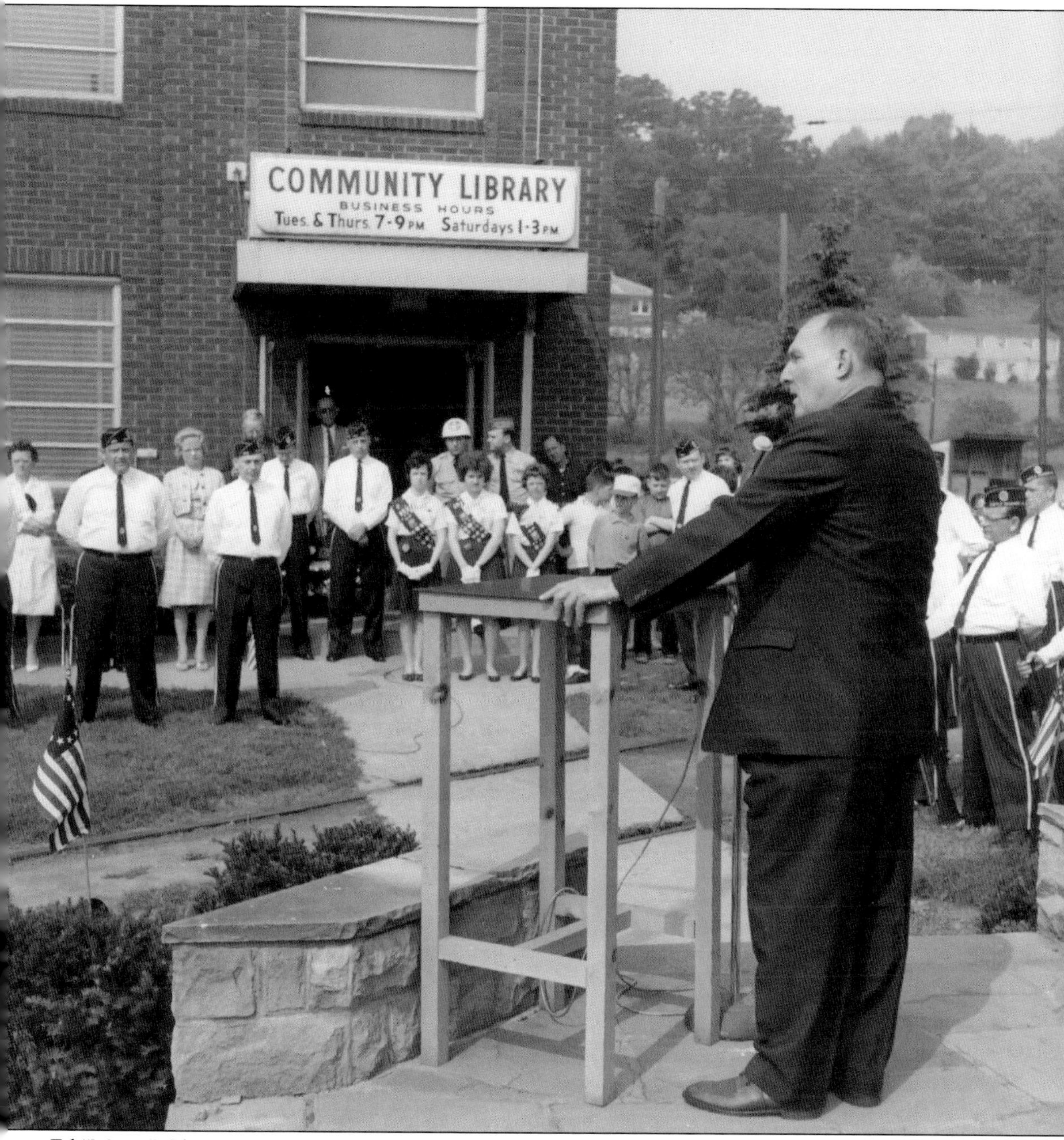

Ed "Moon" Obringer was a colorful part of the Castle Shannon community for many years, first as burgess during the 1950s and later as mayor in the 1960s. Obringer also enjoyed a long career in his day job as a member of the Allegheny County Police Department. A lifelong bachelor, Obringer is seen here addressing a crowd in Castle Shannon during his time as mayor. Carnival-goers may remember him for his work in directing and maintaining order in the firemen's gravel parking lot next to Hamilton School. Obringer presided at a number of borough activities and building dedications, notably the annual Christmas tree burn next to Hamilton School in late December. He also served as an usher at St. Anne Church. (Photograph by George "Jasper" Evans, courtesy of Ric Evans.)

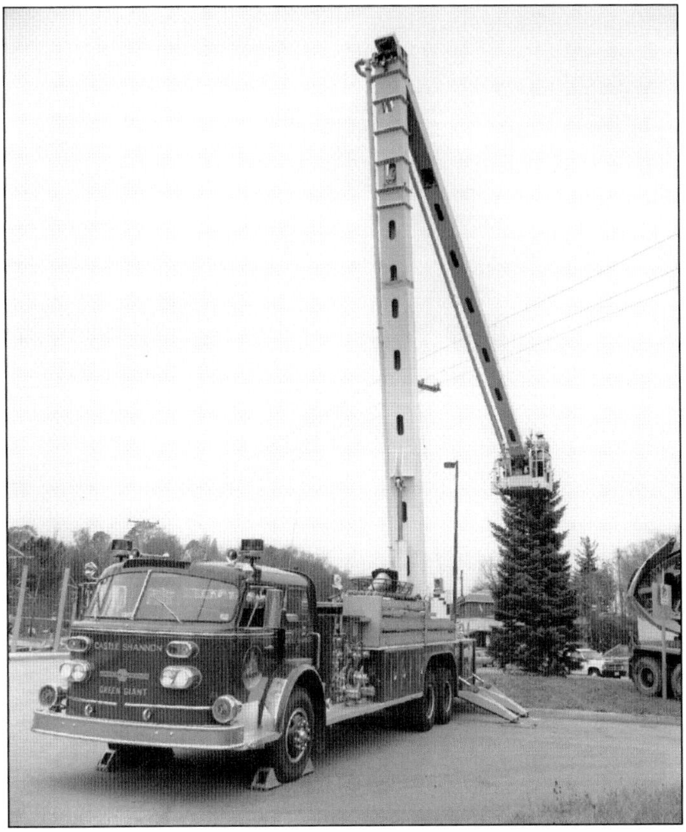

To start the 1987 holiday season on an appropriate note, a Christmas tree was dedicated. Each year, the Castle Shannon Volunteer Fire Department invites everyone to make decorative additions to the tree. With the closings of several elementary schools in the past 25 years, Hamilton Park has become the hub of recreational activities in Castle Shannon. The annual Community Day is held each Memorial Day weekend, and fireworks are generally launched from the park on special occasions. (Photograph by George "Jasper" Evans, courtesy of Ric Evans.)

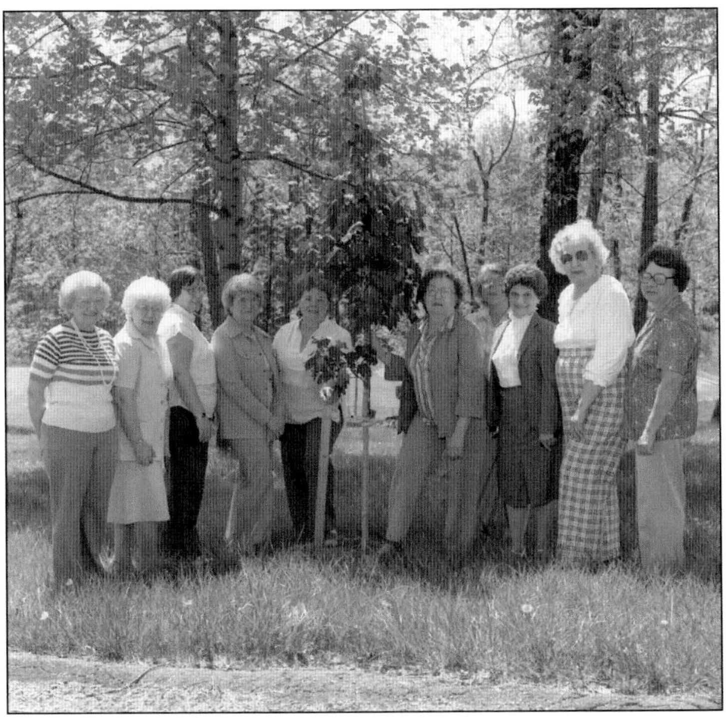

The Women's Club of Castle Shannon planted its own tree at Hamilton Park in 1987 to help commemorate the location as a new center of recreational activity in the borough. The park provides ample space to play ball, ride a bike, or simply while away some time on a pleasant afternoon. (Photograph by George "Jasper" Evans, courtesy of Ric Evans.)

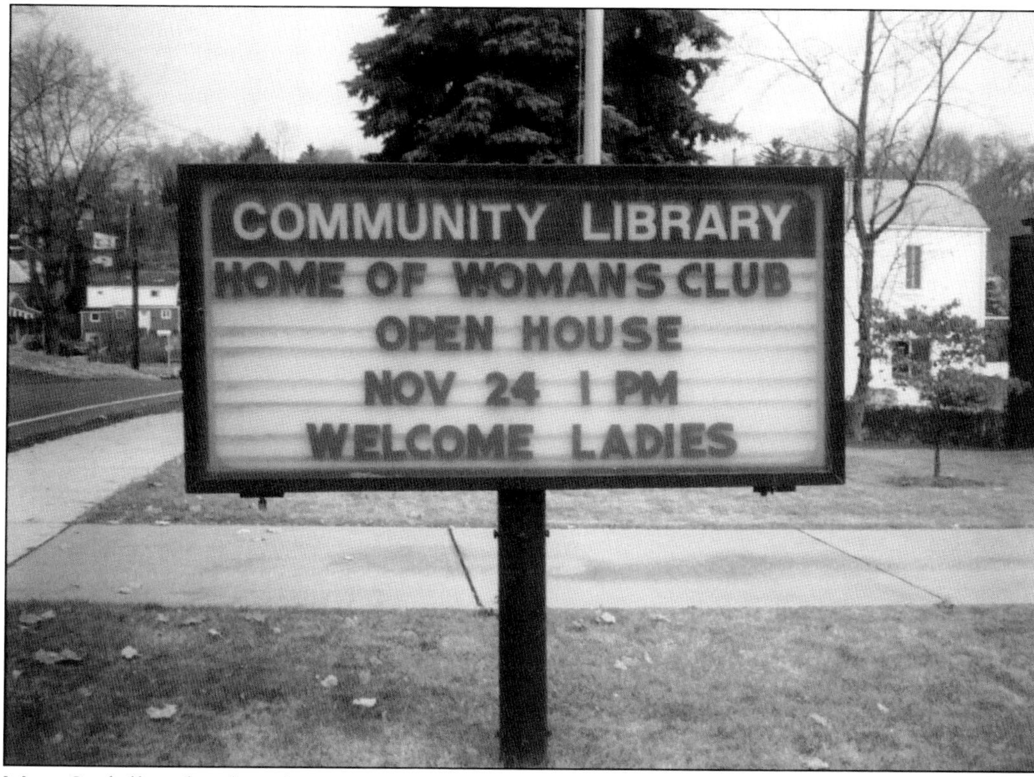

Mary Scabilloni has long been one of Castle Shannon's most respected community leaders. She was a two-time president of the Women's Club of Castle Shannon, serving a total of eight years in that capacity, and also was involved with the local Boy Scouts. The Women's Club used to hold its meetings at Myrtle Avenue School, then later at the old borough building, before moving to the Community Library of Castle Shannon when it opened in 1966. The group also organized and started the kitchen in the lower level of the library. It participated in women's club conferences with other groups from around the state, and was involved with the local arts festival. The monthly meetings generally featured a luncheon and guest speaker. Some meetings would have themes, such as the Titanic or a Hawaiian luau. The marquee in front of the library was donated by the Women's Club. The club disbanded in 2002. (Both photographs courtesy of Mary Scabilloni.)

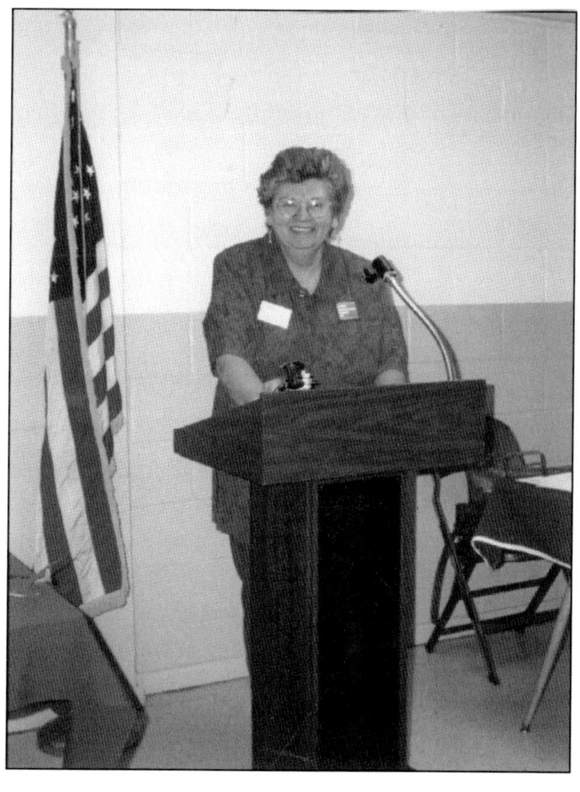

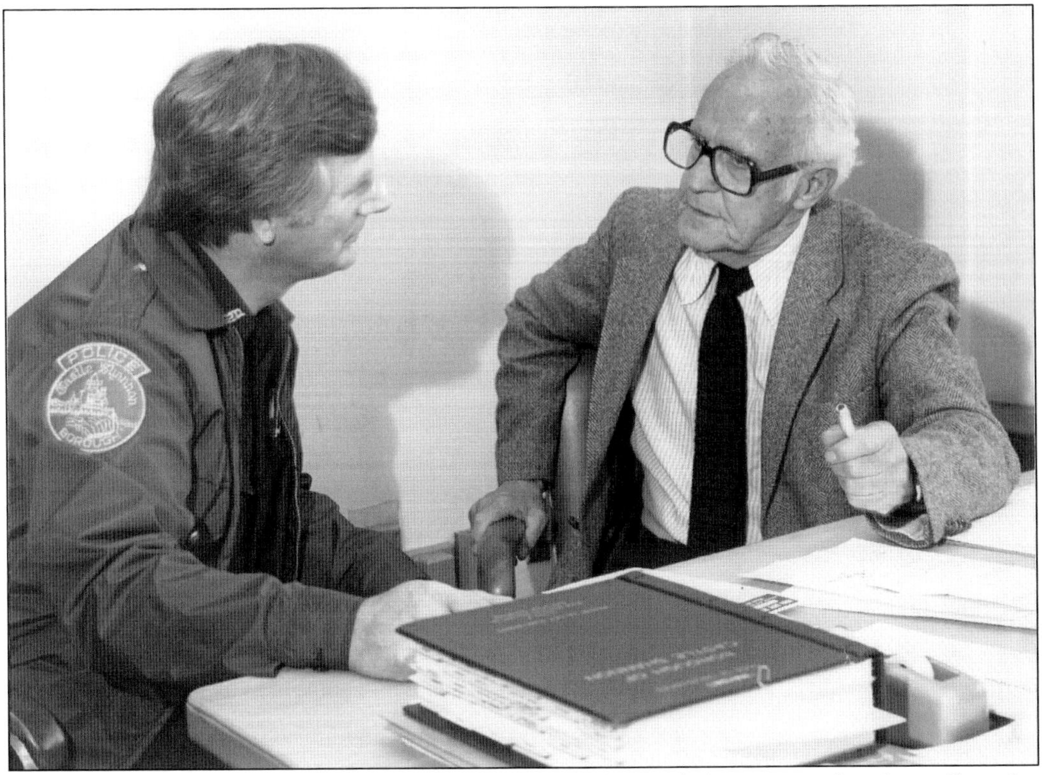

Castle Shannon mayor George Evans (right) discusses borough business with police officer Irv Sniegocki in this mid-1980s photograph. Evans also served as a longtime borough councilman and dabbled in photography. Much of his fine work can be found in these pages. Sniegocki, originally from Pittsburgh's South Side, joined the Castle Shannon police in 1964 and patrolled the beat until 1990. An enthusiastic walker, he can still be seen, in retirement, taking daily walks through Castle Shannon's neighborhoods. (Photograph courtesy of Ric Evans.)

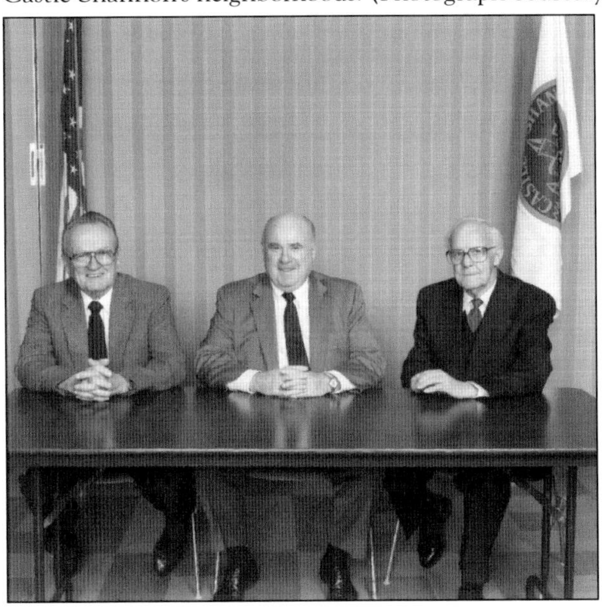

A trio of Castle Shannon mayors sits for this photograph in the mid-1990s. Shown from left to right are, Mike Cheberenchick (1974–1977), Tom O'Malley (1986–2000), and George "Jasper" Evans (1983–1985). All three gentlemen also served as councilmen in Castle Shannon. As of 2012, Cheberenchick still had a seat on the borough council. (Photograph courtesy of Jean O'Malley.)

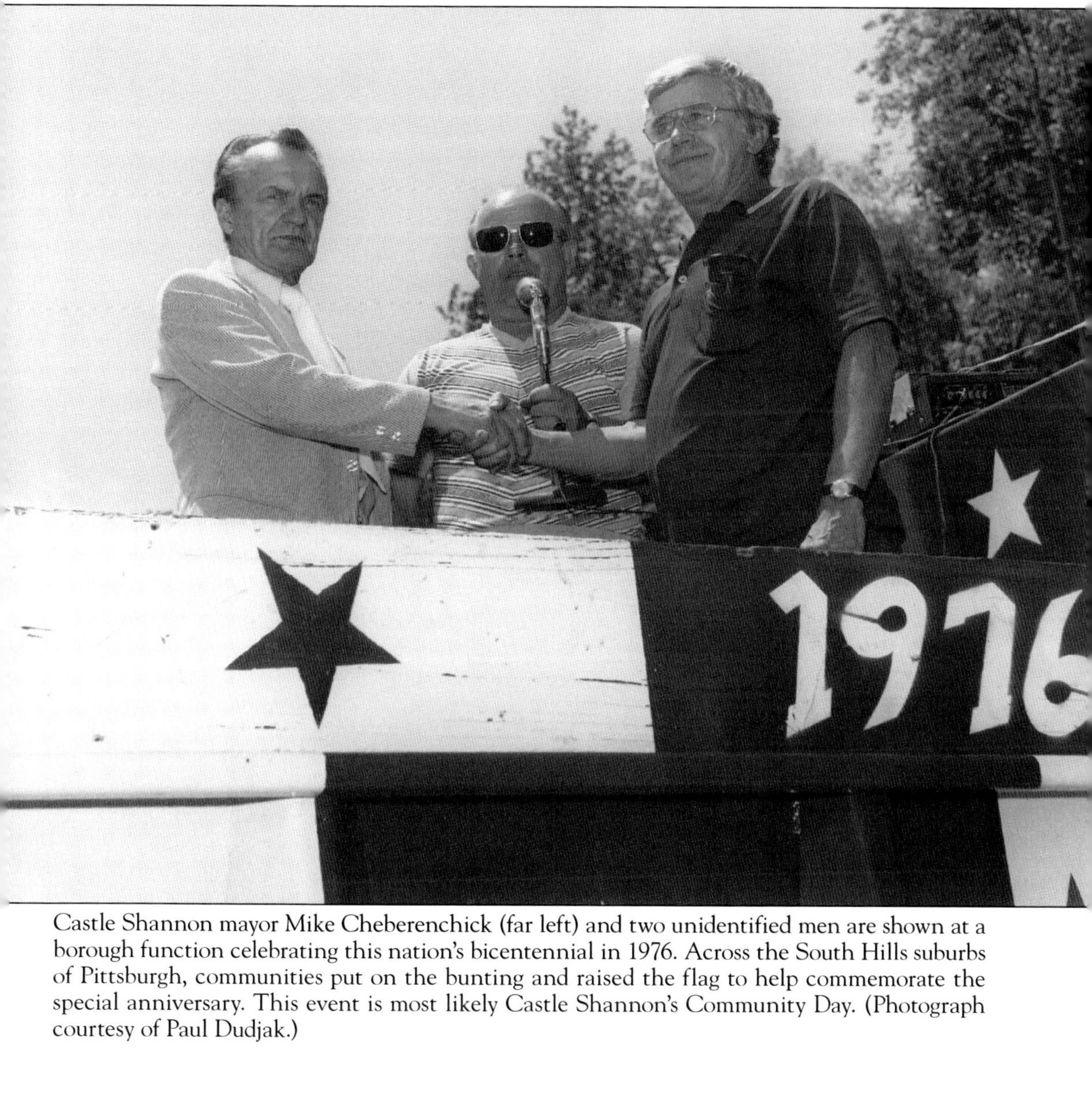

Castle Shannon mayor Mike Cheberenchick (far left) and two unidentified men are shown at a borough function celebrating this nation's bicentennial in 1976. Across the South Hills suburbs of Pittsburgh, communities put on the bunting and raised the flag to help commemorate the special anniversary. This event is most likely Castle Shannon's Community Day. (Photograph courtesy of Paul Dudjak.)

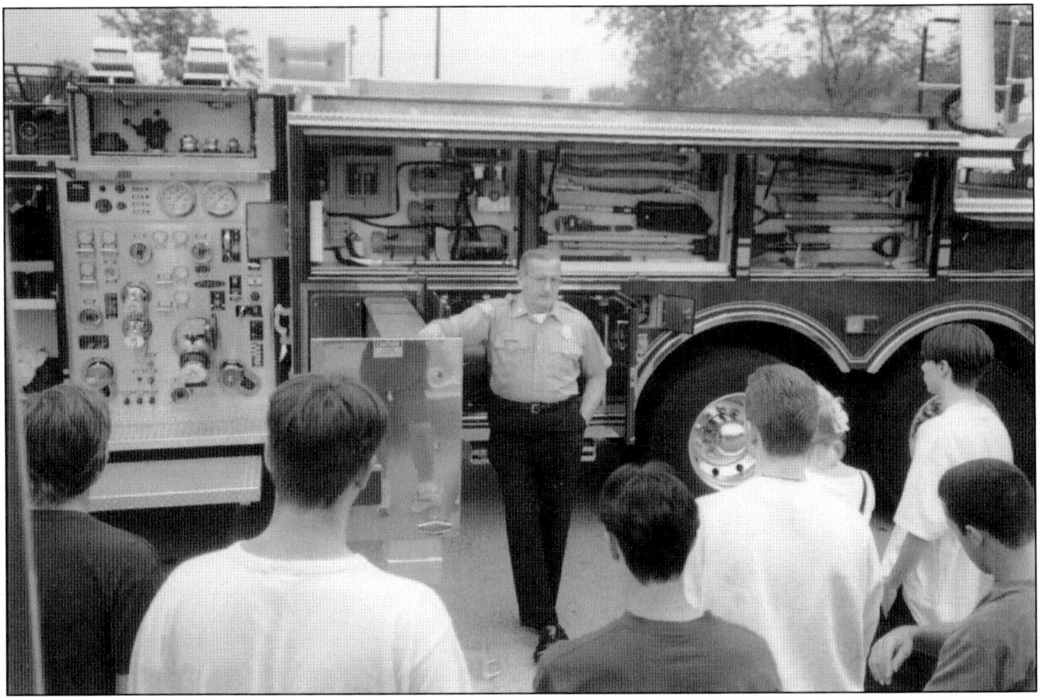

Castle Shannon Volunteer Fire Department chief Jim O'Brien addresses a group of young people about firefighting and fire safety while standing in front of one of Castle Shannon's trucks. O'Brien joined the force in 1966 and became chief in 1976. He is now a life member of the Castle Shannon Volunteer Fire Department. (Photograph courtesy of Castle Shannon Volunteer Fire Department.)

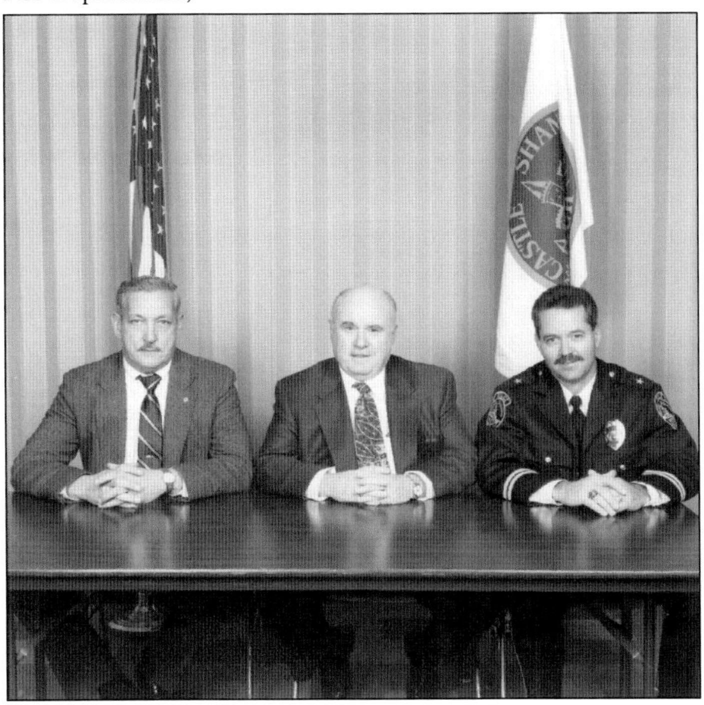

This 1980s photograph at the Castle Shannon Municipal Center shows, from left to right, Fire Chief Jim O'Brien, Mayor Tom O'Malley, and Police Chief Harold Lane. When Castle Shannon moved its municipal building into the refurbished former Highland Elementary School, the mayor's office was relocated as well. (Photograph courtesy of Jean O'Malley.)

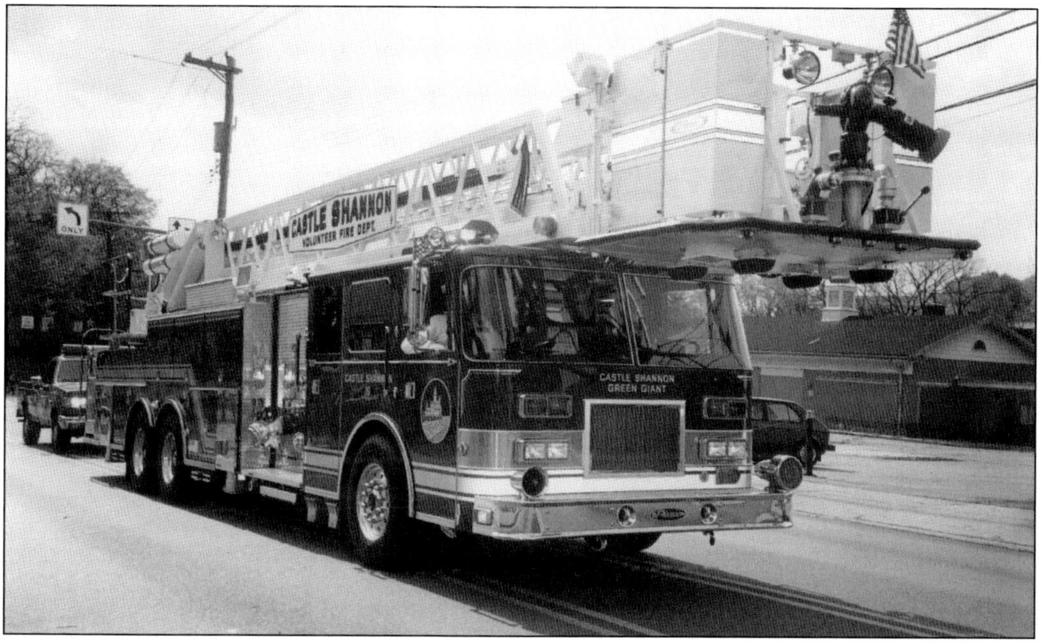

Pictured here is the Castle Shannon Volunteer Fire Department's Green Giant truck. This is the second truck to bear that name. The first was purchased in 1969. One of the unique features of the Green Giant is its 90-foot aerial platform. It also has a 1,000-gallon-per-minute pump. Many aerial trucks did not have pumps at the time. (Photograph courtesy of Mary Scabilloni.)

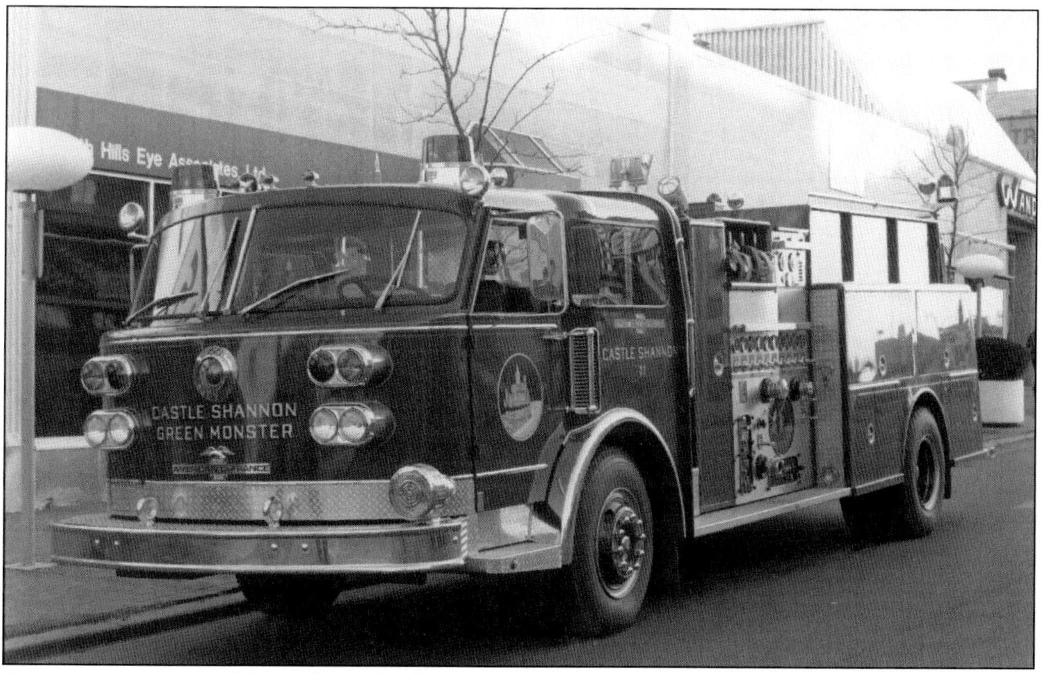

Another in the proud line of Castle Shannon Volunteer Fire Department engines is the Green Monster. Unique to Castle Shannon, and in keeping with its Irish "Shannon" heritage, all of Castle Shannon's fire trucks are green, not the traditional red or yellow that most fire companies in the United States use. (Photograph courtesy of the Castle Shannon Volunteer Fire Department.)

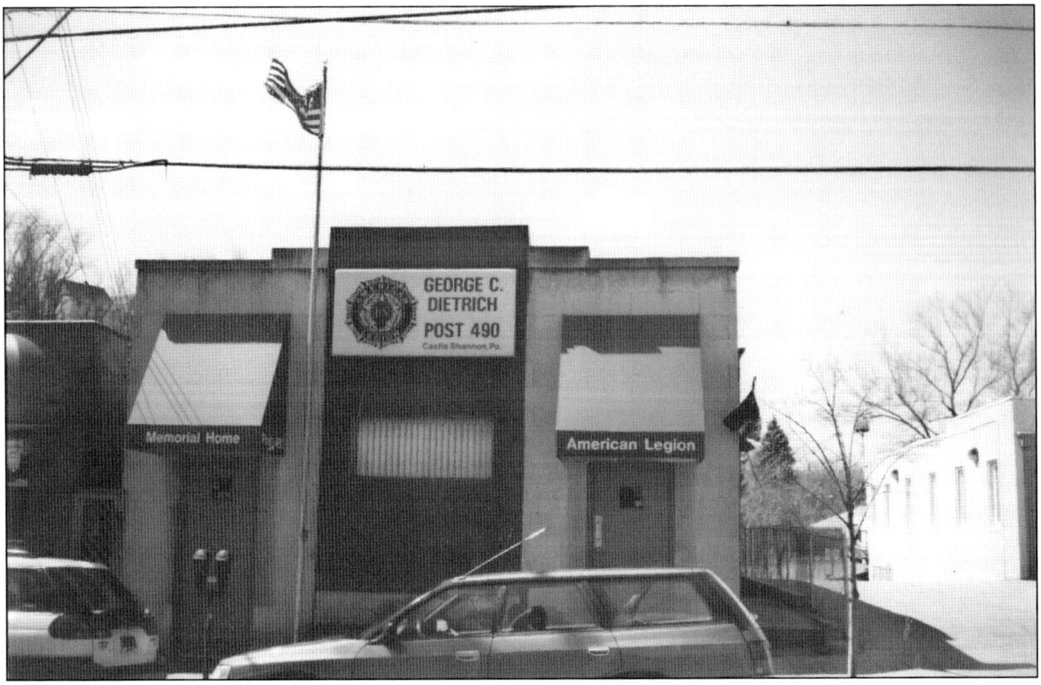

Castle Shannon's American Legion Post 490 was established in April 1930. Its current home on Castle Shannon Boulevard was built in 1949. The post is named for George C. Dietrich (1896–1988), a World War I veteran who organized the American Legion for Castle Shannon. (Photograph courtesy of Mary Scabilloni.)

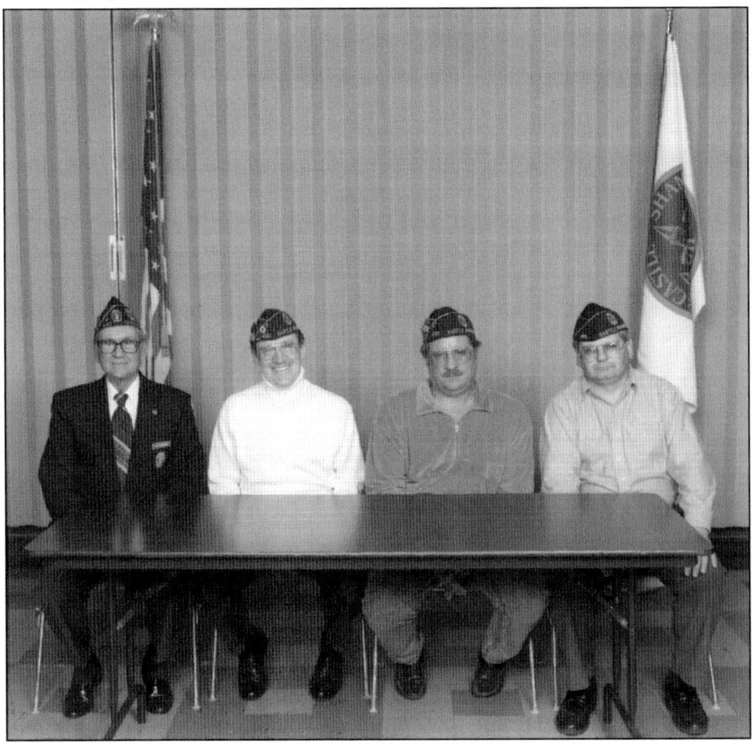

Officers from Castle Shannon's American Legion Post 490 pose for this photograph at the time of Castle Shannon's 75th anniversary celebration in 1994. Shown from left to right are Dan Guerieri, chaplain; Tim Murray, senior vice commandeer; Al Dunn, commandeer; and John Vales, junior vice commander. (Photograph courtesy of Jean O'Malley.)

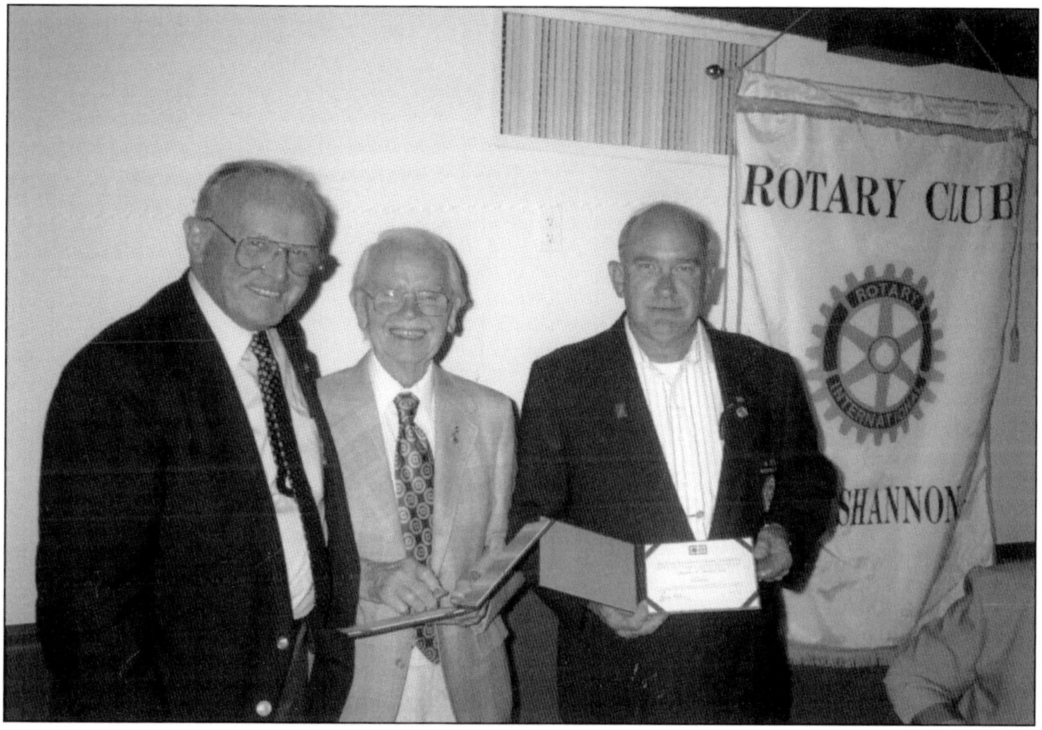

The Castle Shannon Rotary Club was organized in 1943. It later merged with the organizations from neighboring Mt. Lebanon and Dormont. For many years, the group held its meetings at Castle Shannon's Methodist church. Seen in this photograph are officers Mac McDonald (left), Bill Phillips (center), and Chuck McGervey. (Photograph courtesy of Jean O'Malley.)

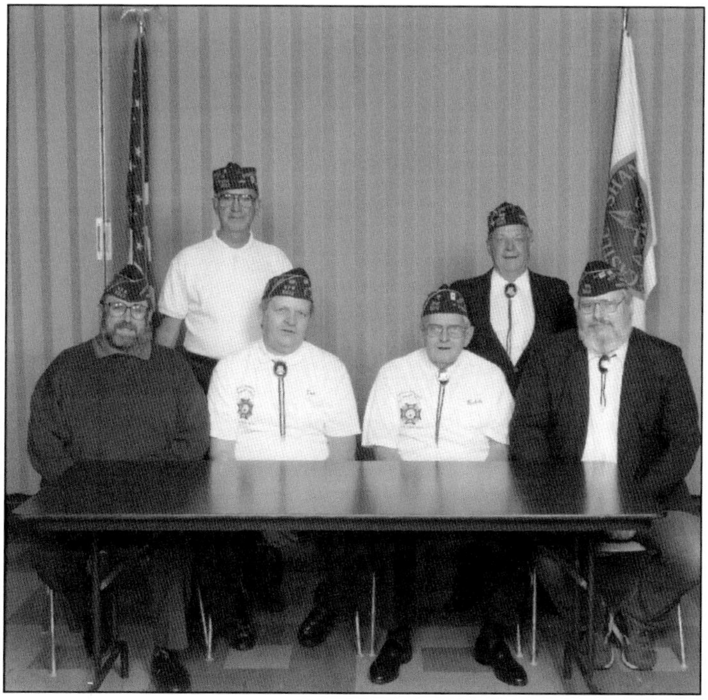

Castle Shannon's branch of the Veterans of Foreign Wars, Post 5012, was established in 1946 by Elmer Zeiler. The group was famous for its outstanding rifle squad. Shown in this mid-1990s photograph are, from left to right, the following officers: (seated) adjutant Dennis McCarthy, senior vice president Tom Clibbens, commandeer Tom O'Donnell, and junior vice president Jim Daube; (standing) quartermaster Vince Davare and chaplain George Oehling. (Photograph courtesy of Jean O'Malley.)

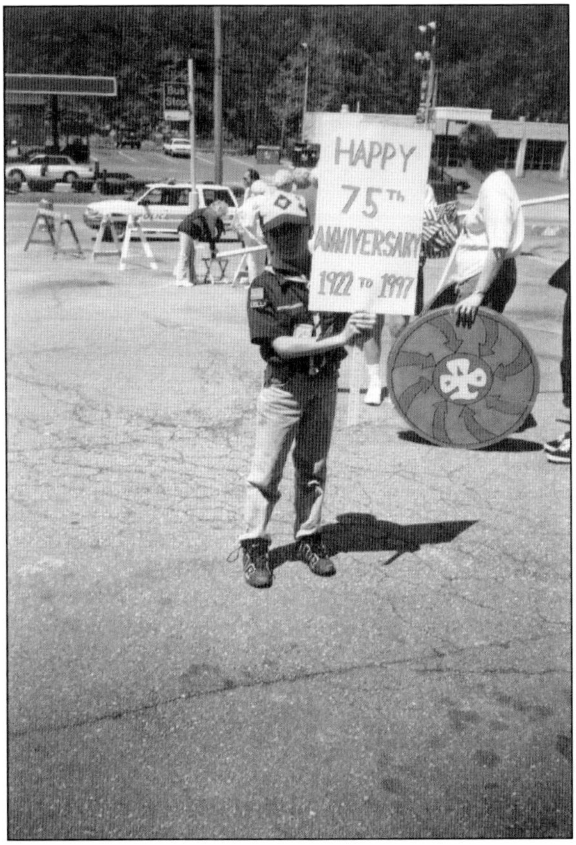

An unidentified Castle Shannon Boy Scout offers his appreciation to the Castle Shannon Volunteer Fire Department on the occasion of its 75th anniversary. The community as a whole showed its support across the two-day celebration on May 17 and 18, 1997. This photograph was taken in the parking lot of the firehouse on Route 88. (Photograph courtesy of Mary Scabilloni.)

The Castle Shannon Volunteer Fire Department marches along Route 88 in the direction of the firehouse in May 1997 as part of its 75th anniversary celebration. Marching to the left side of the group is Jim O'Brien. In the background, behind the telephone pole, is Martin Auto Gallery. Signs along the street advertise the wares of John McGinnis and Company. (Photograph by Mary Scabilloni.)

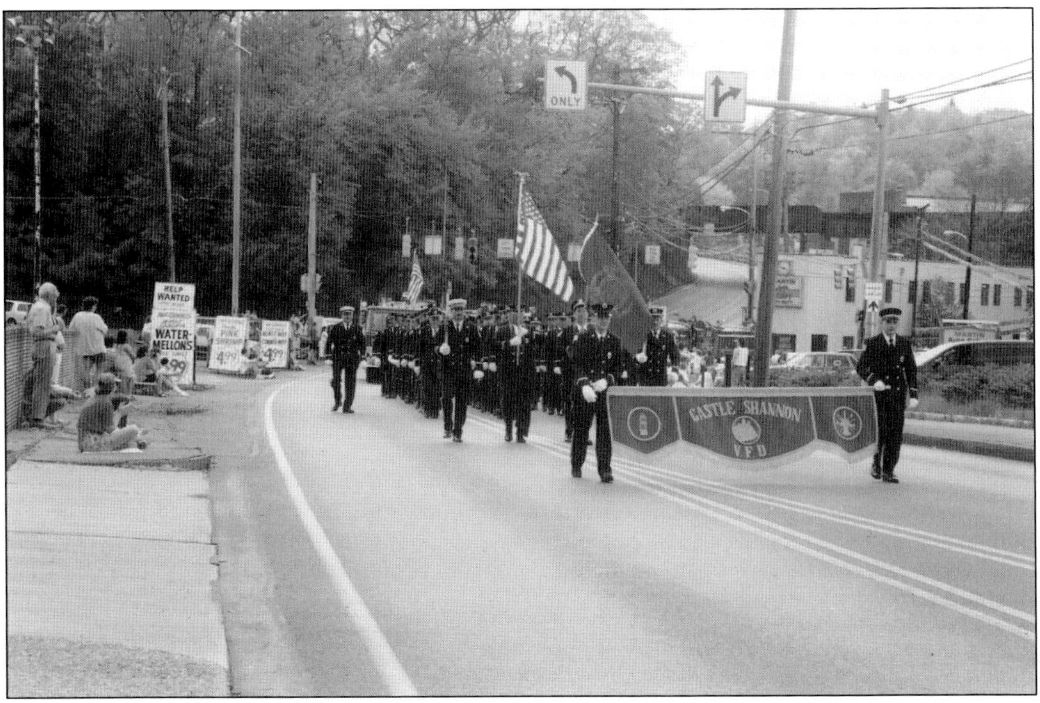

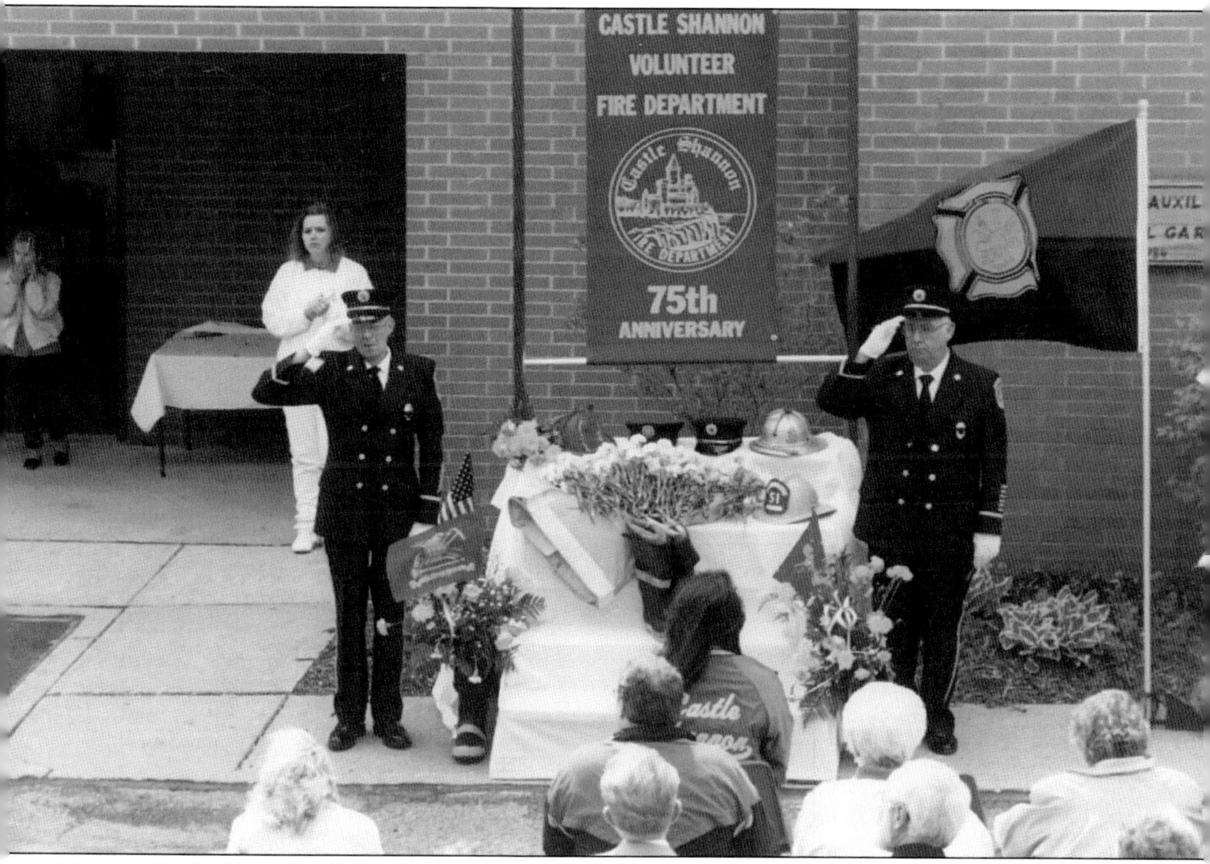

Veteran Castle Shannon Volunteer Fire Department fireman Sam Provost (left) and an unidentified fireman salute during the ceremony honoring the fire department's 75 years of service. The event was staged over the weekend of May 17 and 18, 1997, and included a parade down Route 88 that featured convertibles carrying local community and business leaders. The fire department, which receives no financial aid of any type, is completely self-sufficient. Its annual summer carnival, which starts on the last Monday in July, is one of the most popular events in Castle Shannon. The fire department also hosts bingo games on Tuesday evenings as well as themed parties for its membership. Firemen must be residents of Castle Shannon and at least 18 years of age, but they do not have to be property owners. All members undergo extensive classroom and on-site firefighting training sessions. (Photograph courtesy of Castle Shannon Volunteer Fire Department.)

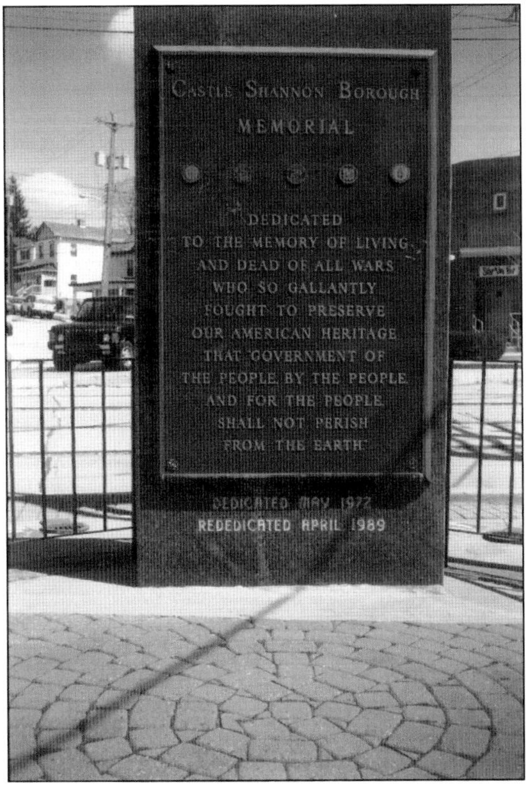

The Castle Shannon Borough Memorial, first dedicated in May 1972, was located behind the old borough building. When that building was removed, the memorial was shifted not too far away, to a more central location in the center of town. The plaque reads: "Dedicated to the memory of living and dead of all wars who so gallantly fought to preserve our American heritage that 'government of the people, by the people, and for the people, shall not perish from the Earth.'" (Photograph by Mary Scabilloni.)

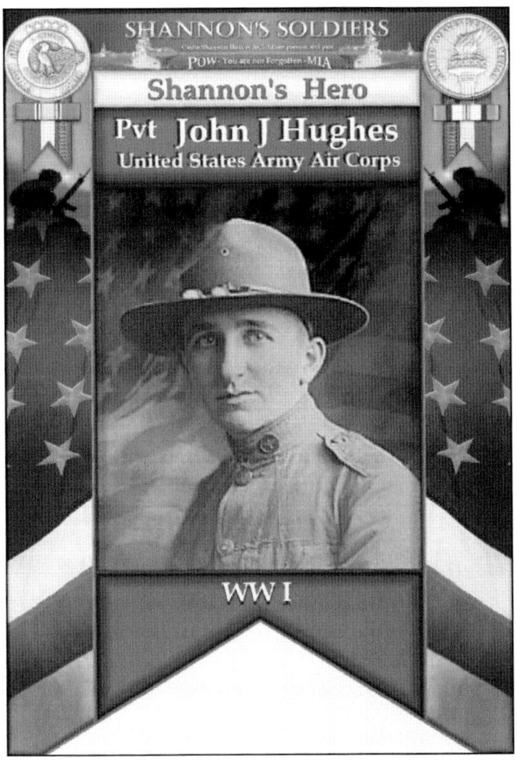

Castle Shannon's John J. Hughes appears on one of the banners along Willow Avenue and Castle Shannon Boulevard honoring war veterans who came from the borough. A World War I veteran, Private Hughes served in the United States Army Air Corps's 9th Division. (Photograph courtesy of Castle Shannon Revitalization Corporation.)

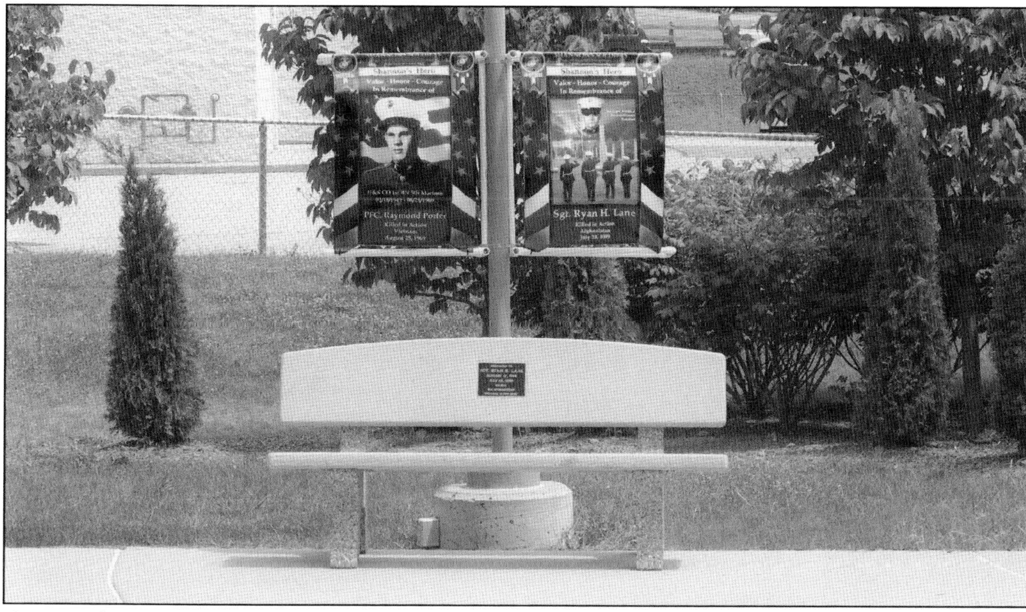

A special set of memorial banners was made for two of Castle Shannon's most heroic sons—Marine Pfc. Raymond Porter (left) and Marine Sgt. Ryan Lane (right). A Keystone Oaks High School graduate, Porter had served less than two years in Vietnam when he was killed at the age of 20 during a mortar attack in Quang Nam on August 25, 1969. Lane, the son of former Castle Shannon police chief Harold Lane, also graduated from Keystone Oaks. He died July 23, 2009, in the Helmand province of Afghanistan of wounds sustained while supporting combat operations. (Photograph courtesy of Castle Shannon Revitalization Corporation.)

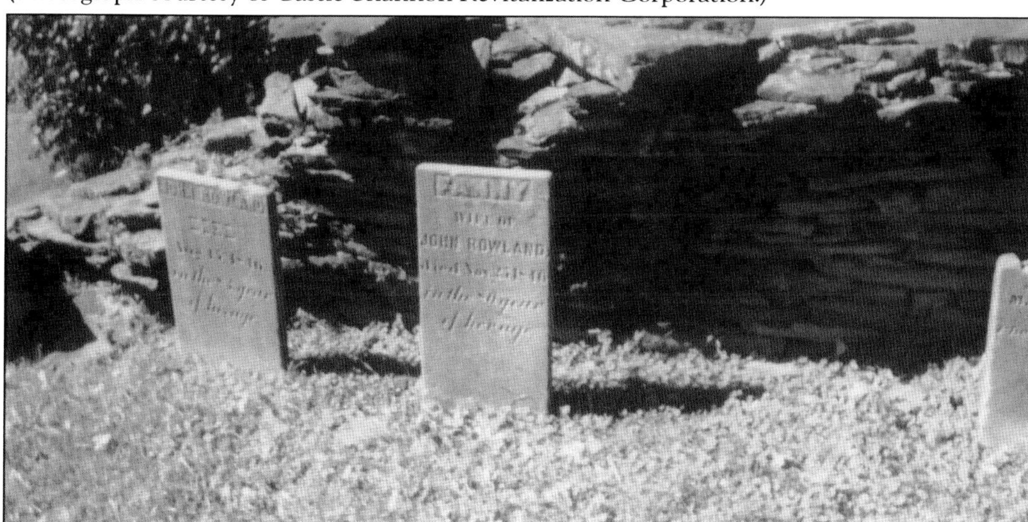

The oldest graves in Castle Shannon have no particular military connection, but they do remain a little-known Castle Shannon oddity. The Rowland graves are located behind Castle Shannon Auto Body on Castle Shannon Boulevard. The stones date back to the 1840s. The date of death for John Rowland reads November 25, 1846. The graves are most visible by looking over the hill along the first-base line from the far baseball diamond at O'Malley Field at Myrtle School. (Photograph courtesy of Mary Scabilloni.)

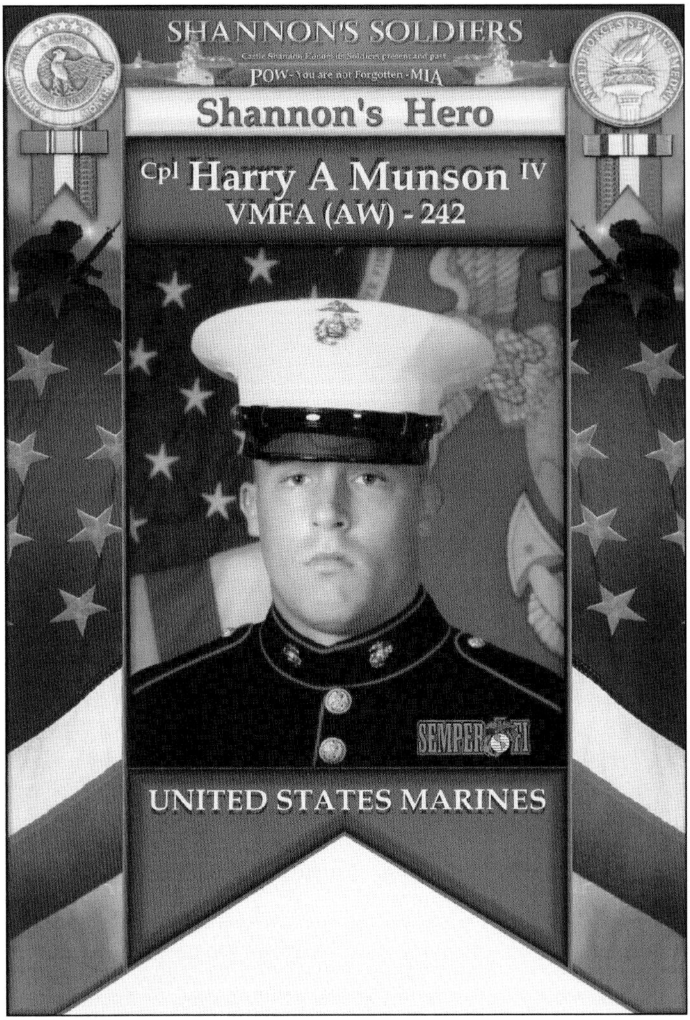

Lt. Cpl. Harry Munson IV, United States Marine Corps, is another Castle Shannon soldier honored by the borough as part of the Revitalization Corporation's "Shannon's Hero" program. He has been stationed in Japan. (Photograph courtesy of Castle Shannon Revitalization Corporation.)

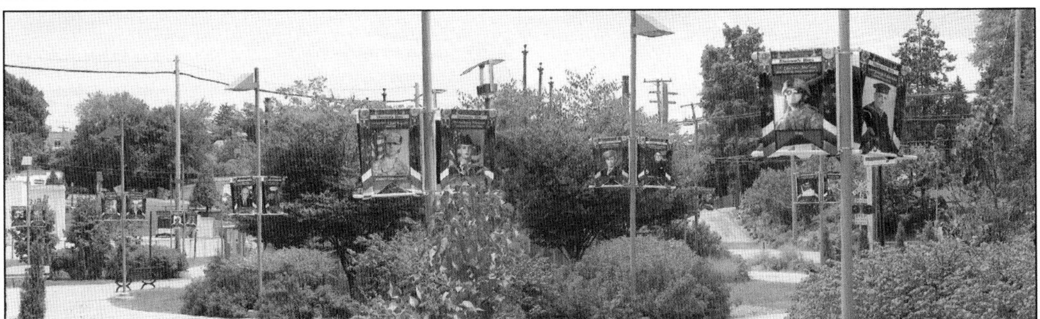

One of the first projects undertaken by the Castle Shannon Revitalization Corporation, established in 2009, was to construct a lasting tribute to the soldiers from Castle Shannon who had served their country in wars. Each memorial banner is devoted to an individual service member. The Revitalization Corporation's effort has been written up by the Veterans Administration and has received other accolades of appreciation. (Photograph courtesy of Castle Shannon Revitalization Corporation.)

Cpl. Sam Sciullo, United States Army, served three years during World War II. Attached to the military government, he spent time in London, Paris, and Berlin. After returning from the war, he graduated from the University of Pittsburgh and went to Pitt's law school on the GI Bill. He practiced law for 52 years, with offices in Castle Shannon and downtown Pittsburgh, and was a Castle Shannon councilman, fireman, and Rotarian. (Photograph courtesy of Castle Shannon Revitalization Corporation.)

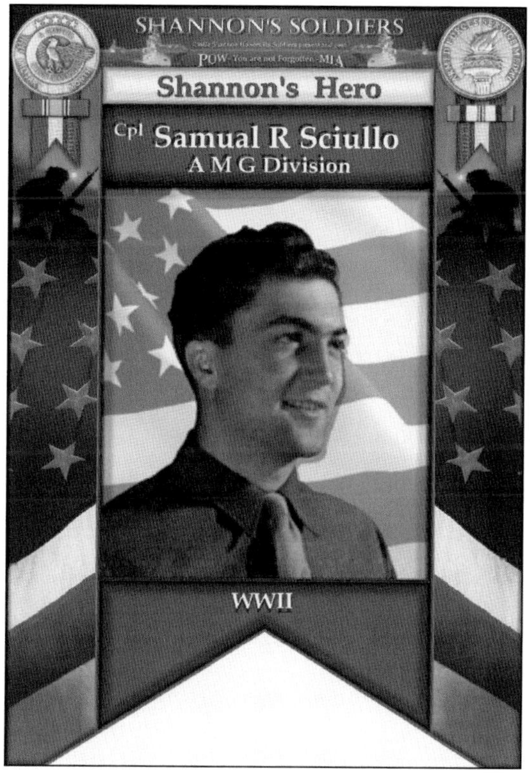

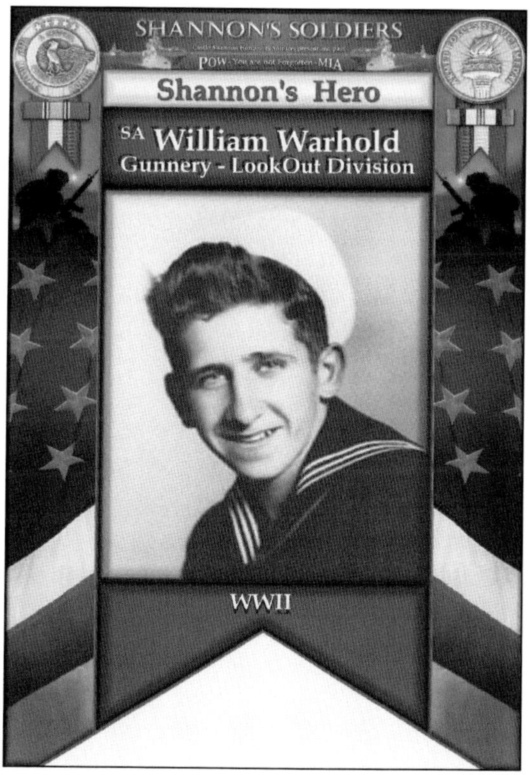

William Warhold served on the USS *Sangamon* (CVE-26), Air Group 26.33.37. The ship was commissioned on August 25, 1942, and decommissioned on October 24, 1945. It later received the Presidential Unit Citation. A lookout, Warhold received the Purple Heart when a Japanese kamikaze pilot crashed into the ship. Warhold later worked in sales and servicing for reproducing equipment. He also managed the Elks Club in Bethel Park for 20 years. (Photograph courtesy of Castle Shannon Revitalization Corporation.)

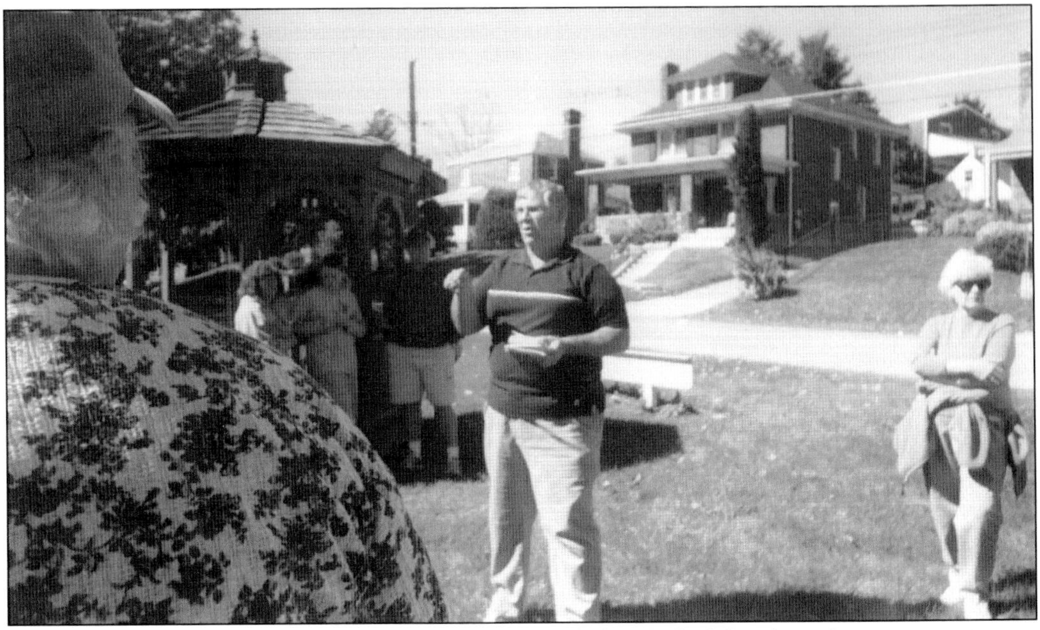

Paul Dudjak, a retired letter carrier and Keystone Oaks High School graduate, is passionate about Castle Shannon history. He maintains a thorough collection of articles and photographs chronicling the borough's history at the Community Library. In the fall of 2004, Dudjak conducted a walking tour of Castle Shannon. (Photograph courtesy of Mary Scabilloni.)

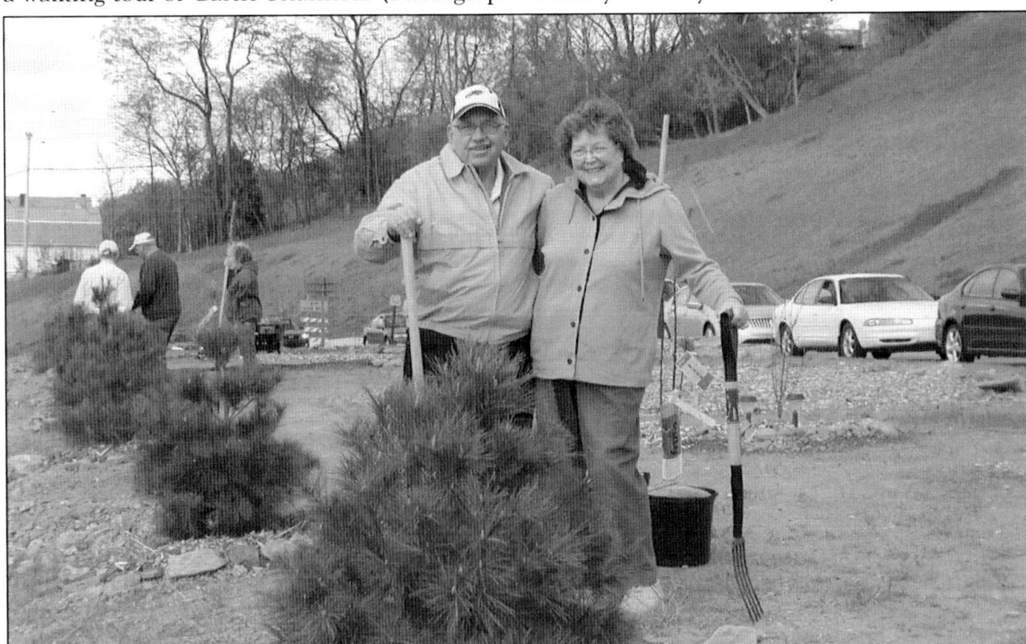

Mayor Donald Baumgarten and his wife, Ruth, have shovels in hand at a tree-planting event in Castle Shannon. Baumgarten has served the borough as auditor, councilman, president of council, and, currently, mayor. He also sponsors a booth at the annual St. Anne Parish Fair held each June on the St. Anne School grounds. (Photograph courtesy of Castle Shannon Revitalization Corporation.)

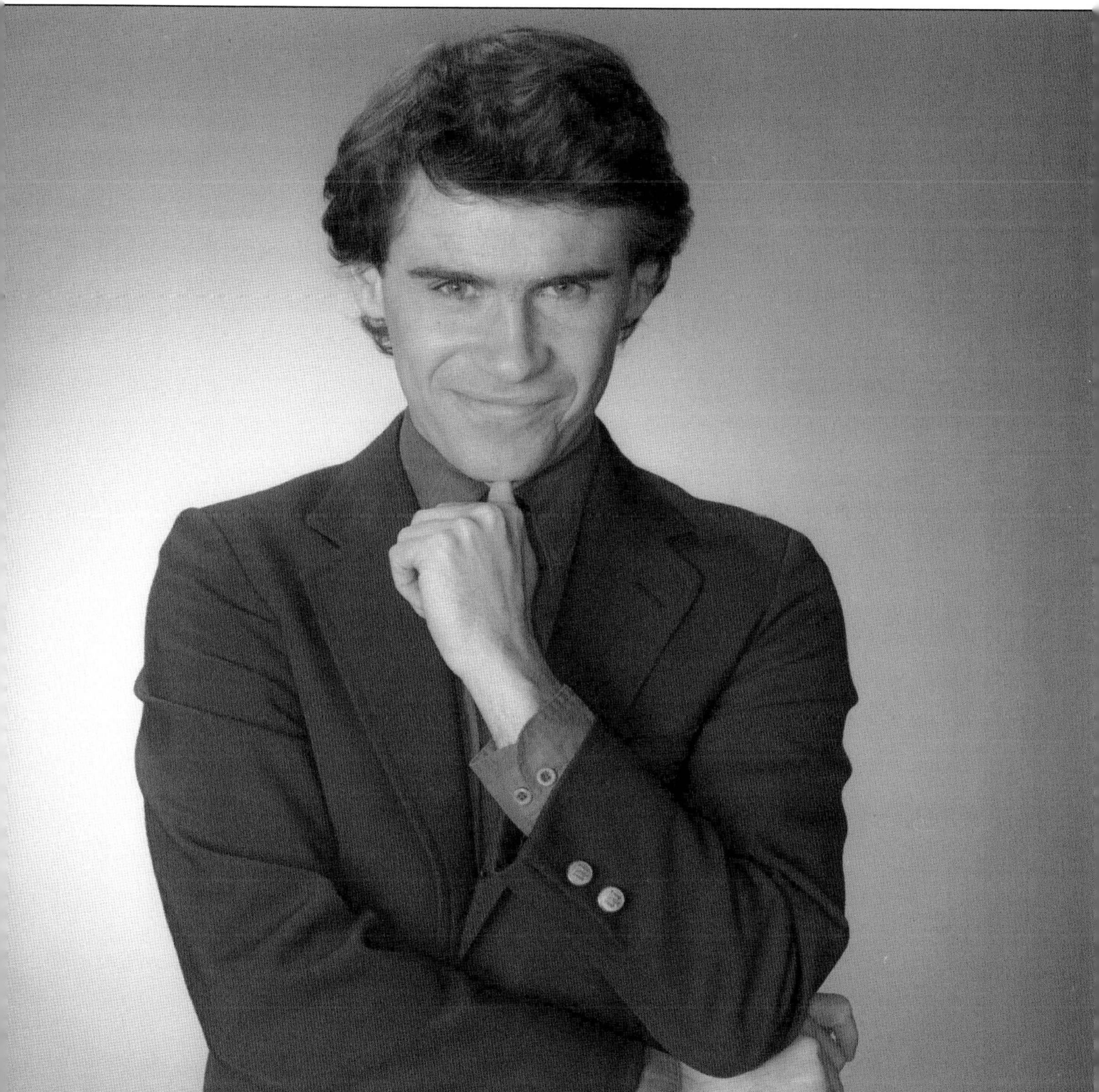

Before Dennis Miller was Dennis Miller, he was spending part of his teenage years working behind the counter at the old Village Dairy in the Lebanon Shops on Mt. Lebanon Boulevard. Miller was born November 3, 1953, in Pittsburgh and grew up in Castle Shannon. He graduated from Keystone Oaks High School in 1971. With a major in journalism, he graduated from what was then called Point Park College in 1976. He got an early introduction to the television business when he hosted a show on KDKA Channel 2 titled *The Trolley Show*, a program aimed at teenagers. He also did funny essays for Channel 2's more serious evening news program, *Evening Magazine*. Miller joined the cast of NBC's *Saturday Night Live* in the mid-1980s, and his professional career skyrocketed from there. He hosted *The Dennis Miller Show* on HBO in 1992, then *Dennis Miller Live* from 1994 to 2002. He was part of ABC's *Monday Night Football* broadcast crew from 2000 to 2001. He has since appeared in a number of films and HBO specials. (Photograph by Ric Evans.)

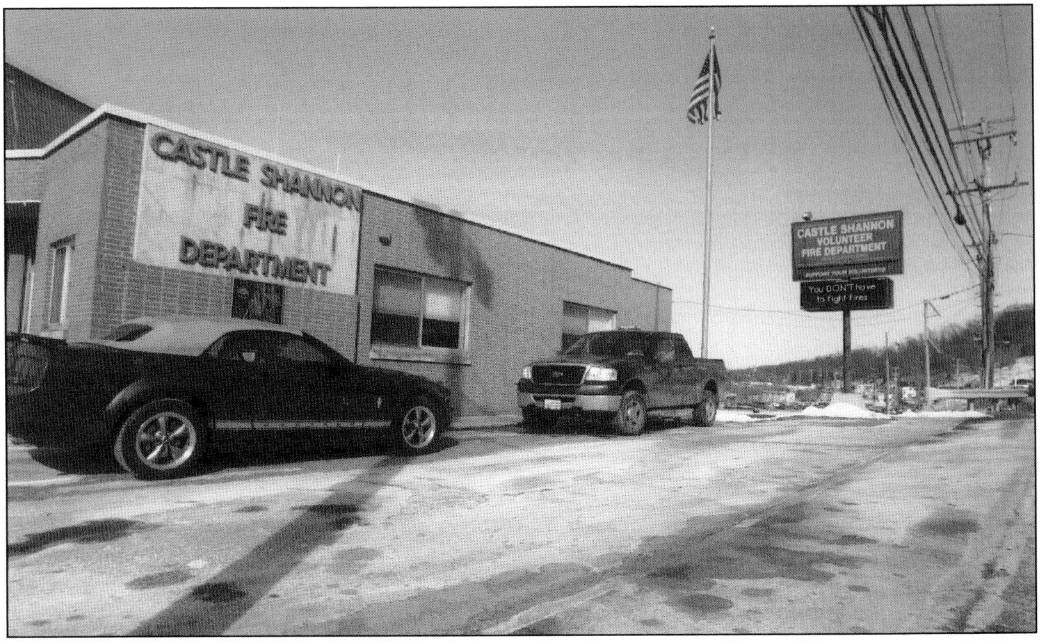

The Castle Shannon Volunteer Fire Department headquarters on Route 88 was a natural place for the organization to build when it looked to abandon its former house on Park Avenue. The current building is adjacent to where the old Hamilton School building stood and is right next to Memorial Hall, which hosts many events sponsored by the fire department. (Photograph by Charles LeClaire.)

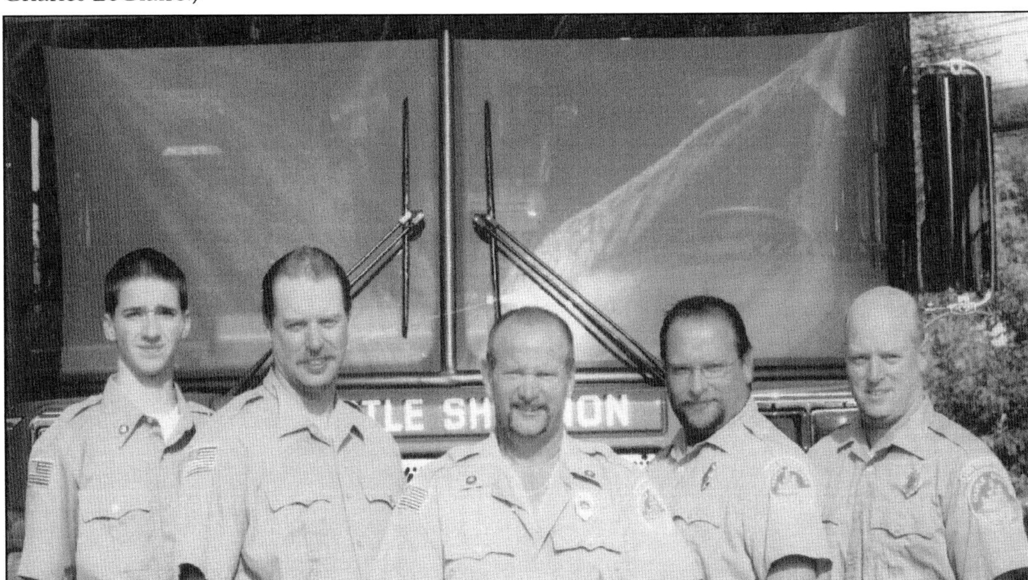

Joining the Castle Shannon Volunteer Fire Department is a family tradition for the Brannons. Pictured are, from left to right, Patrick Brannon, Shawn Brannon, Kevin Brannon, Keith Brannon, and Brian Brannon. Four other members of the family—Ed Brannon, John Brannon, Charles Brannon, and Ed Brannon—plus extended family members Joe Baldauf and James McMonagle, also were members of the department. (Photograph courtesy of Kevin Brannon.)

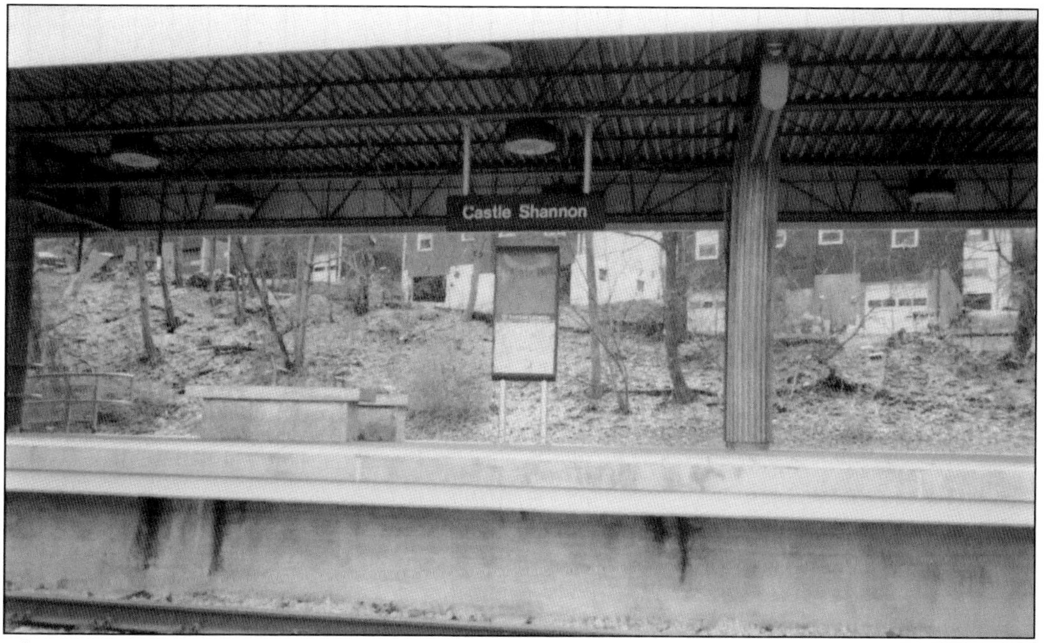

The Castle Shannon trolley stop is used daily by hundreds of workers commuting between their home neighborhoods, downtown Pittsburgh, and points in between. This stop is situated next to a large Port Authority parking lot. The residential area behind the platform shows the back ends of several of the duplexes that line that street. (Photograph by Mary Scabilloni.)

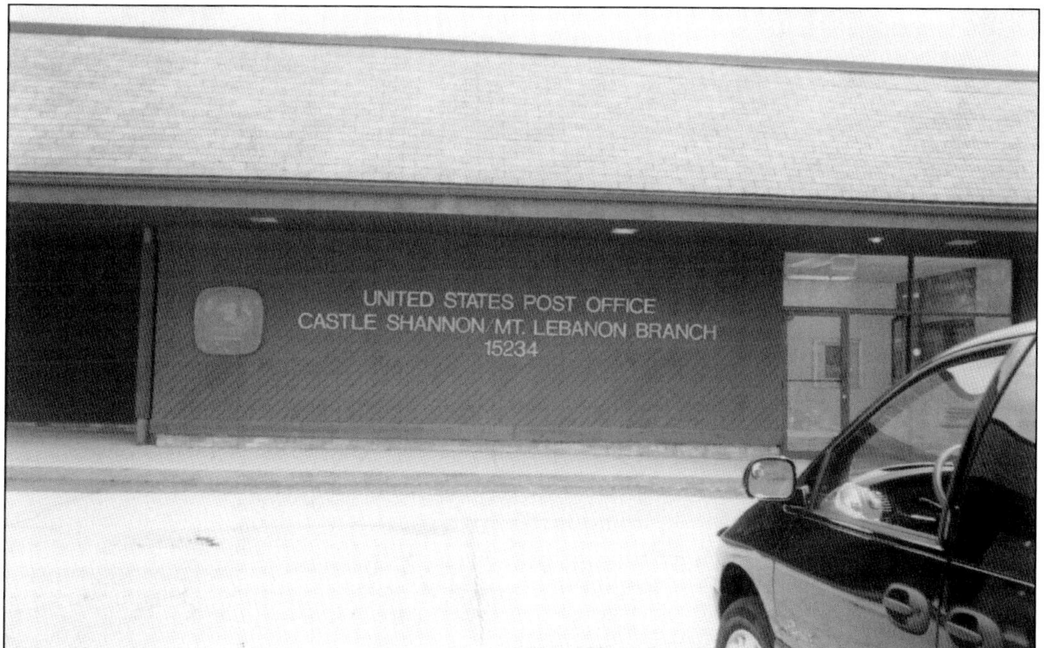

This photograph shows the Castle Shannon/Mt. Lebanon Branch United States Post Office, located at 370 Castle Shannon Boulevard. Castle Shannon originally had its own branch office on Willow Avenue, and Mt. Lebanon had its own on Washington Road, before the neighboring towns merged their post offices into one in August 1983. (Photograph by Mary Scabilloni.)

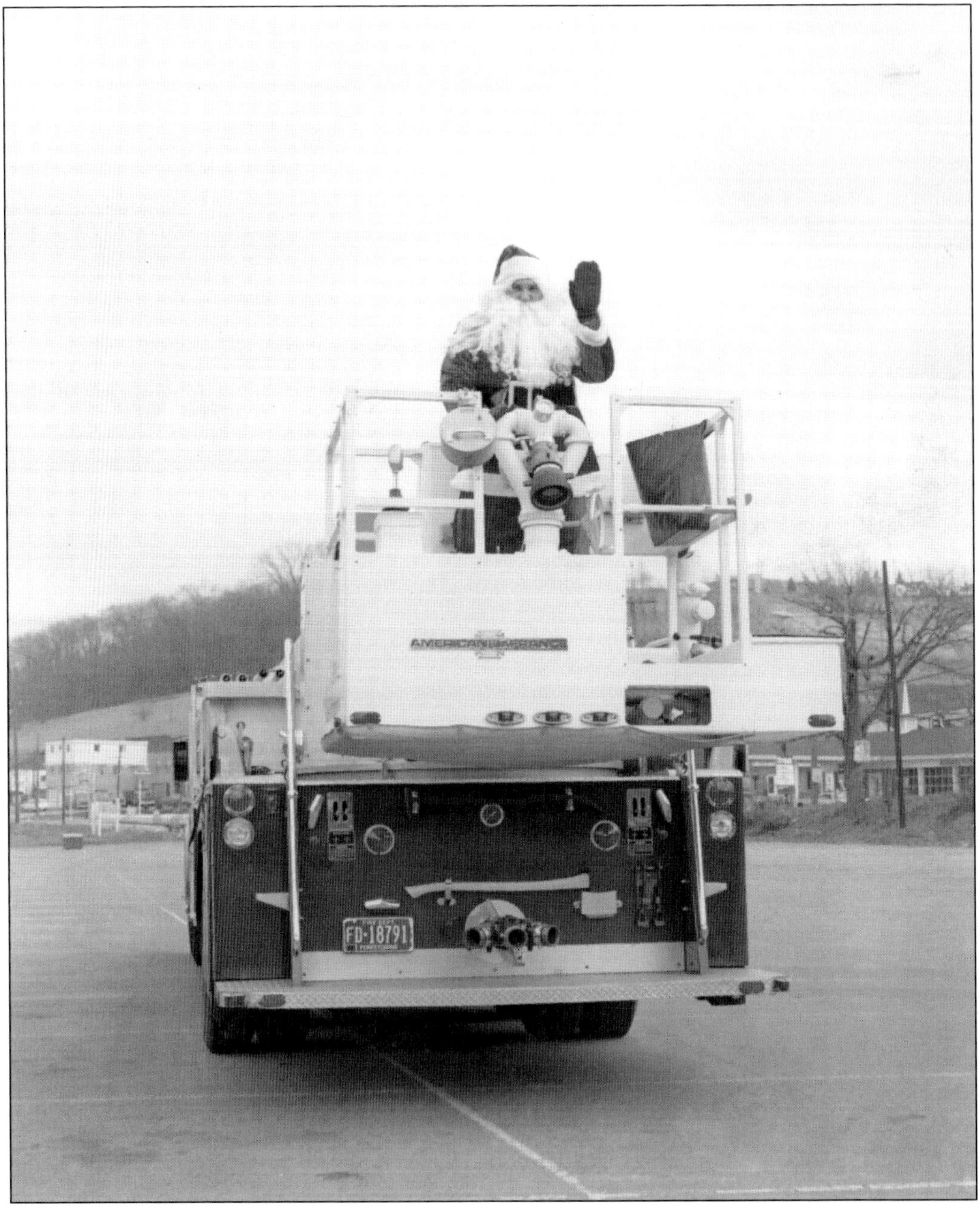

One of the highlights of the Castle Shannon holiday season is when Santa Claus makes his annual run through the borough on the Sunday before Christmas. Armed with a bullhorn and transported by one of the Castle Shannon Volunteer Fire Department's fire trucks, Santa dispenses holiday greetings and lots of sweets and goodies to local youngsters. (Photograph courtesy of Castle Shannon Volunteer Fire Department.)

Three

Commerce

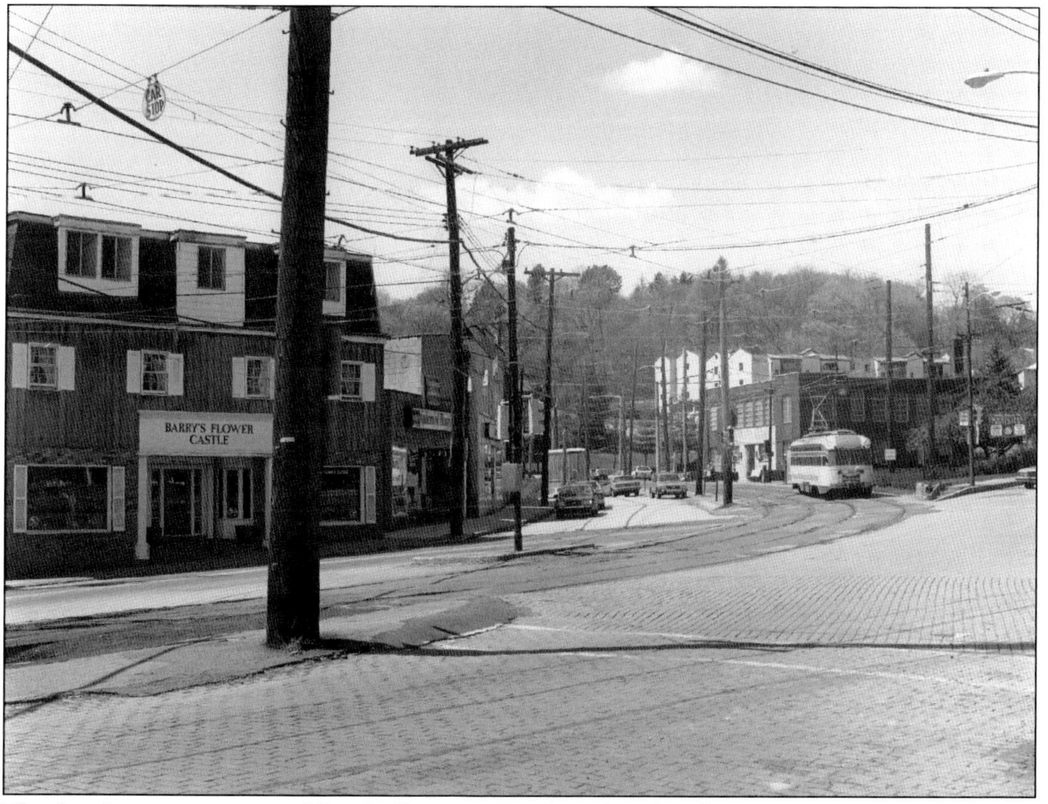

The familiar intersection of Castle Shannon Boulevard and Willow Avenue is depicted in this April 1987 photograph. The trolley car is headed toward the Castle Shannon Municipal Building. The Place SeVille Apartments on Bockstoce Street can be seen above the borough headquarters. At left is Barry's Flower Castle, the last business in the old Castle Shannon Hotel before that building was eventually demolished. (Photograph by George "Jasper" Evans.)

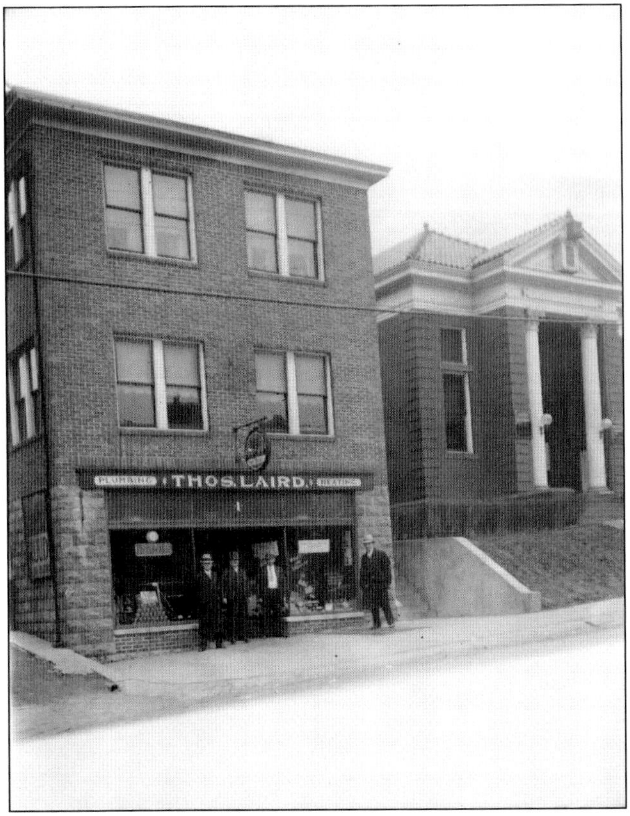

This photograph shows the old Thomas Laird Plumbing and Heating Building on Poplar Street. Laird also did work as a blacksmith. His tombstone in Bethel Cemetery notes his emigration from his native Scotland to Castle Shannon. Next to Laird's building is the bank that was the scene of the infamous 1917 robbery. (Photograph by George "Jasper" Evans, courtesy of Ric Evans.)

Fritz's Market, located on Library Road near Castle Shannon Boulevard, was one of several independently owned and operated grocery stores that existed around Castle Shannon during the first half of the 20th century. Later residents of the borough will remember the Willow Superette, located not too far from where Fritz's business once operated. (Photograph by George "Jasper" Evans, courtesy of Ric Evans.)

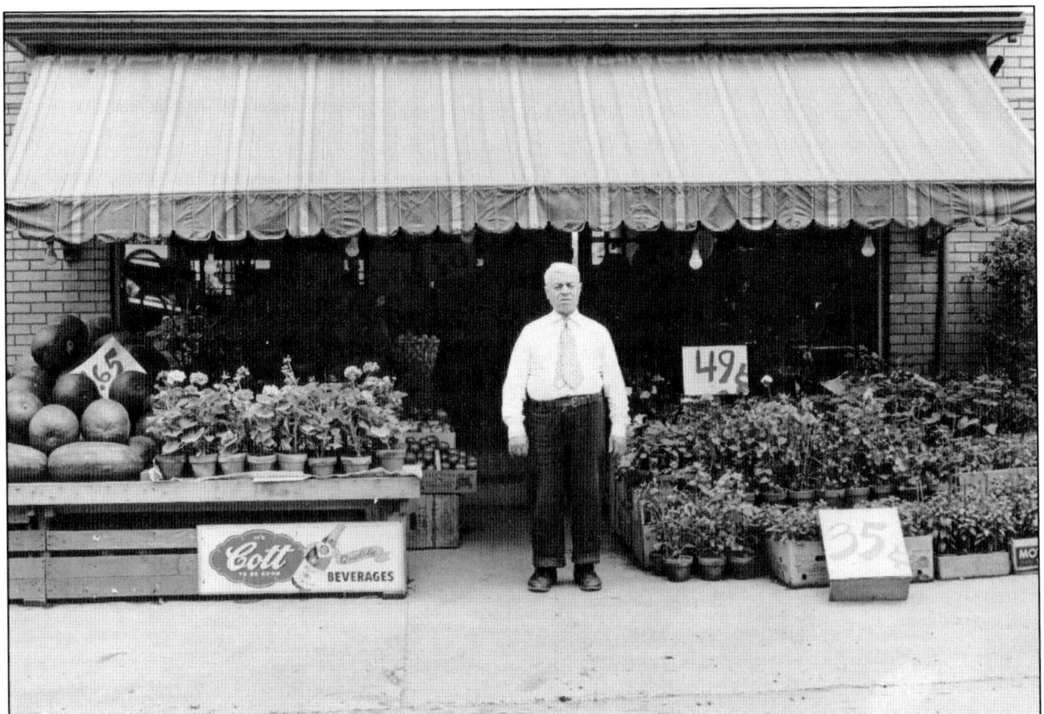

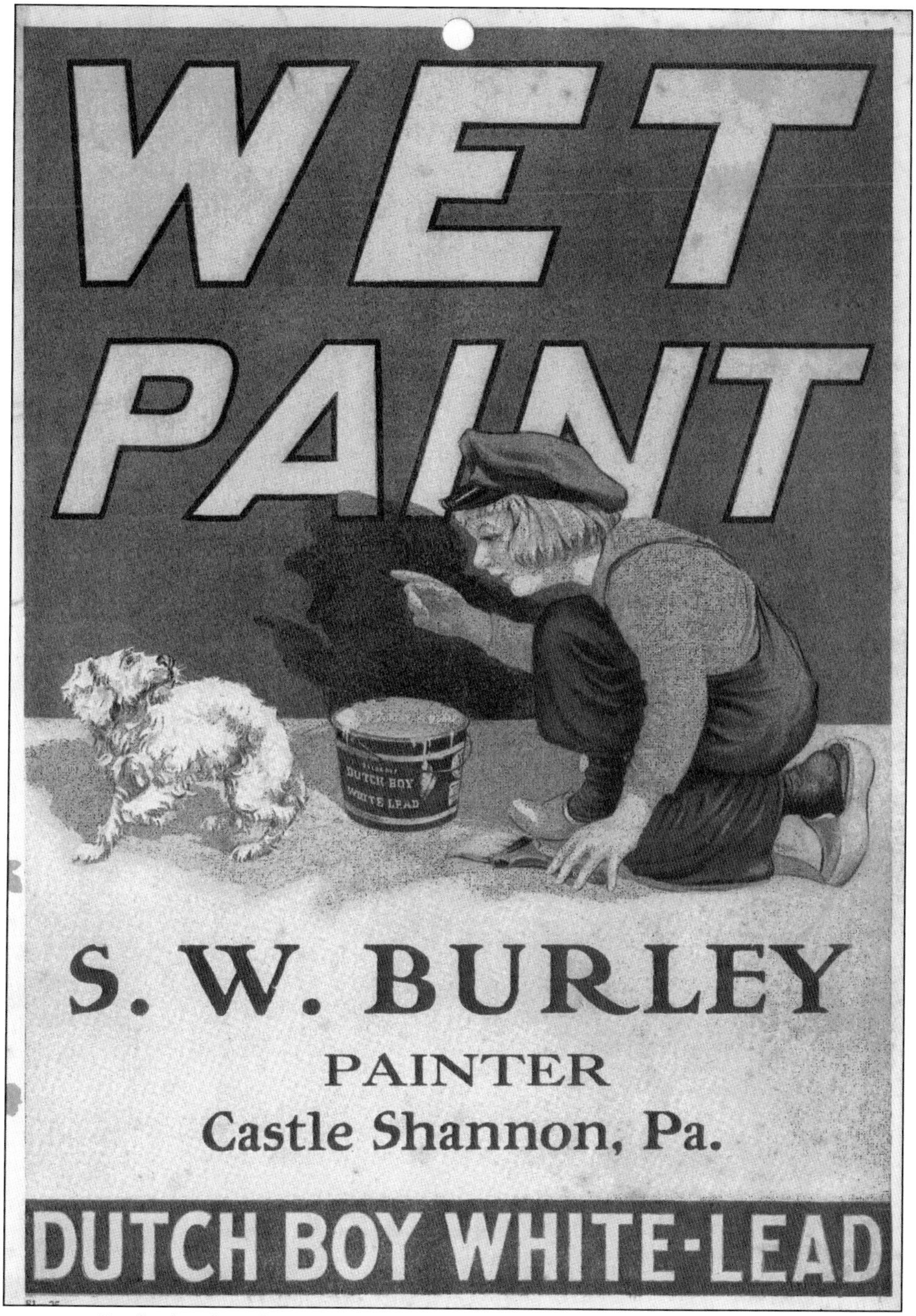

The surname Burley has long been connected with Castle Shannon commerce. Samuel W. Burley was a commercial painter who lived in Castle Shannon in the early 1900s. Another Burley, Jack, was a Castle Shannon contractor. Commercial painting was especially important to Castle Shannon business during its earliest years, as many of the businesses were made of wood. A few relics of the "Wooden Age" can still be seen in parts of Castle Shannon on Willow Avenue. (Photograph courtesy of Paul Fey.)

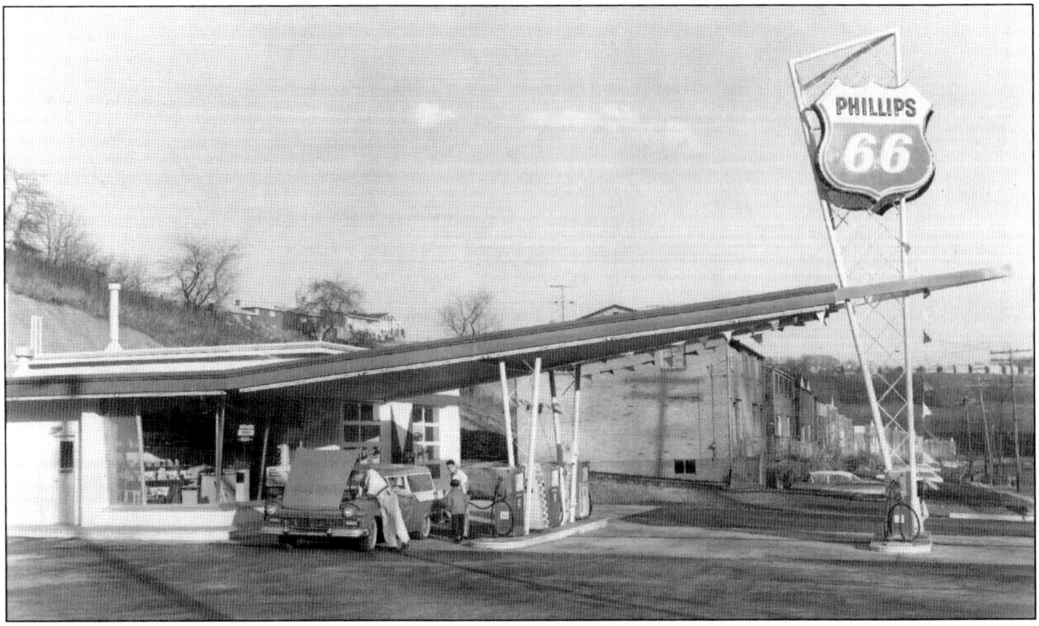

Castle Shannon has always had a reputation for having quite a few bars and gas stations. Shown here in the 1960s is a Phillips 66 service station that was located at the corner of Sleepy Hollow Road and Columbia Street near the Sleepy Hollow Shopping Center. The row of duplexes that lines that street still remains. (Photograph by George "Jasper" Evans, courtesy of Ric Evans.)

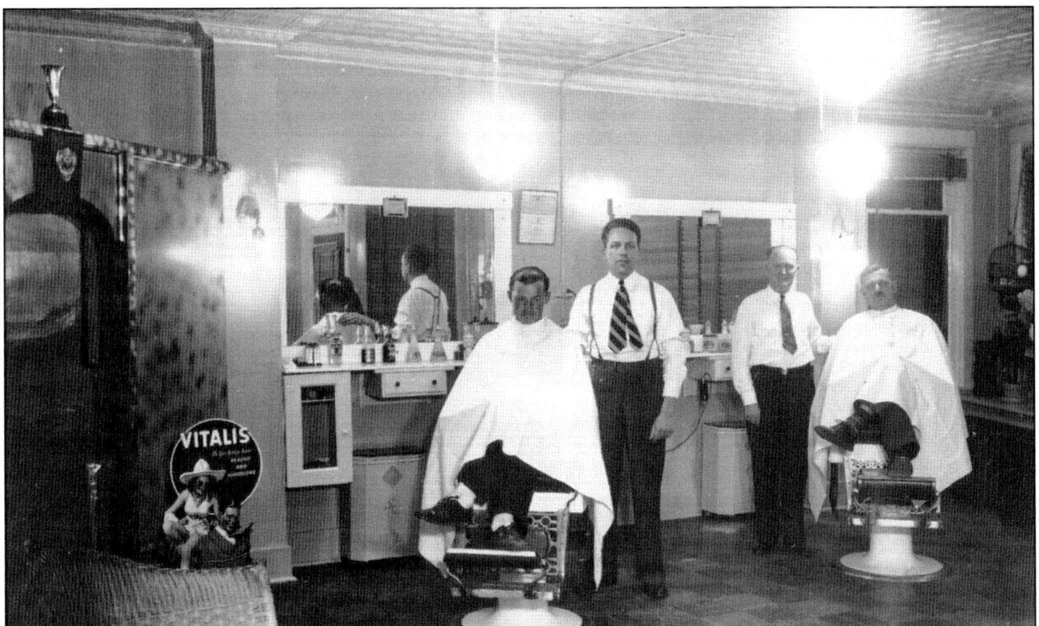

This is the interior of the Willow Avenue Barber Shop. Castle Shannon has had a number of barbershops and beauty parlors over the years, many concentrated in the main business district of Willow Avenue and exclusively privately owned and operated. A husband and wife, Ron and Sue Carpenter, ran hair-service businesses in different parts of the same building for many years. (Photograph by George "Jasper" Evans, courtesy of Ric Evans.)

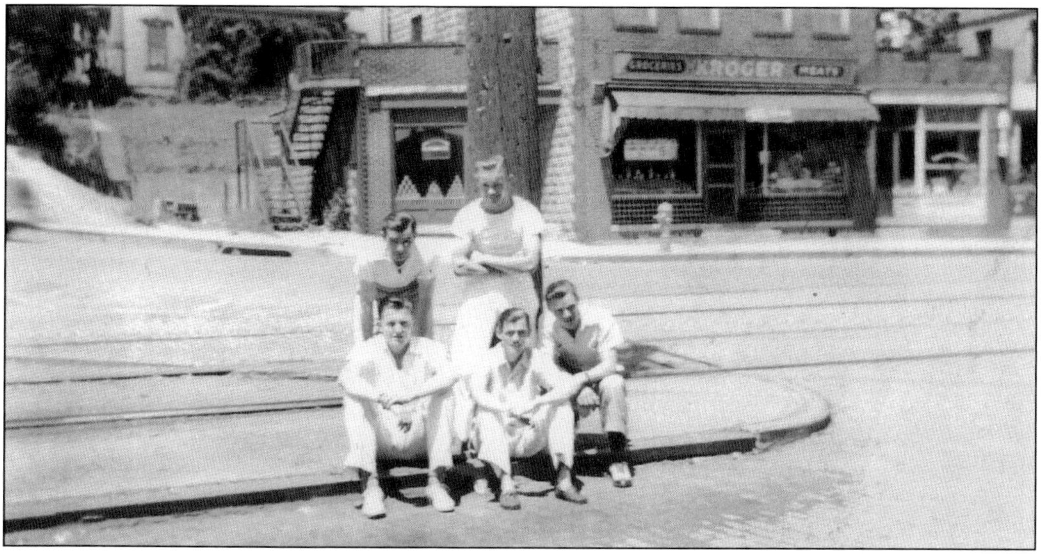

The traffic stop at the corner of Willow Avenue and Castle Shannon Boulevard was a good resting place for these Castle Shannon gentlemen. They are, from left to right, (seated) Frank Beatty, Francis "Slick" Creehan, and Frank Gill; (standing) Regis Creehan and unidentified. In the background is a Kroger grocery store. Kroger later relocated to the far end of the Lebanon Shops Shopping Center. The same building that housed Kroger is seen in the photograph below. It has served many business interests in its lifetime. Here, it is Castle Shannon Plumbing and Heating. It was also Troy Campbell's Barber Shop. Castle Shannon resident and attorney Sam Sciullo used the upper level as a night office for more than 50 years. (Above photograph, courtesy of Paul Dudjak; below photograph, courtesy of Paul Fey.)

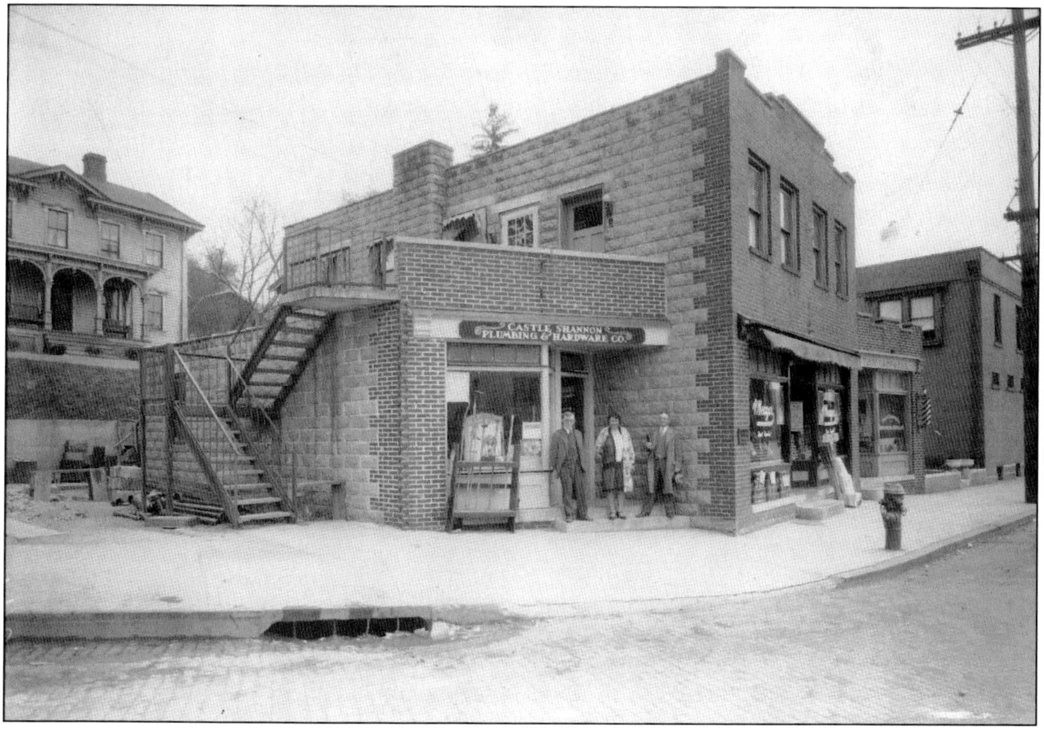

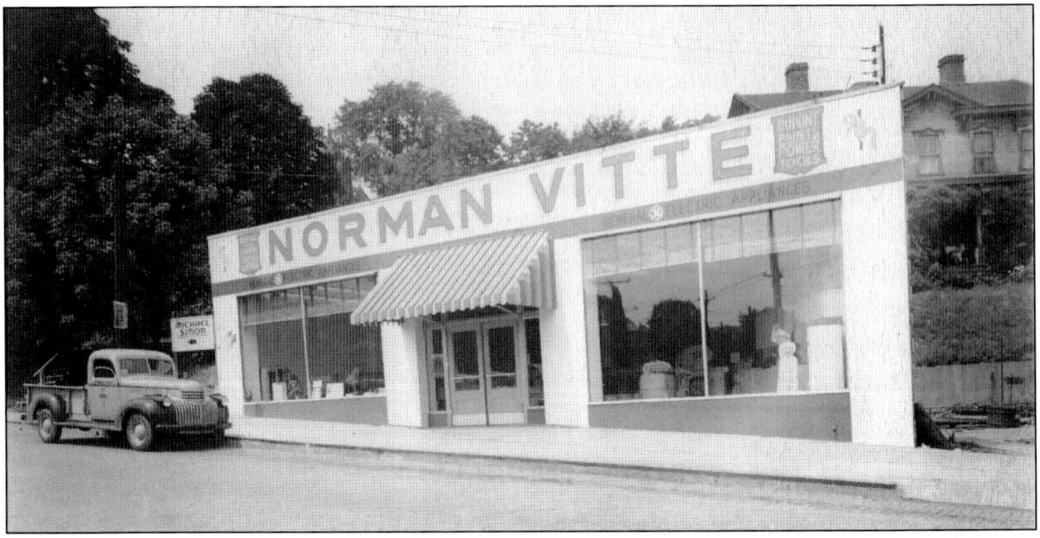

The original Norman Vitte hardware store is shown here along the familiar brick road that is Castle Shannon Boulevard. The building was later expanded to two floors, and the store eventually added unfinished furniture to its wares. Another Vitte store, dealing in lawn mowers and repairs, operated on Rockwood Avenue in Castle Shannon from 1968 to 1977. (Photograph by George "Jasper" Evans, courtesy of Ric Evans.)

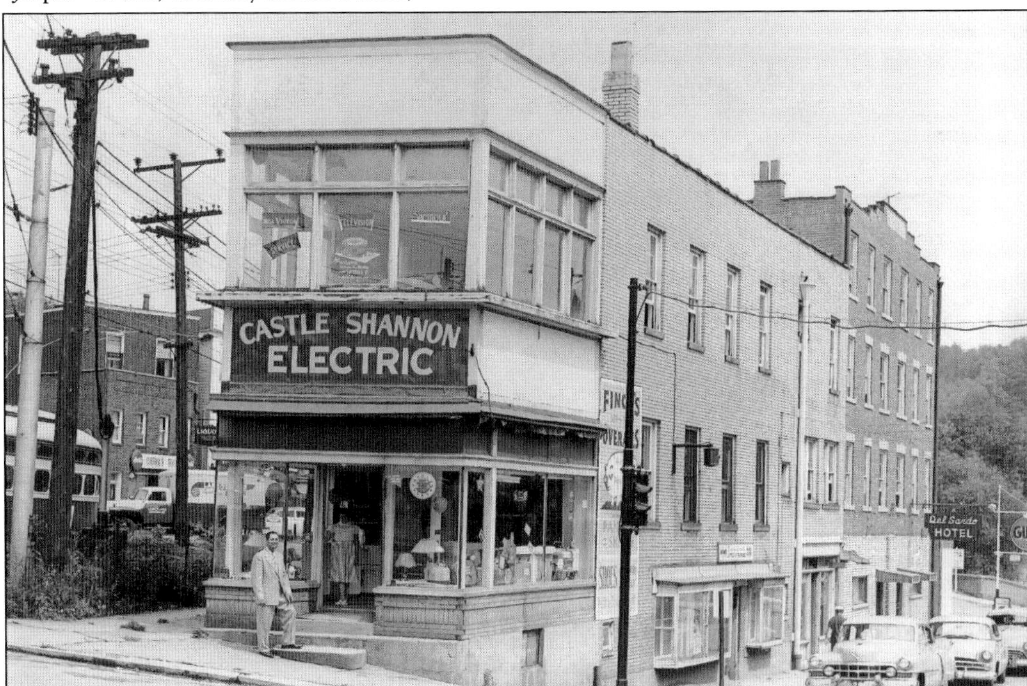

Though on a much smaller scale, of course, the design of this familiar building is to Castle Shannon residents what the electronic message board at Times Square is to New Yorkers. In the 1940s, it was Castle Shannon Electric. In the far right portion of the photograph is the old Del Sardo Hotel, next to a Gulf service station. (Photograph by George "Jasper" Evans, courtesy of Ric Evans.)

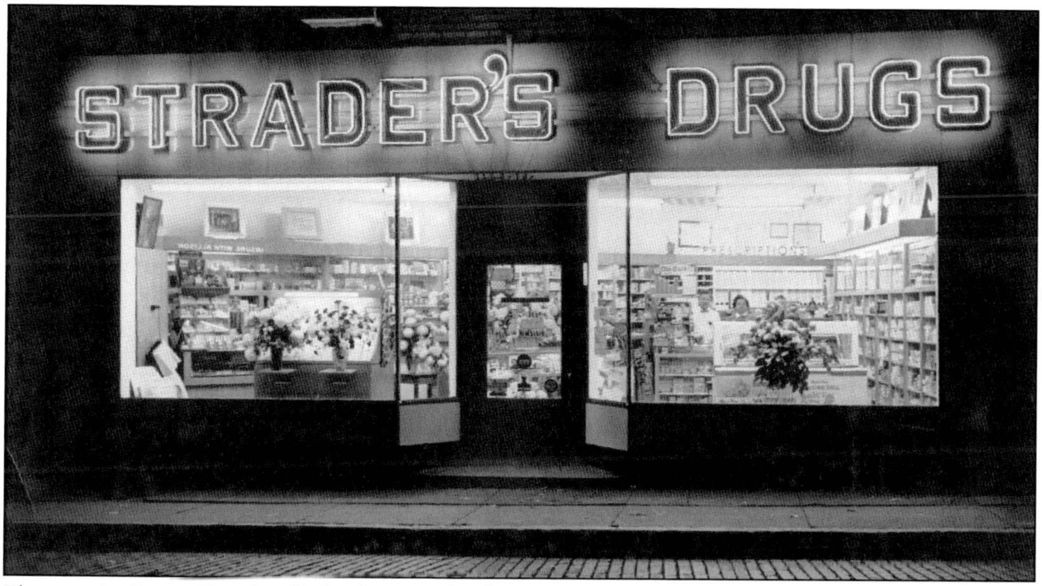

Pharmacist James Strader (below) opened a drugstore in 1929 on what was then called Railroad Street. The road later became Willow Avenue. The neon sign (above) was later removed. The store was conveniently located in the heart of Castle Shannon's business district and served the purposes of area physicians, whose offices were usually located a short distance from the drugstore. Patients needing to have prescriptions filled could make the easy walk to Strader's. Students walking home from nearby Myrtle School found the store handy for purchasing an after-school candy bar or batteries for a new transistor radio. After Strader's closed, the building saw a number of businesses come and go. Most recently, it has been a pizza shop and a tattoo parlor. (Both photographs by George "Jasper" Evans, courtesy of Ric Evans.)

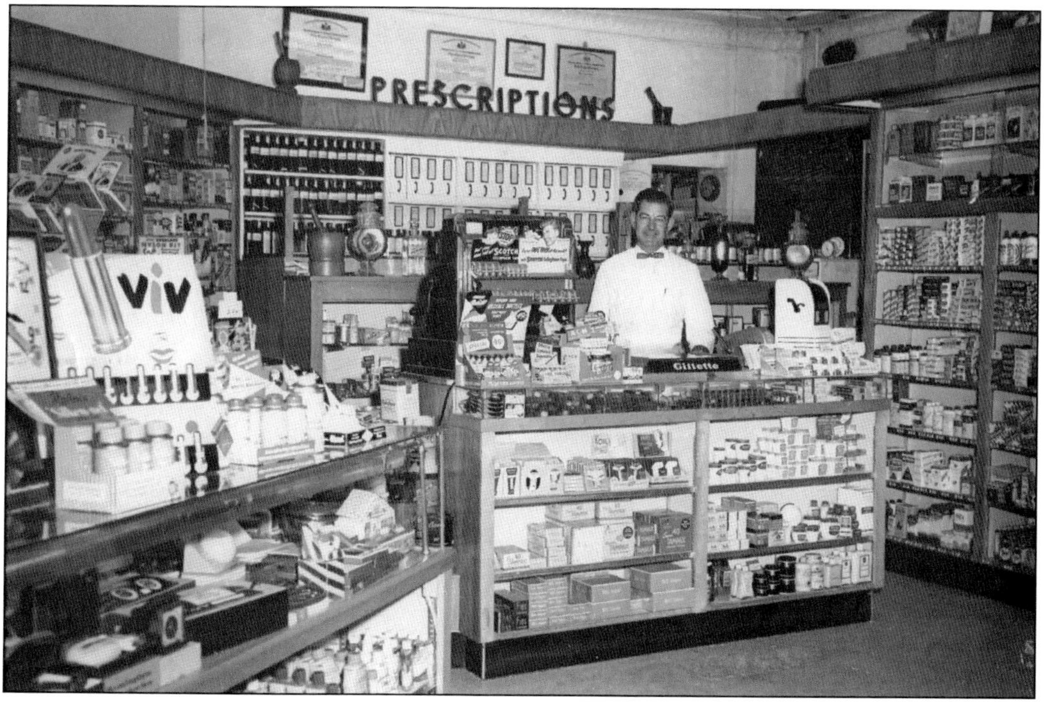

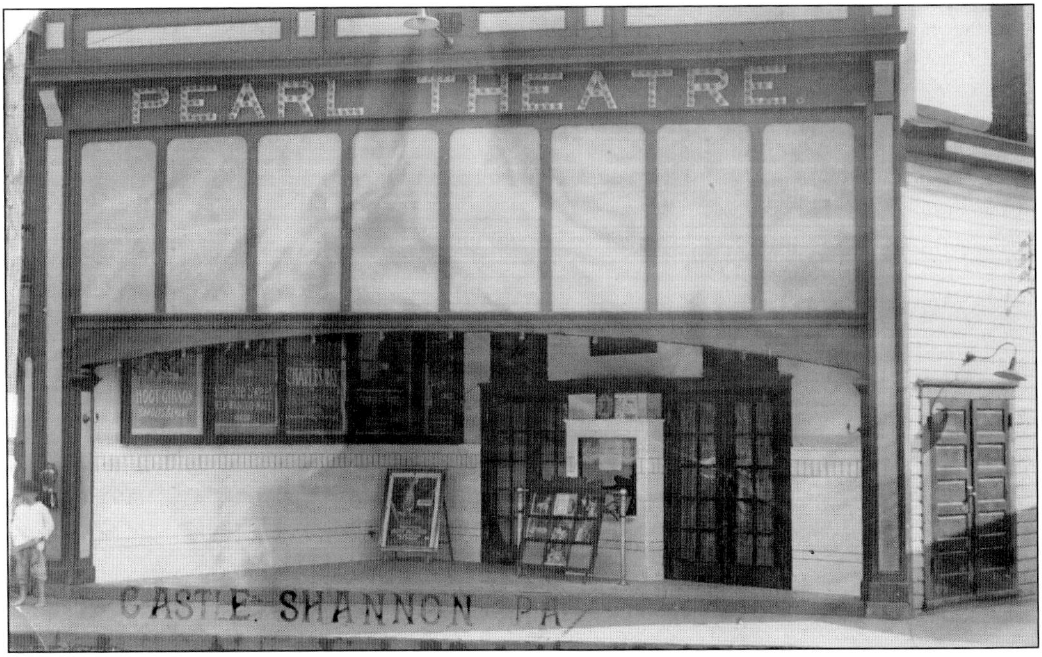

The original Pearl Theatre was built in the late 1910s by Mary Ann Schenot. It was located at the corner of Railroad Street (later Willow Avenue) and Castle Shannon Boulevard. Schenot also owned the Castle Shannon Hotel, which can be seen next door in the picture below. It was later called the Castle Theatre and remained so from 1939 until December 1951, when it was destroyed by a fire that started in the projection room. One of the unique features of the theater was that its proprietress unleashed a dog to go through the aisles following each viewing to pick up discarded items left by patrons, which were then placed in a lost-and-found bin. (Above photograph, courtesy of Paul Fey; below photograph, courtesy of Castle Shannon Volunteer Fire Department.)

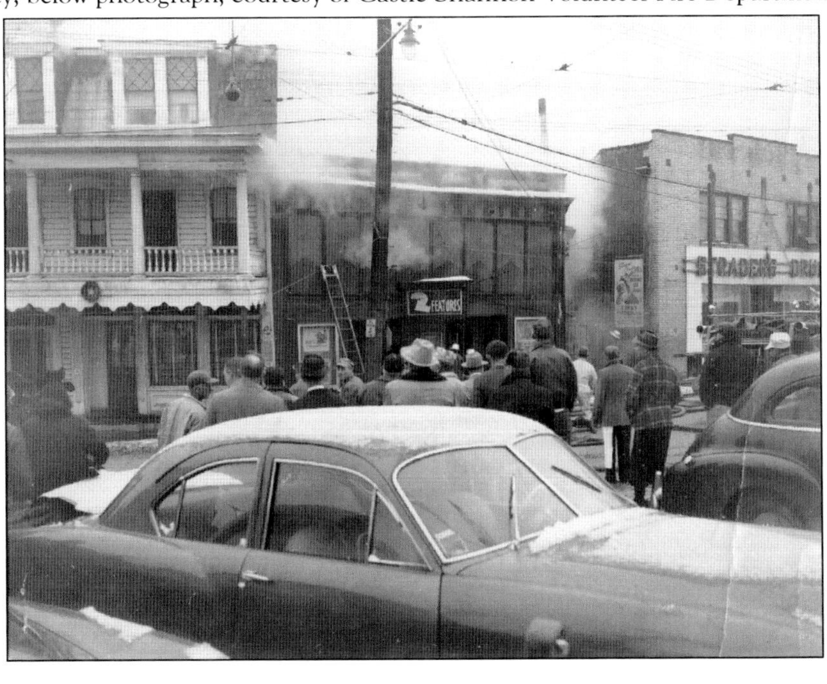

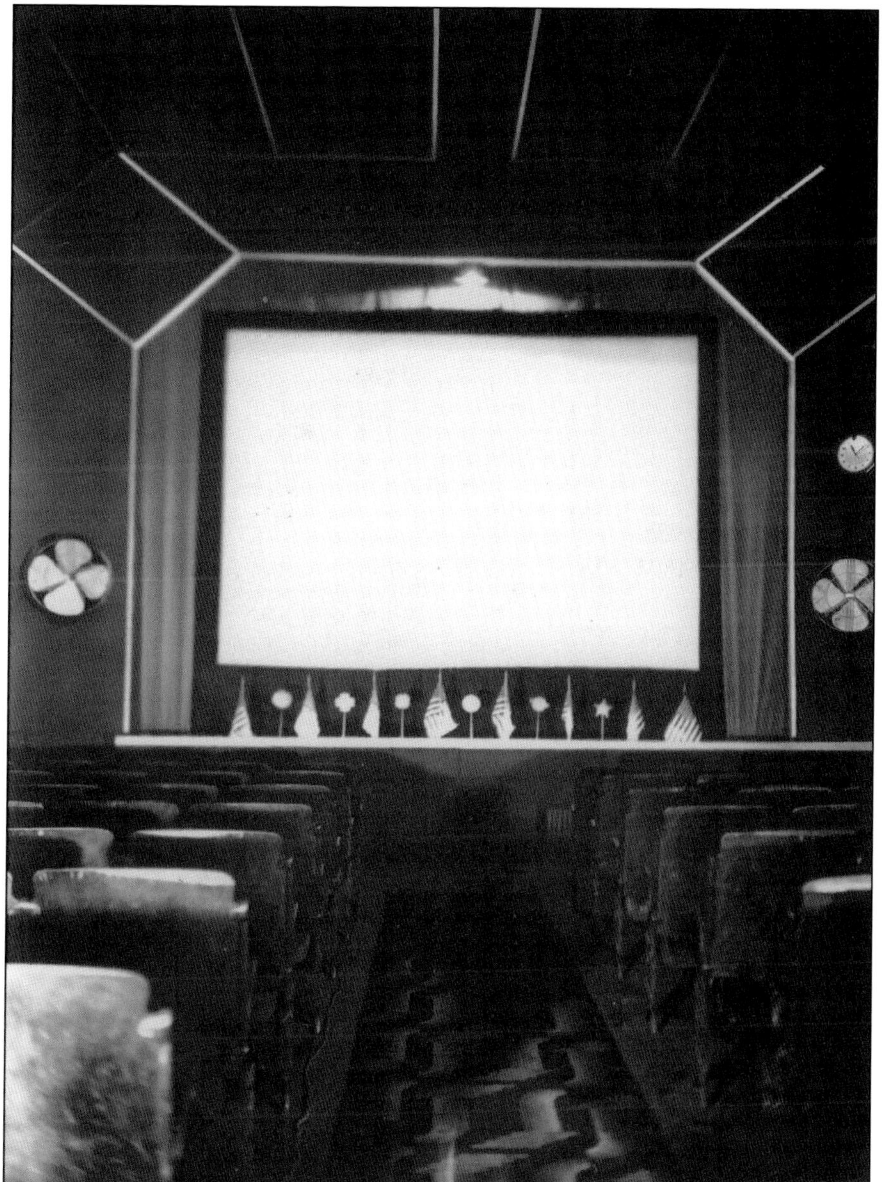

This is an interior photograph of the auditorium portion of the Pearl/Castle Theatre on Castle Shannon's Willow Avenue. Note the wall clock on the far right side and air fans on each side of the screen. The theater never had air-conditioning. The Pearl Theatre featured both silent and talkies, and a folding billboard customarily stood in front of the entrance advertising the current features that were running inside. Hoot Gibson films were popular at the theater. Newsreels were often played before the start of the feature. During the 1930s and 1940s, newsreels in movie houses often were the only news-related moving images people in the United States received from around the country and the world. The theater was standard and comparable in size to other theaters in suburban Pittsburgh communities from 1920 to 1950. In those days, the largest theaters were located in metropolitan areas. The Pearl and Castle Theatres would have been similar in size to a theater found in today's multiplexes. (Photograph by George "Jasper" Evans, courtesy of Ric Evans.)

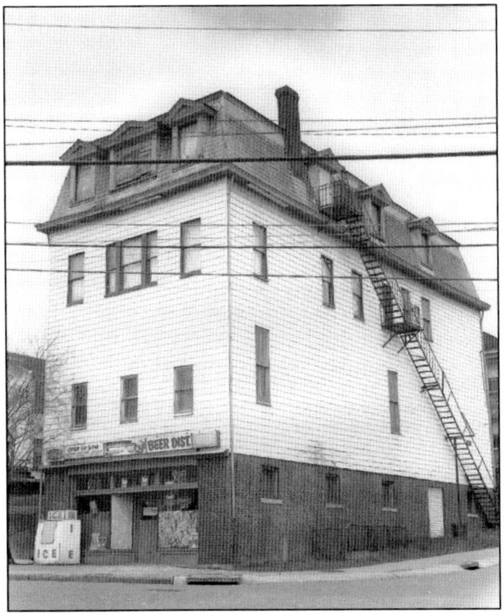

The Trance Beer Distributorship at the corner of Poplar Street and Willow Avenue sold beer and soft drinks to Castle Shannon residents for many years. It was also the Fisher Beer Distributorship. In its earlier heyday, it was a store supplying plumbing and hardware services. The trolley line ran across the street from the building, and the old Pittsburgh National Bank Building was just up Poplar Street. (Photograph by George "Jasper" Evans, courtesy of Ric Evans.)

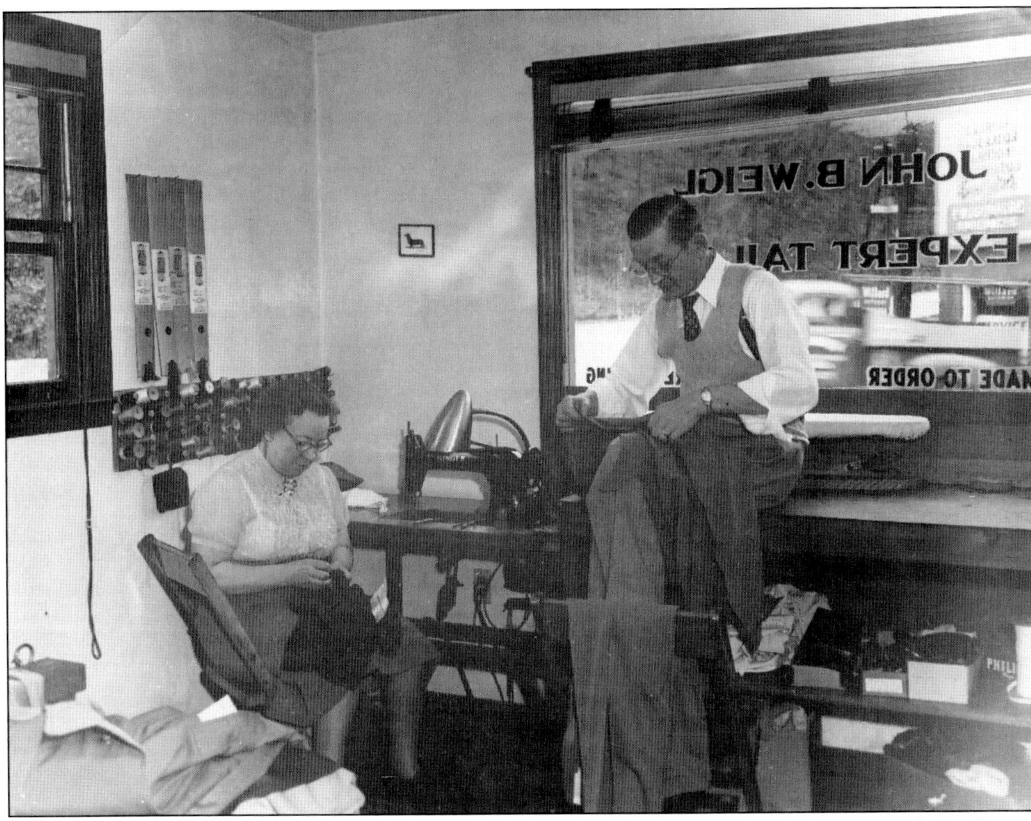

John B. Weigl, "Expert Tailor" had a little shop at the end of Castle Shannon Boulevard near Library Road. Customers from around the South Hills suburbs brought their clothes to Weigl, whose "made to order" promise was as good as advertised. (Photograph by George "Jasper" Evans, courtesy of Ric Evans.)

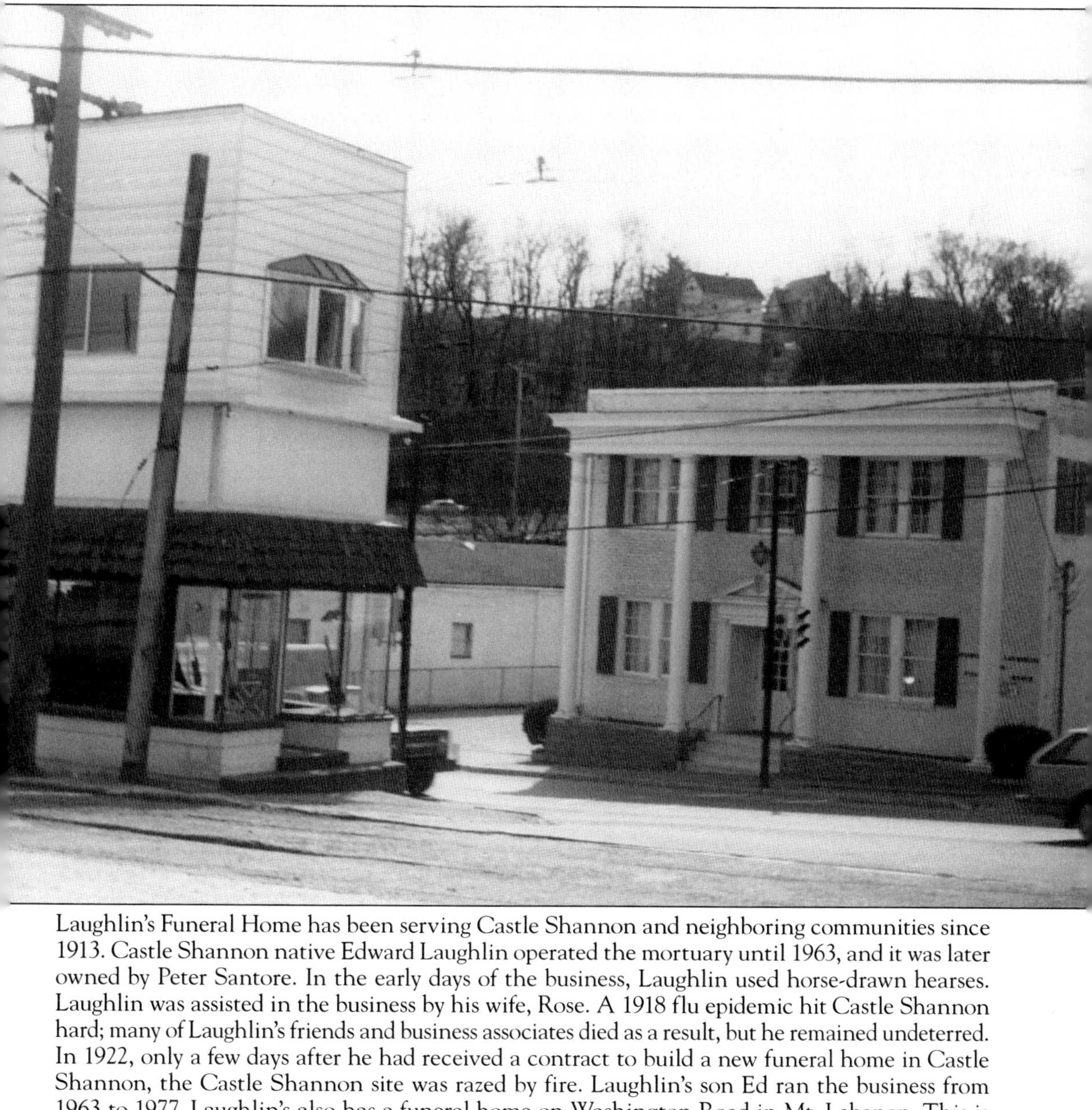

Laughlin's Funeral Home has been serving Castle Shannon and neighboring communities since 1913. Castle Shannon native Edward Laughlin operated the mortuary until 1963, and it was later owned by Peter Santore. In the early days of the business, Laughlin used horse-drawn hearses. Laughlin was assisted in the business by his wife, Rose. A 1918 flu epidemic hit Castle Shannon hard; many of Laughlin's friends and business associates died as a result, but he remained undeterred. In 1922, only a few days after he had received a contract to build a new funeral home in Castle Shannon, the Castle Shannon site was razed by fire. Laughlin's son Ed ran the business from 1963 to 1977. Laughlin's also has a funeral home on Washington Road in Mt. Lebanon. This is a photograph of the front of the Castle Shannon home, taken from the sidewalk in front of the Vic Lawrence Music Studio. (Photograph courtesy of Mary Scabilloni.)

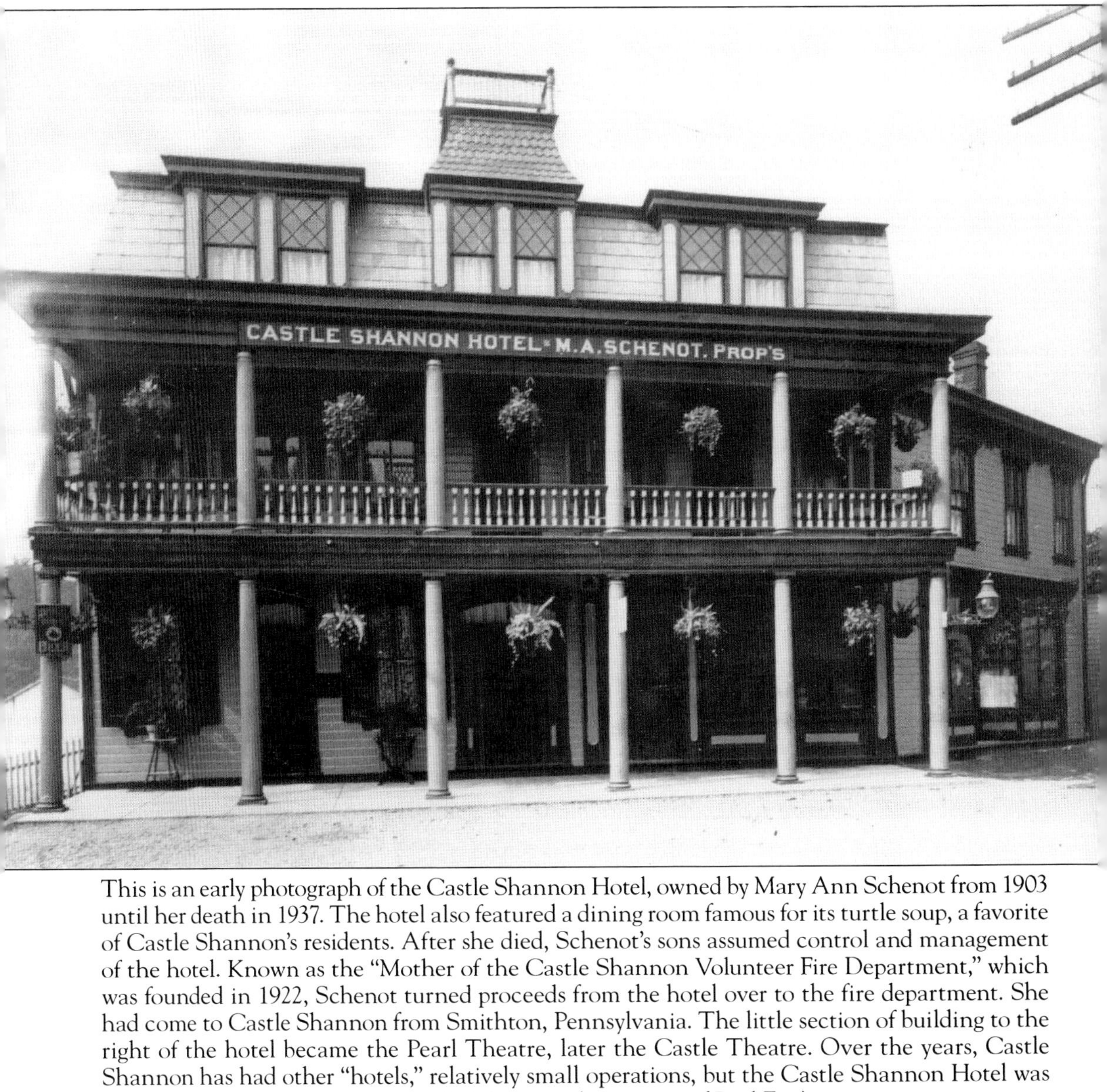

This is an early photograph of the Castle Shannon Hotel, owned by Mary Ann Schenot from 1903 until her death in 1937. The hotel also featured a dining room famous for its turtle soup, a favorite of Castle Shannon's residents. After she died, Schenot's sons assumed control and management of the hotel. Known as the "Mother of the Castle Shannon Volunteer Fire Department," which was founded in 1922, Schenot turned proceeds from the hotel over to the fire department. She had come to Castle Shannon from Smithton, Pennsylvania. The little section of building to the right of the hotel became the Pearl Theatre, later the Castle Theatre. Over the years, Castle Shannon has had other "hotels," relatively small operations, but the Castle Shannon Hotel was regarded as the grandest of them all. (Photograph courtesy of Paul Fey.)

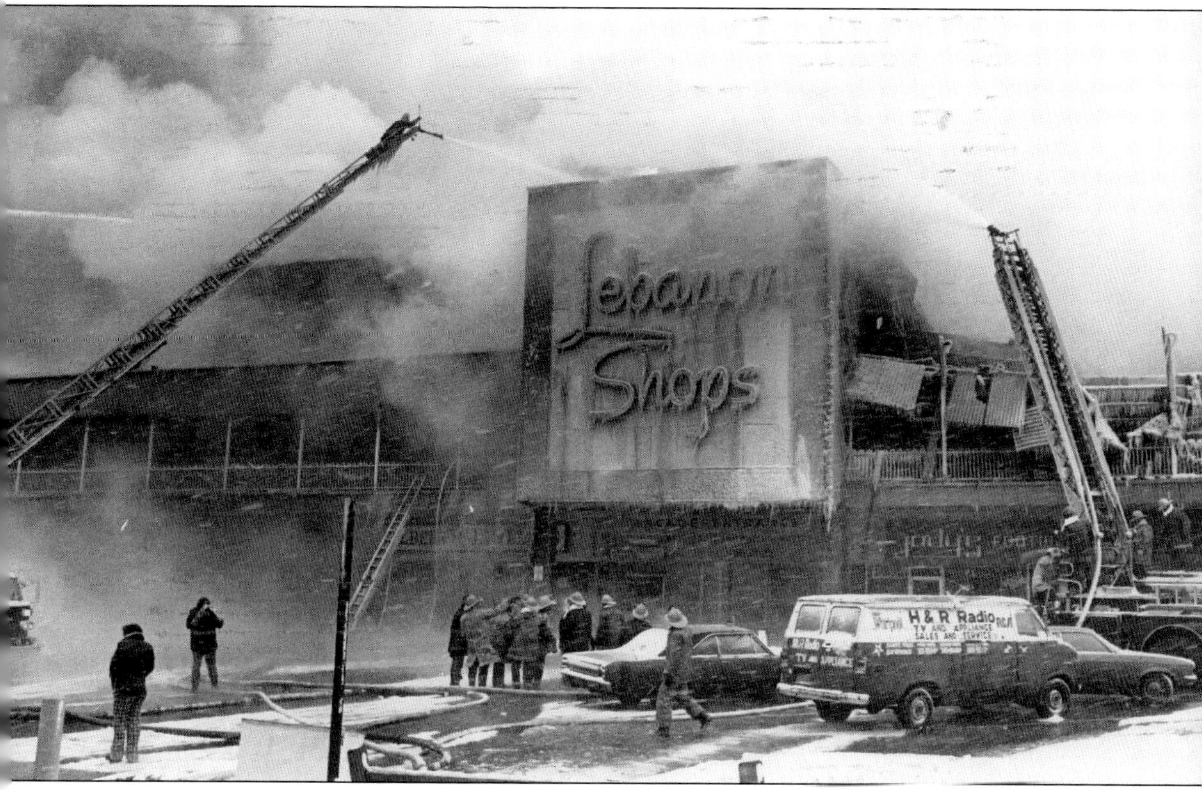

January 1977 was in the midst of a particularly harsh winter in Pennsylvania, but it became much hotter around 4:20 a.m. when Castle Shannon Volunteer Fire Department chief Jim O'Brien was the first man to arrive at a major fire at the Lebanon Shops on Mt. Lebanon Boulevard. "It was already going pretty good by the time I got there," O'Brien recalled in a 2012 interview. "We had help from about seven or eight different [fire] companies. That was certainly the most spectacular fire I saw during my time as an active member of the department." The fire was believed to have started in a space heater or pipe leading up through the second story of the G.C. Murphy store at the shopping center. Fortunately, because of the hour, no people were in the structure at the time of the fire's outbreak. Stockers had just left the Kroger grocery store at the far end of the Lebanon Shops, and some recall they may have smelled smoke, but no alert was given to authorities. Kroger left the Lebanon Shops shortly after the fire and never returned. Many offices located on the second (balcony) level of the building sustained heavy damages. (Copyright *Pittsburgh Post-Gazette*, 2012, all rights reserved. Reprinted with permission.)

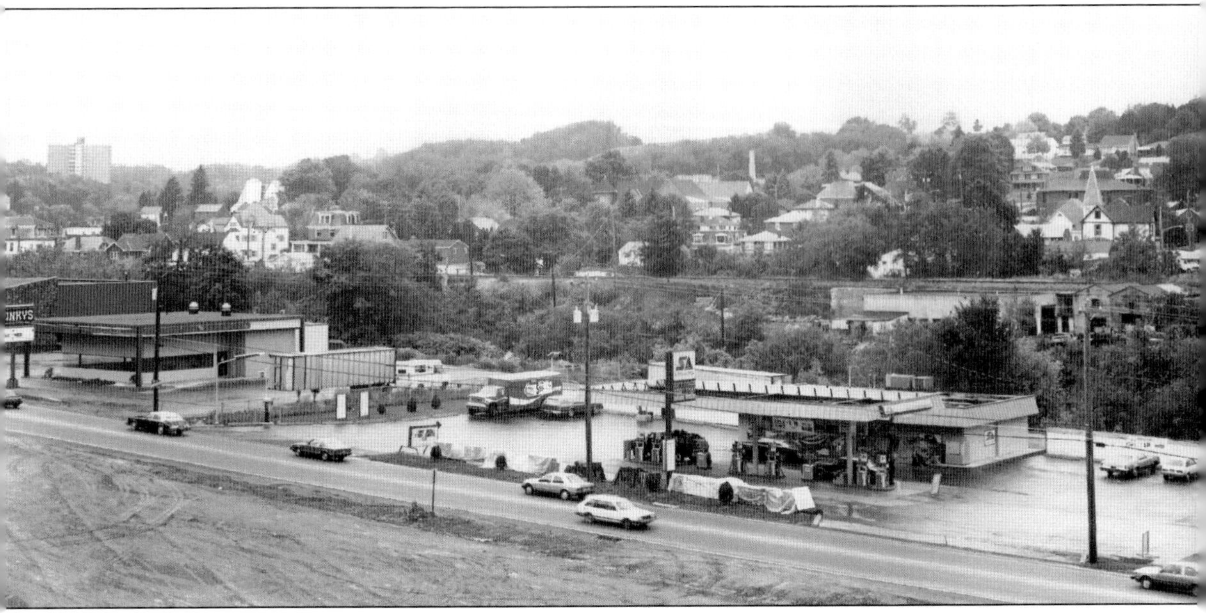

Fast-food restaurants can be found almost everywhere today, but it was not until the 1970s that they appeared all over, and Castle Shannon was no exception. Winky's restaurant, at far left, was the first fast-food establishment in Castle Shannon. It opened in the 1960s, before a McDonald's arrived across town on Mt. Lebanon Boulevard. Winky's was similar to McDonald's in terms of menu offerings and price. It was a chain that had other restaurants in the Pittsburgh area before going under. As of 2012, the building had been an Arby's for many years. Next to Winky's in this photograph is a Hi Fi gas station that by 2012 was a Marathon gas and convenience store. The convenience store remains much as it appears in this picture. Note that the area across the street was undeveloped at the time. (Photograph by George "Jasper" Evans, courtesy of Ric Evans.)

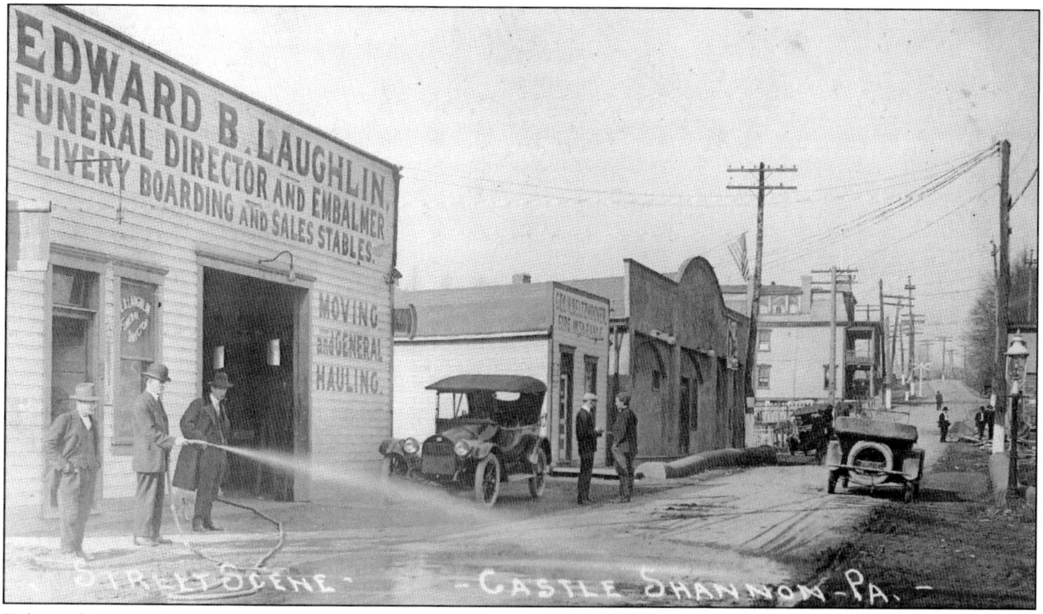

Edward Laughlin can be seen hosing off the area in front of Edward B. Laughlin, Funeral Director and Embalmer. He also provided livery boarding and sales stables. Laughlin also moved and hauled items. His original building, seen here, was located down the street, toward Route 88, from where the current funeral home stands on Willow Avenue. (Photograph courtesy of Paul Fey.)

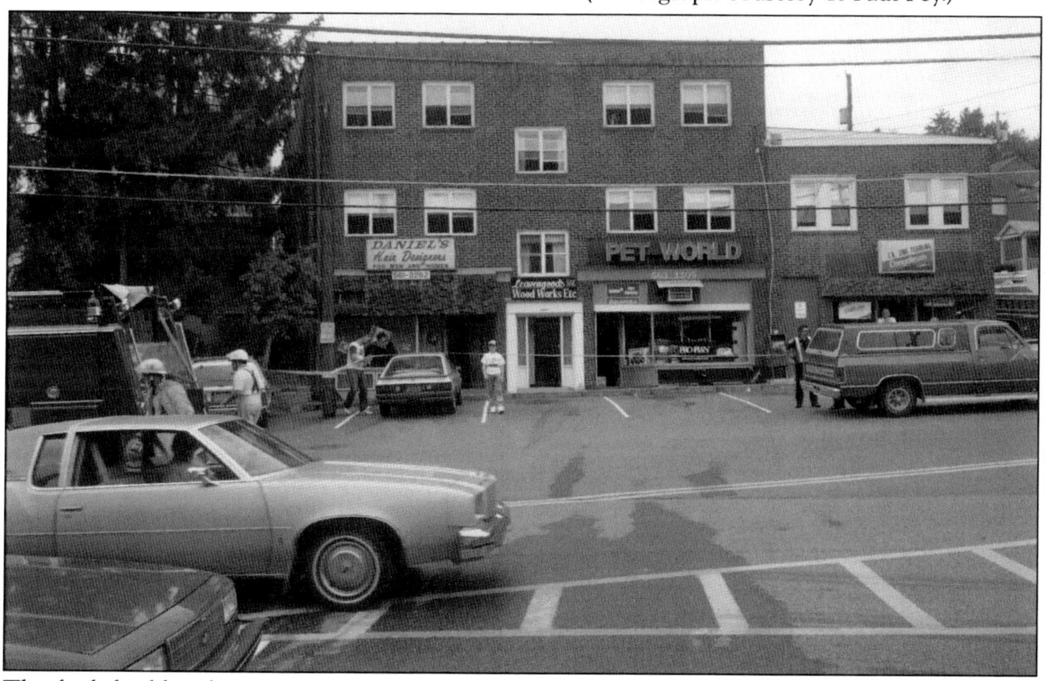

This little building has seen any number of businesses come and go in Castle Shannon. This 1980s photograph features Pet World in the center, but for many years students leaving school in the afternoon headed to it when it was KK's, a popular destination for soft drinks and candy, plus other baking and kitchen needs, owned by the Kletter family. It later housed Sole Survivor and currently is home to a yoga studio. (Photograph courtesy of Castle Shannon Volunteer Fire Department.)

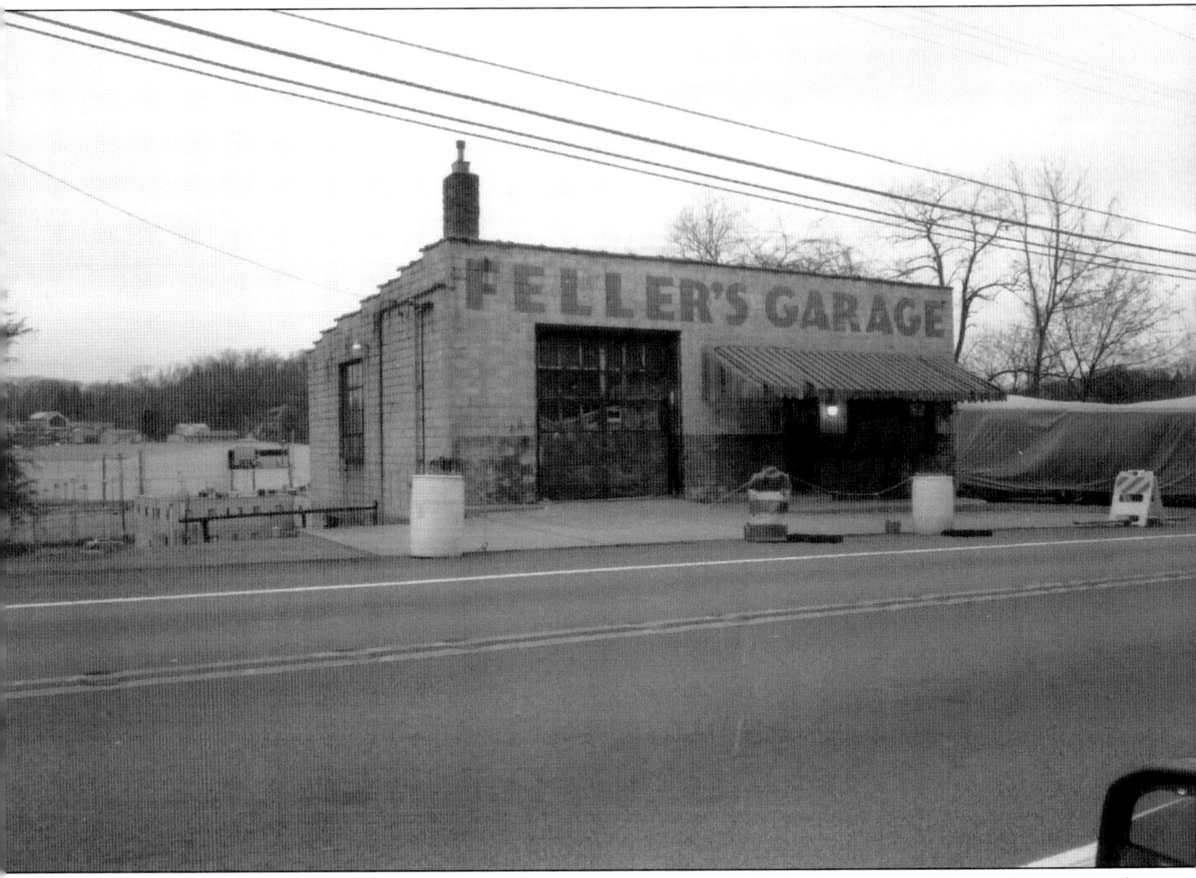

This photograph from November 2011 shows a desolate Feller's Garage on Route 88 in Castle Shannon, several years after owner Jim Feller retired from the business. Feller's Garage was an institution in the South Hills of Pittsburgh. Folks from the community would take their cars to Feller's for simple repairs and state inspections. The establishment also sold Atlantic gasoline for a short period. The business was founded by Al Feller, the longtime Castle Shannon Volunteer Fire Department chief. When he died in 1981, son Jim took over the business. But with the advent of computerized dashboards and engines, the range of Feller's service became limited. Castle Shannon old-timers, however, remained loyal to the business, and Feller's Garage will always be a place that brings a smile to the people of the borough. Jim Feller passed away in February 2012. (Photograph by Sam Sciullo Jr.)

Four

Church and School

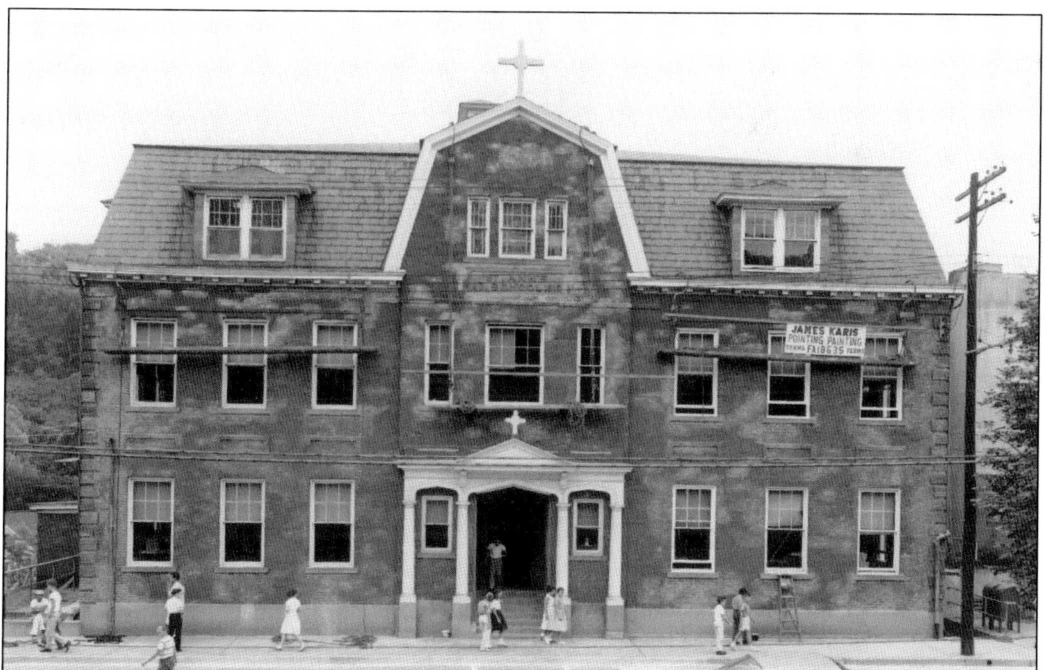

The old St. Anne School on Willow Avenue was directly across the street from the church. This photograph is from the late 1950s, several years after the new school was built adjacent to it. Both school buildings were used simultaneously for many years. (Photograph courtesy of St. Anne School.)

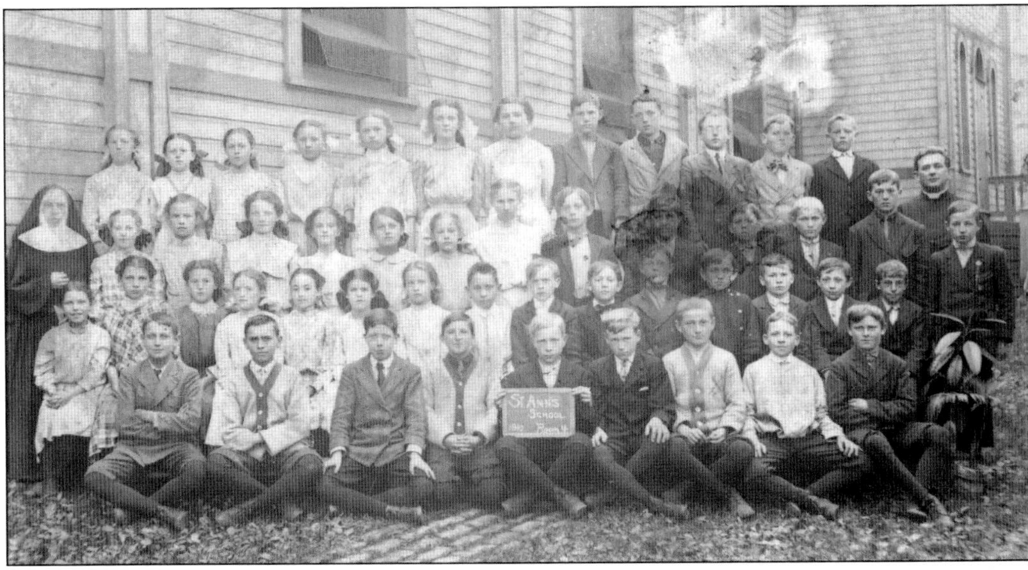

This undated photograph from the early 20th century shows St. Anne School students in front of the school building. The school was dedicated in October 1912. It included eight well-equipped classrooms, an auditorium, meeting room, pool hall, and amusement room, a forerunner to the more modern gymnasium. A nun (at left) and priest (far right) keep the children settled for the picture. (Photograph courtesy of St. Anne School.)

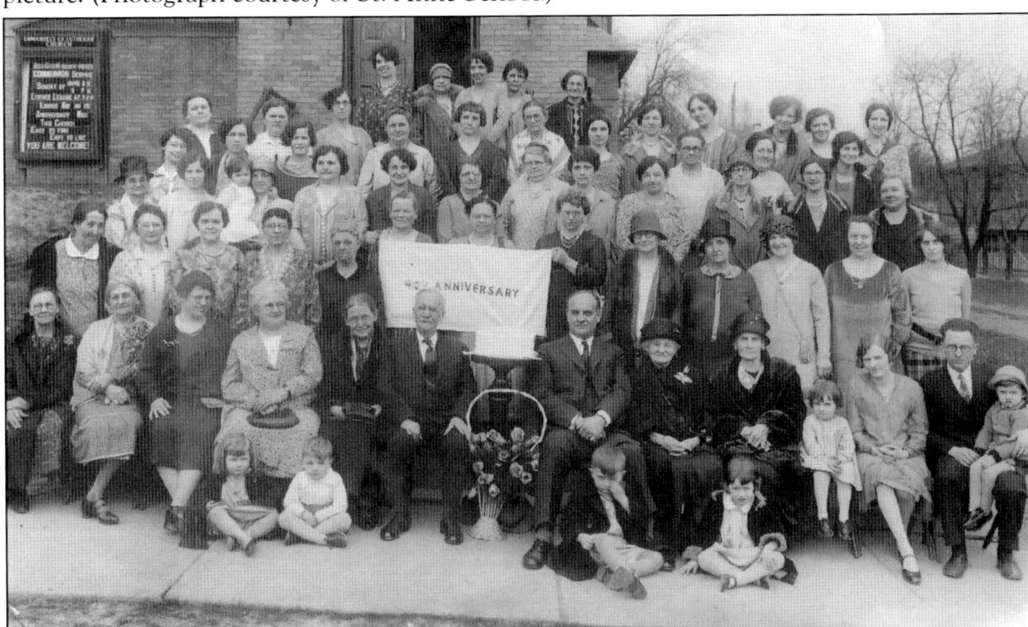

The congregation of Castle Shannon's Emmanuel Evangelical Lutheran Church assembles on April 4, 1929, to celebrate the 40th anniversary of the Ladies Aid. The photograph was taken in front of the steps of the old church, which still stands, although a new church has since been constructed adjacent to this one. Doris Harbaugh, the little girl in the fourth row, third from left (in a woman's arms), was the only surviving member of this group as of 2012. (Photograph courtesy of Emmanuel Evangelical Lutheran Church.)

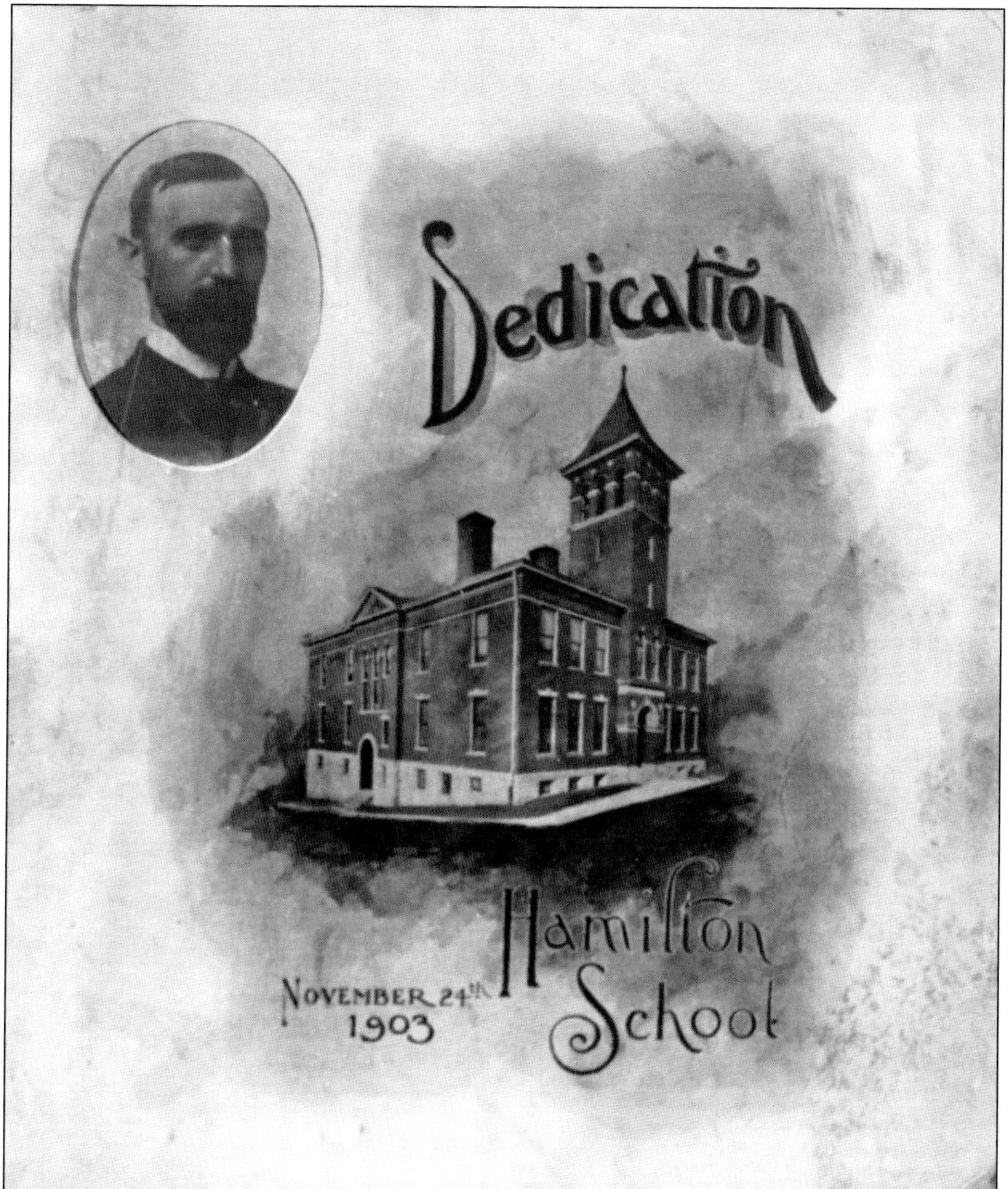

This is the official program from the dedication of Hamilton School on November 24, 1903. It was not until 1919 that Castle Shannon was incorporated as a borough from sections of Baldwin, Mt. Lebanon, and what was then called Bethel Township. Hamilton School, at its inception, was part of the Baldwin School District. It was, however, the oldest school building in what would eventually become Castle Shannon. The unidentified man on the program cover was most likely a professor who taught at the school. Hamilton School was located on Library Road, more commonly known later as Route 88, in an area of land that the Castle Shannon Volunteer Fire Department would come to utilize extensively. The fire department also used Hamilton School in various ways during its annual carnival week and, in its final years, for fundraising purposes. (Photograph courtesy of Ric Evans.)

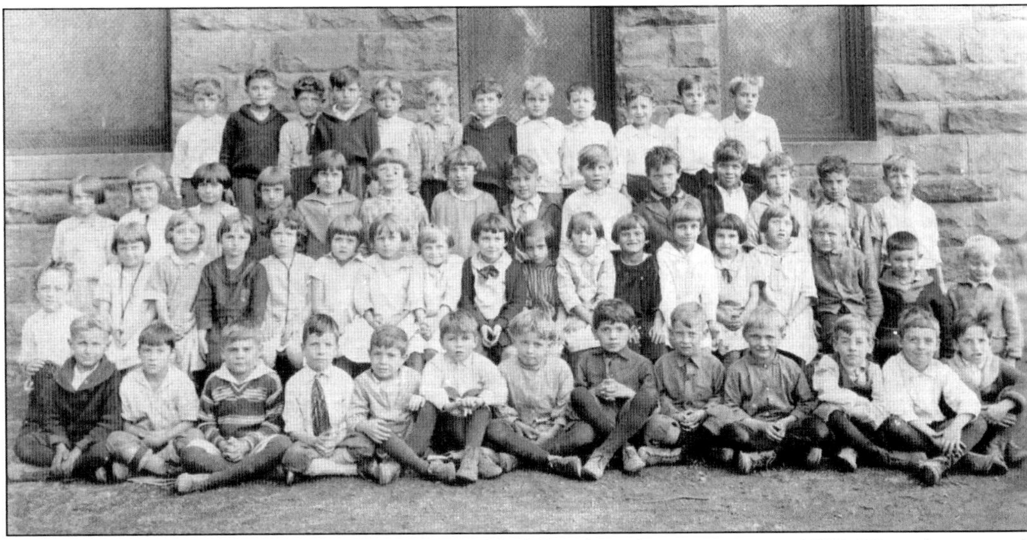

Students from Hamilton School have assembled for this class picture in 1927. The photograph was taken along one of the sides of the building. Note that, much like in the previous picture from an early St. Anne class, the boys and girls are positioned into groups, rather than mixed. One boy, in the first row, fourth from left, even put on a tie for the event. In later years, Keystone Oaks elementary school boys were urged to wear a tie for all of their class pictures. (Photograph by George "Jasper" Evans, courtesy of Ric Evans.)

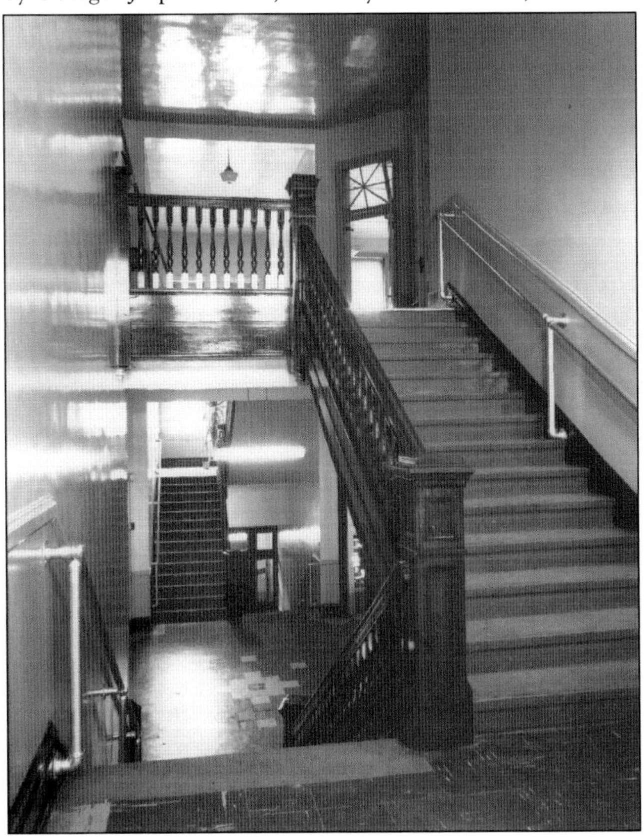

This interior view of Hamilton School, which had two floors and a basement level, shows the beautiful wooden railings along the wide staircase. The school also had an impressive bell tower, which can be seen in many photographs. The bell itself was later moved to Myrtle Elementary School in Castle Shannon. (Photograph by George "Jasper" Evans, courtesy of Ric Evans.)

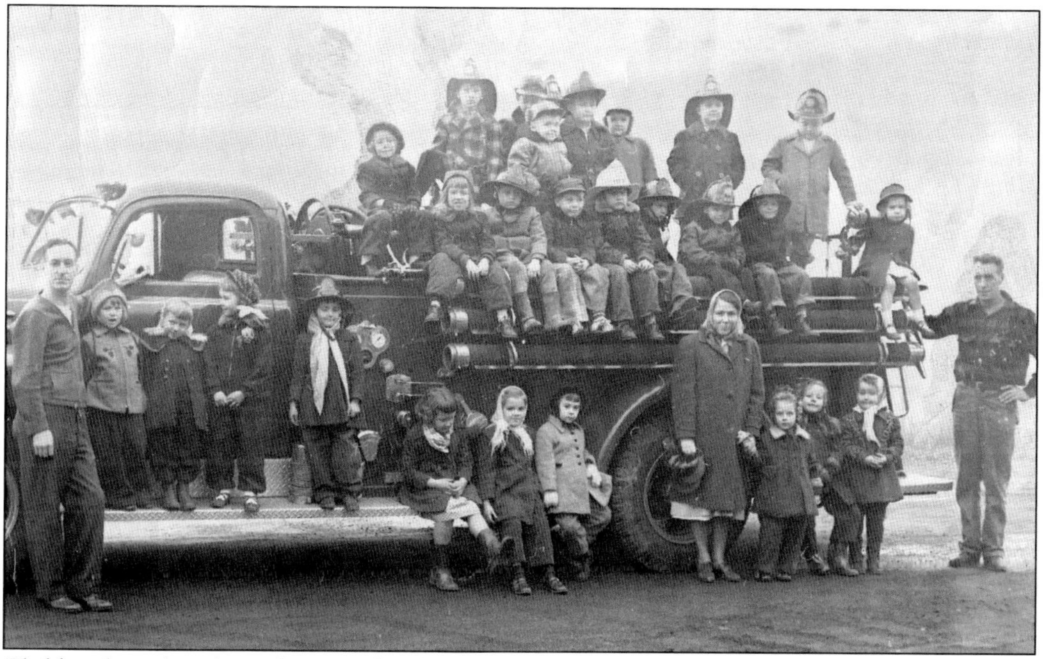

Children have long been fascinated with fire trucks, and this 1951 Hamilton School kindergarten class is no different. The Castle Shannon Volunteer Fire Department often let kids climb aboard the trucks and check out the various gadgets and fancy instruments that go into fighting fires. (Photograph courtesy of Castle Shannon Volunteer Fire Department.)

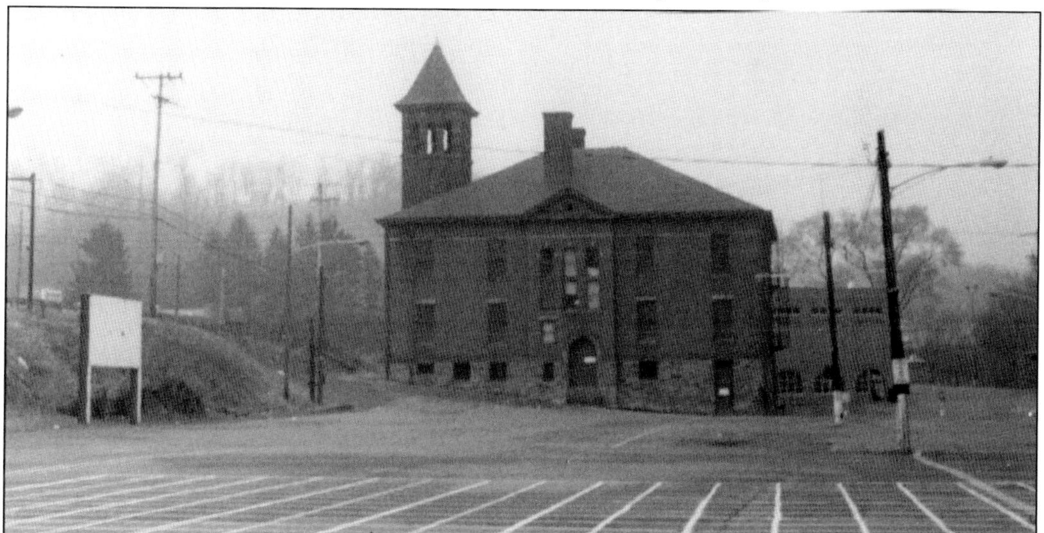

Hamilton School, lonely and abandoned, is seen on a foggy day in Castle Shannon in the 1970s. The school closed its doors in 1969. The new Castle Shannon Volunteer Fire Department building can be seen behind the school. Note that many of the school's windows have been shuttered. The backboard at extreme left accommodated two hoops for a basketball shooting attraction during the firemen's carnival. In its final years, the building was used by the fire department as a "haunted school" attraction in the weeks leading up to Halloween. (Photograph courtesy of Mary Scabilloni.)

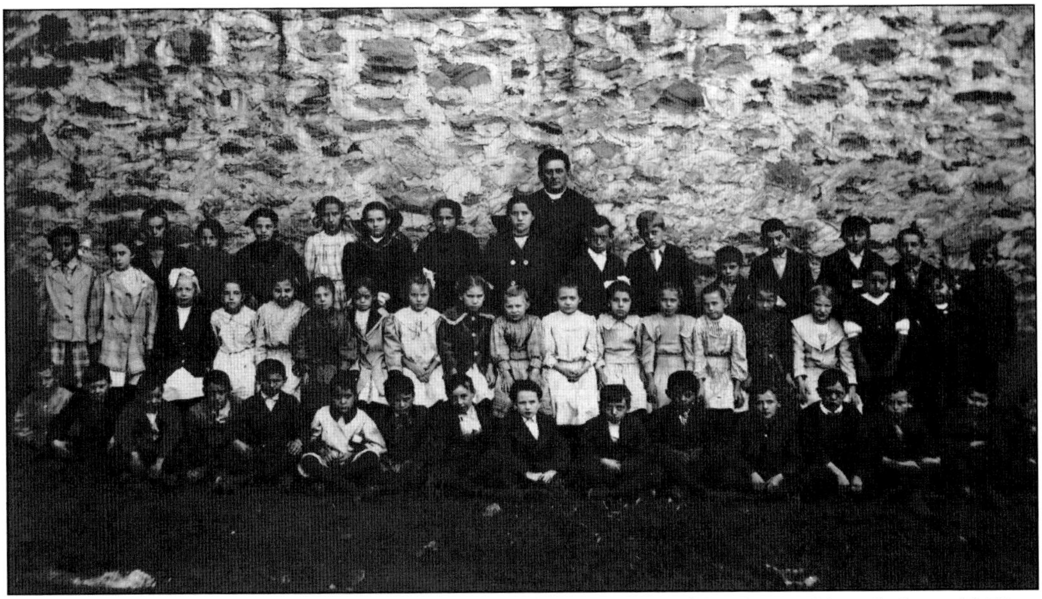

The Reverend Charles Hipp (in back, by himself) was rector of St. Anne Church from 1907 to 1918. He was ordained in 1899. Born in 1867, Father Hipp died in 1918 and is buried in St. Anne Cemetery. (Photograph courtesy of St. Anne School.)

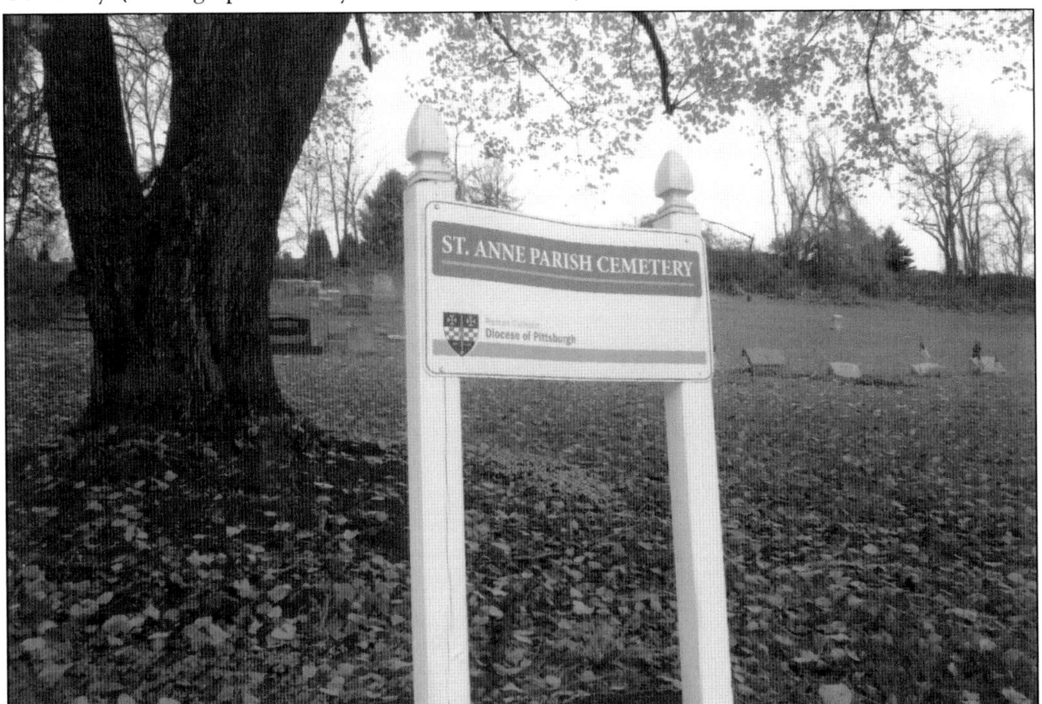

This modern-day photograph shows the lower, smaller portion of St. Anne Cemetery. It is located next to where the old church and parish house stood. The old church property remains undeveloped. This cemetery was dedicated on July 26, 1893, the Feast of St. Anne Day. Although the upper, much larger portion of St. Anne Cemetery is the burial ground most people are familiar with, services are still held in this part of the cemetery. (Photograph by Sam Sciullo Jr.)

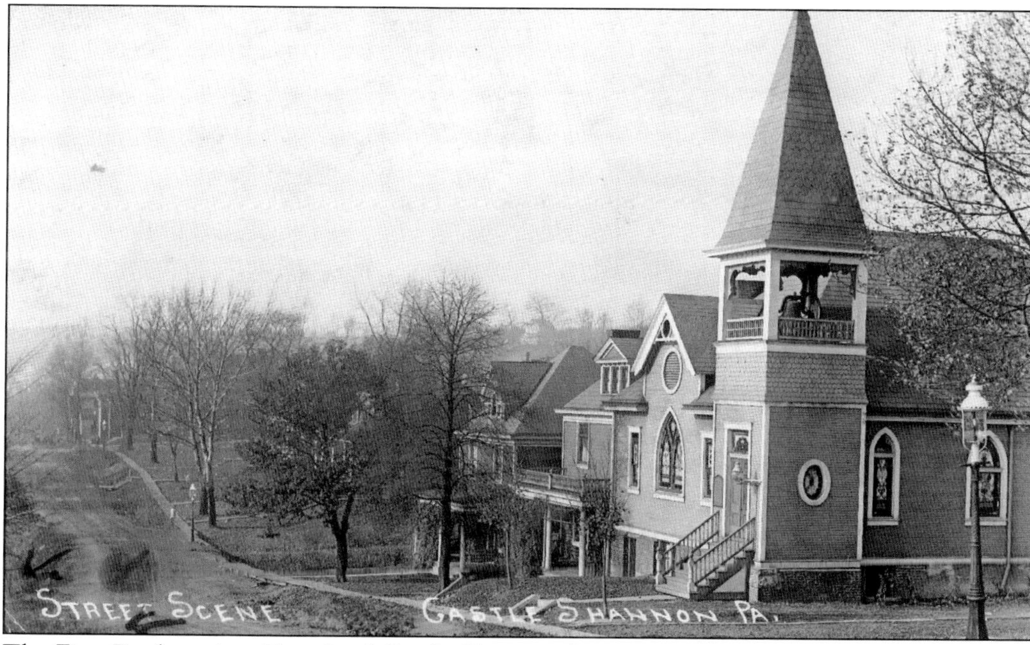

The First Presbyterian Church of Castle Shannon has an interesting past. This building was originally located several blocks away, on a hill along Lebanon Avenue. In June 1911, it was actually lifted off the ground and moved to its current site on Poplar Avenue. Even during the move, worship services continued uninterrupted; they were held wherever the church happened to be on the way to its new location. The church celebrated its 100th anniversary in 1998. (Photograph courtesy of Paul Fey.)

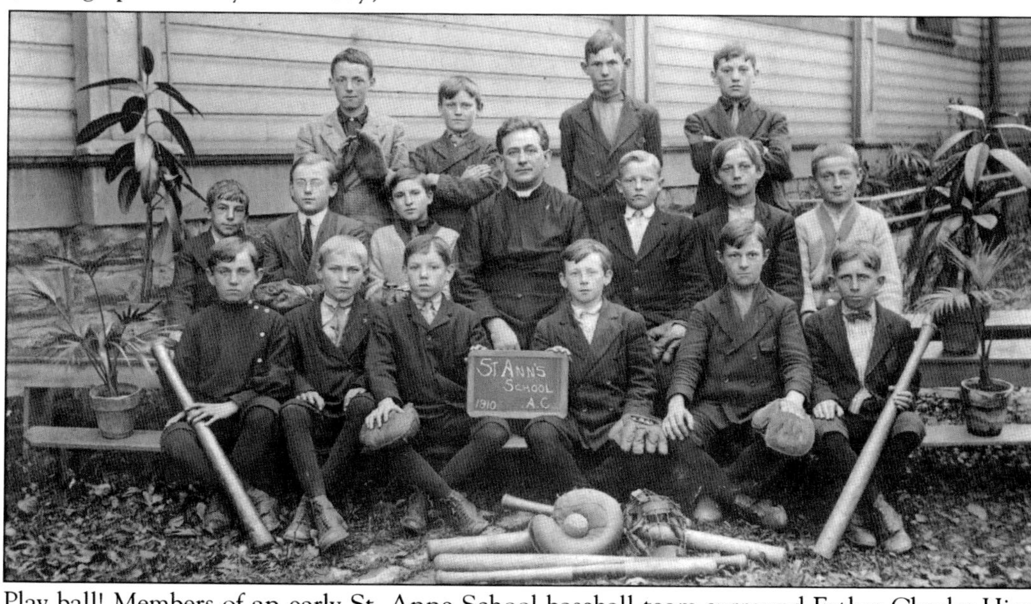

Play ball! Members of an early St. Anne School baseball team surround Father Charles Hipp in this 1910 photograph in front of the old school on Willow Avenue. The sign indicates "St. Ann's School," and "A.C." for athletic club, so it is unknown if all the boys were students at the school. While some may have been parishioners only, most likely these are students exclusively. (Photograph courtesy of St. Anne School.)

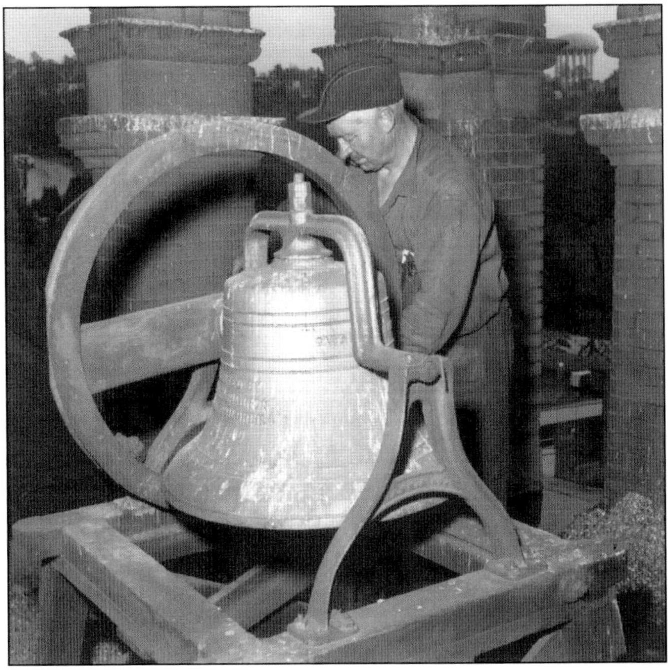

Castle Shannon Volunteer Fire Department chief Al Feller is in the bell tower of Hamilton School for this 1969 photograph. The inscription on the bell indicates that it was a gift from the students of Castle Shannon to the school on February 22, 1900, the anniversary of George Washington's birthday. (Photograph by George "Jasper" Evans, courtesy of the Feller family.)

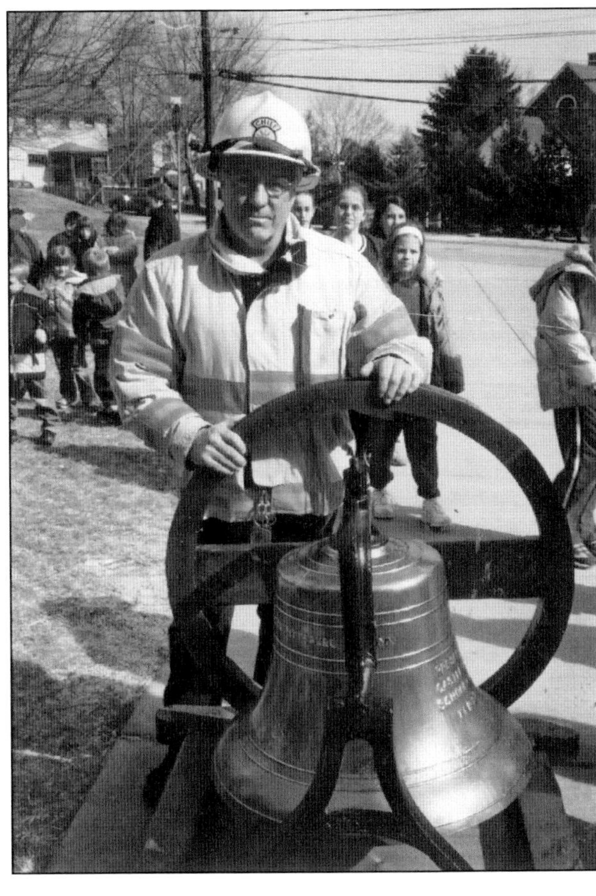

Castle Shannon Volunteer Fire Department chief Bill Reffner stands with the bell from Hamilton School. It was retrieved from its tower before Hamilton was torn down. The bell was then given a good makeover and presented to Myrtle Elementary School, where it now stands. Note the Myrtle students in the background. (Photograph courtesy of Castle Shannon Volunteer Fire Department.)

St. Anne School fielded its first football team in 1950. This team photograph was taken in front of the old school on Willow Avenue. The school's chief football rival was St. Bernard's, located a few miles away in Mt. Lebanon. In its heyday, St. Anne used Vernridge Elementary School's expansive fields for after-school practice sessions. (Photograph courtesy of St. Anne School.)

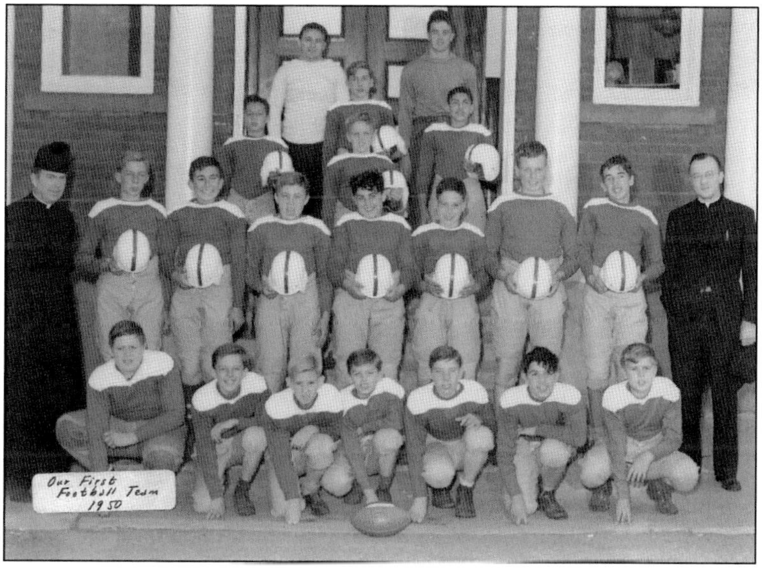

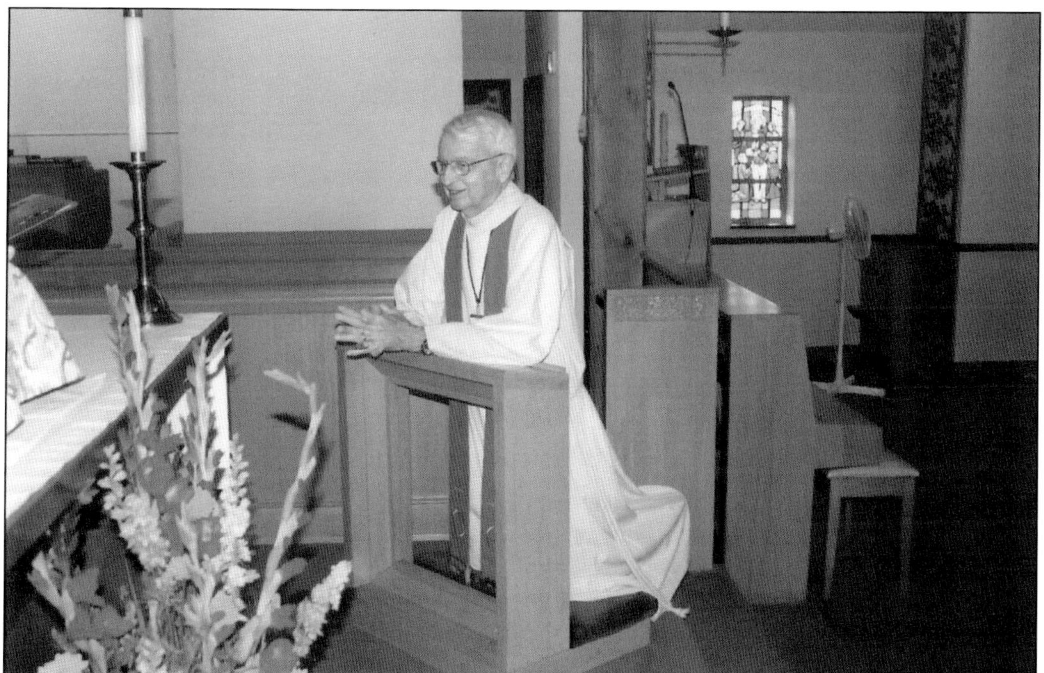

This photograph, taken on September 12, 2010, shows the Reverend James Graeser on the same kneeler on which he was ordained pastor at Emmanuel Evangelical Lutheran Church on June 19, 1960. Emmanuel Lutheran is located on Pine Avenue in Castle Shannon. It celebrated its 100th anniversary in 1985. (Photograph by Joyce Lynn Johnson, courtesy of Emmanuel Evangelical Lutheran Church.)

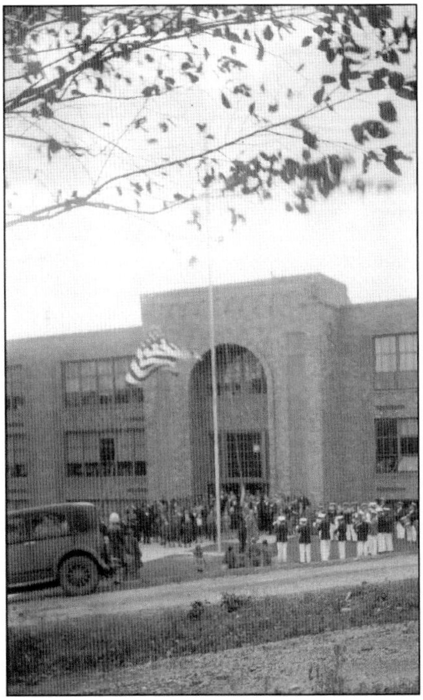

The Myrtle Avenue School is shown on its Dedication Day, October 18, 1930. The property, originally owned by the Smith family, was sold to the Castle Shannon School District. Two holes of the Castle Shannon Golf Club actually occupied part of the property. C.E. Dickey, superintendent of Allegheny County Schools, made the dedication address. (Photograph by George "Jasper" Evans, courtesy of Ric Evans.)

The Castle Shannon Junior High School Marching Band poses in front of Myrtle School in this undated photograph. The band was founded and directed by Leo Yagello (1915–1977), who later was heavily involved with the music program in the Keystone Oaks School District. The Castle Shannon Junior High Band marched in parades in town as well as in the St. Patrick's Day Parade in downtown Pittsburgh. (Photograph by George "Jasper" Evans.)

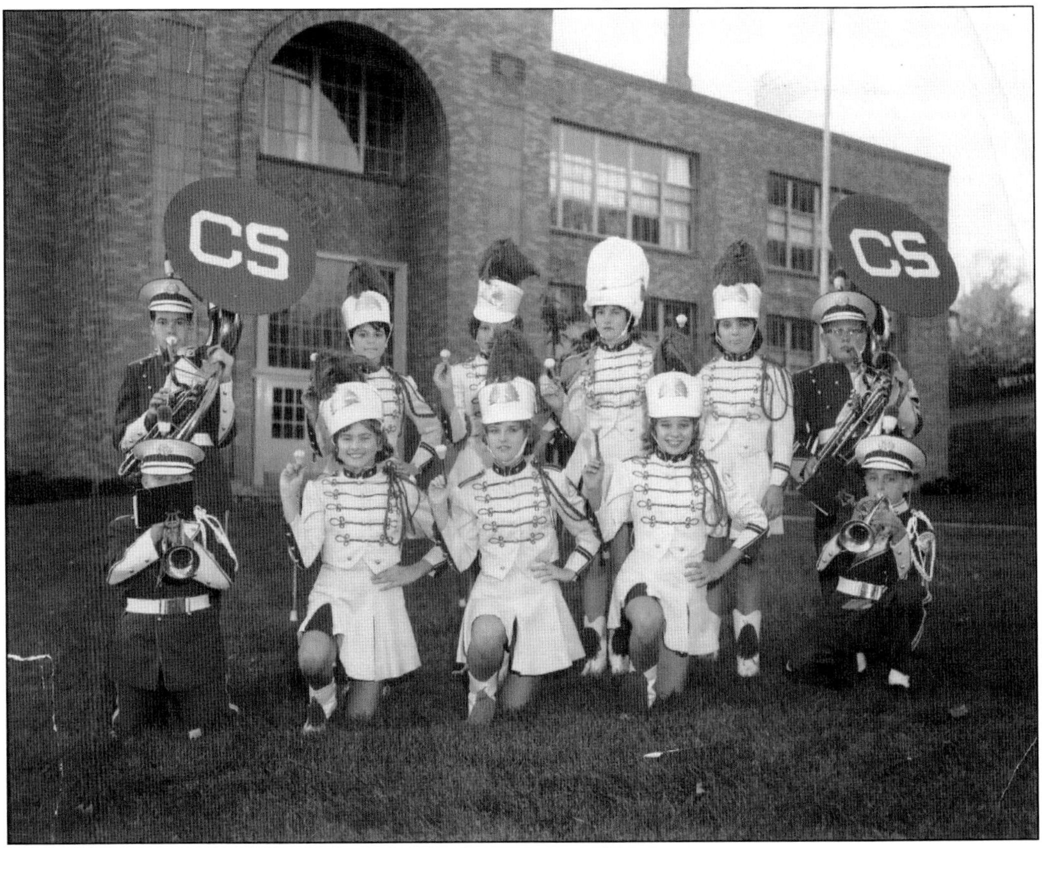

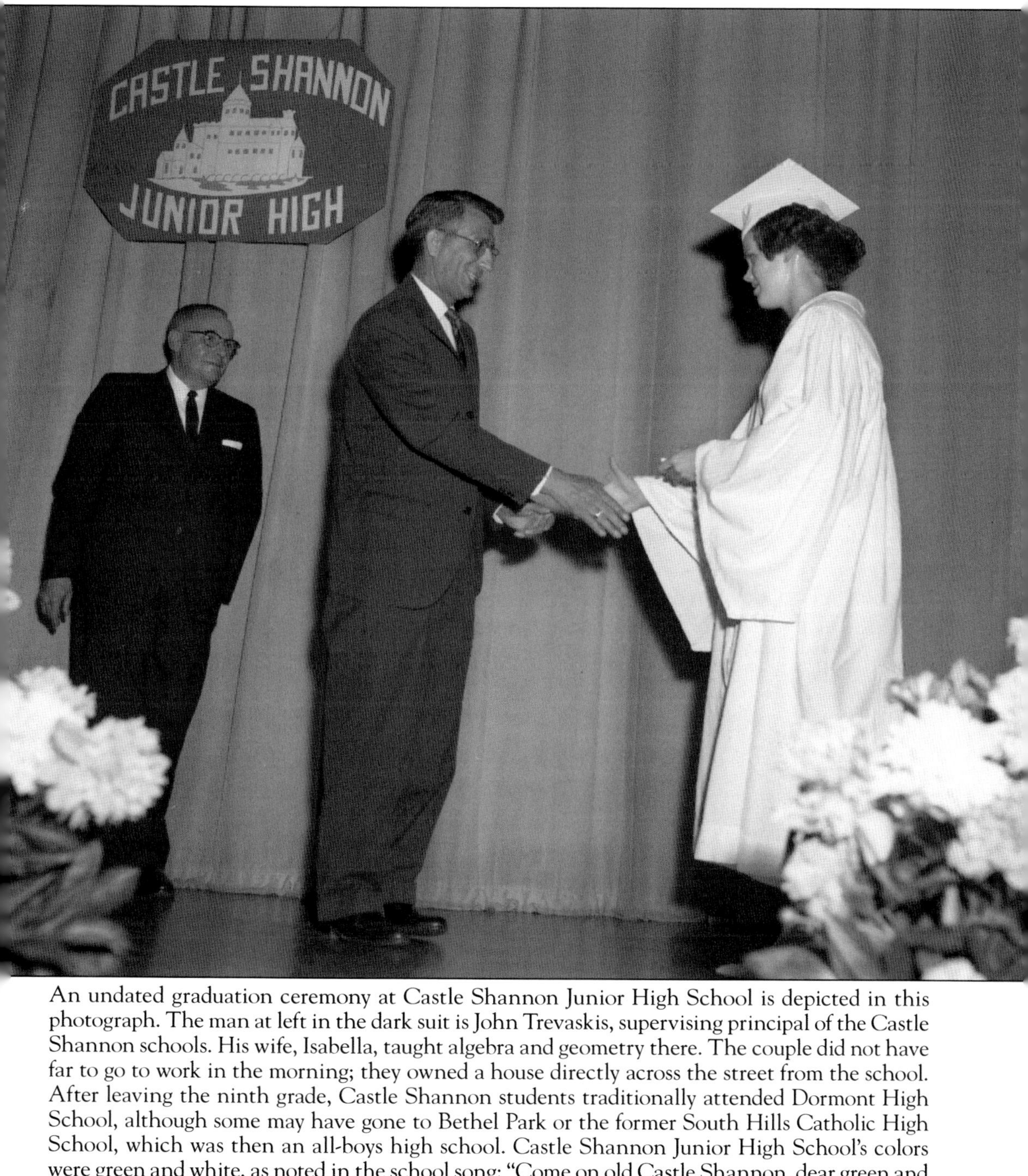

An undated graduation ceremony at Castle Shannon Junior High School is depicted in this photograph. The man at left in the dark suit is John Trevaskis, supervising principal of the Castle Shannon schools. His wife, Isabella, taught algebra and geometry there. The couple did not have far to go to work in the morning; they owned a house directly across the street from the school. After leaving the ninth grade, Castle Shannon students traditionally attended Dormont High School, although some may have gone to Bethel Park or the former South Hills Catholic High School, which was then an all-boys high school. Castle Shannon Junior High School's colors were green and white, as noted in the school song: "Come on old Castle Shannon, dear green and white / We'll show the other teams how to fight, fair and square with courage too / We need the help of you and you. / Wipe off that frown and put on a grin / Give us your best boys so we can win / Castle Shannon Junior High / Shall march on to victory." (Photograph by George "Jasper" Evans, courtesy of Ric Evans.)

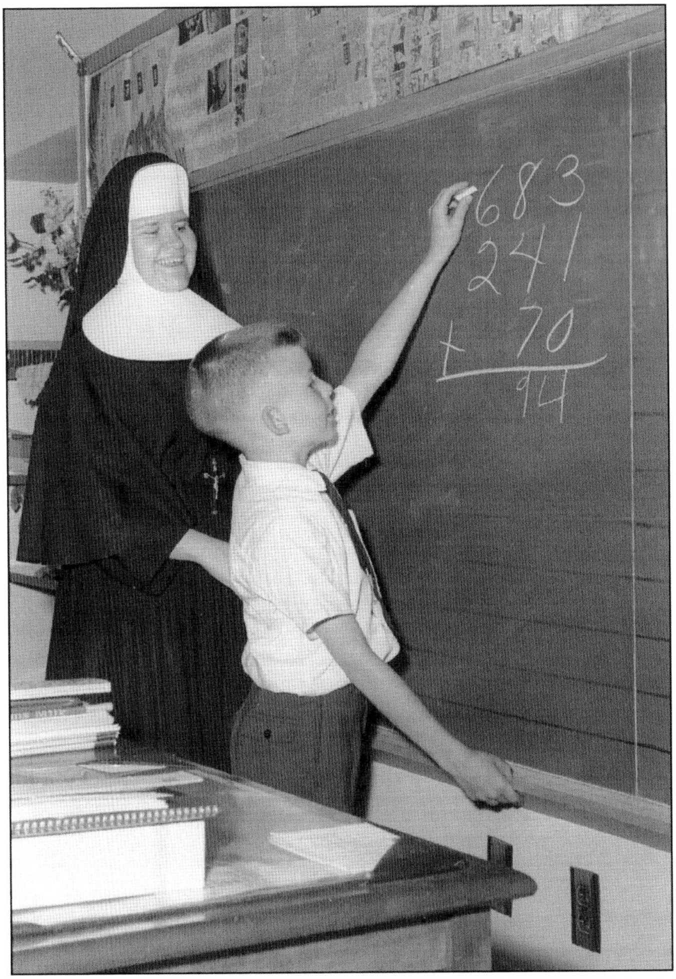

Sister Joachim is overseeing an unidentified student working on a math problem at the chalkboard at St. Anne School. The youngster seems to have learned his lessons well. Note the tie that is worn by the boy. The dress code for students has been relaxed since the 1950s, when the new school was built, but boys and girls still dress uniformly for school. (Photograph courtesy of St. Anne School.)

The new St. Anne School, photographed here from Route 88, was dedicated on March 20, 1954. Bishop John F. Dearden of the Pittsburgh Diocese observed the actual dedication. Part of the old school, adjacent to the new one, can be seen to the right. The trolley stop in the lower right portion of the photograph is no longer there. (Photograph courtesy of St. Anne School.)

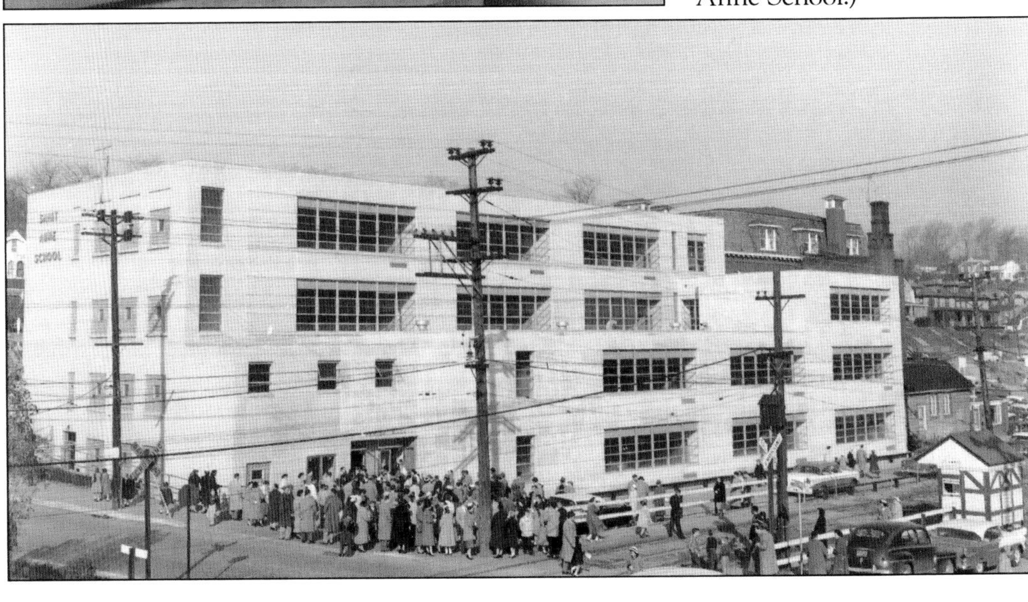

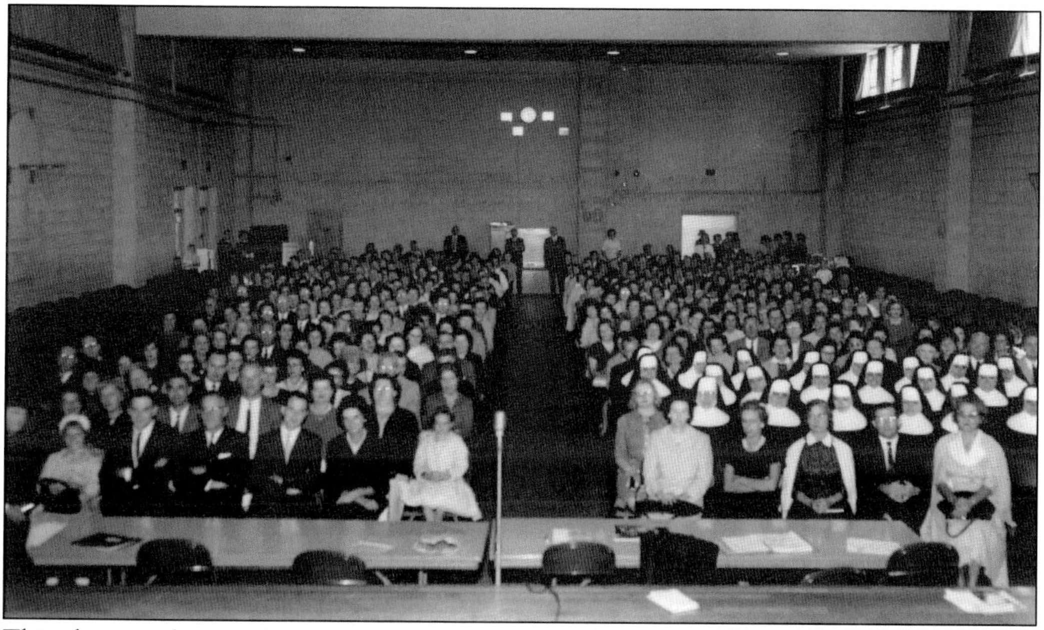

This photograph was taken inside the gymnasium at the new St. Anne School. The large area was often used for meetings and even mass. During the annual St. Anne Parish Fair in June, it becomes the site of a popular flea market. The St. Anne Cyclones boys' and girls' basketball teams play their home games in the gym. (Photograph courtesy of St. Anne School.)

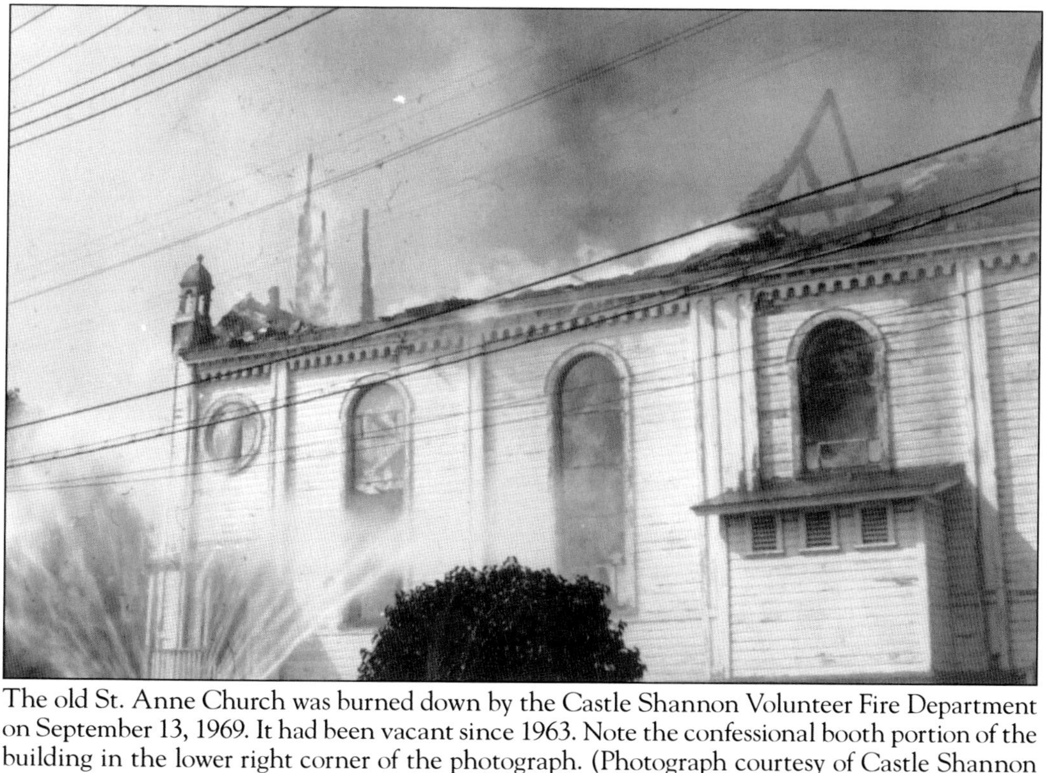

The old St. Anne Church was burned down by the Castle Shannon Volunteer Fire Department on September 13, 1969. It had been vacant since 1963. Note the confessional booth portion of the building in the lower right corner of the photograph. (Photograph courtesy of Castle Shannon Volunteer Fire Department.)

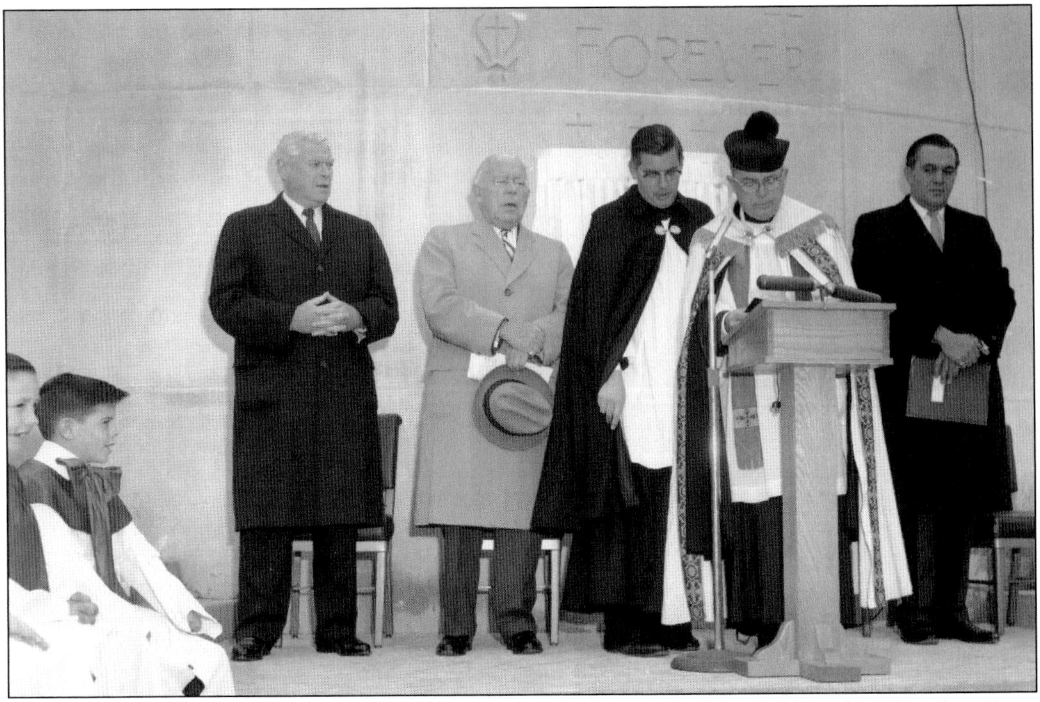

The bell tower at the new St. Anne Church was dedicated a few months after the church in April 1963. The tower was named in memory of labor leader Philip Murray. Shown here, from left to right, are David McDonald (president of the Steelworkers union), David L. Lawrence (Pennsylvania's governor and the former mayor of Pittsburgh), Father Richard Scherer, the Reverend Eugene Harkins (St. Anne's pastor at the time), and an unidentified man. (Photograph by George "Jasper" Evans, courtesy of Ric Evans.)

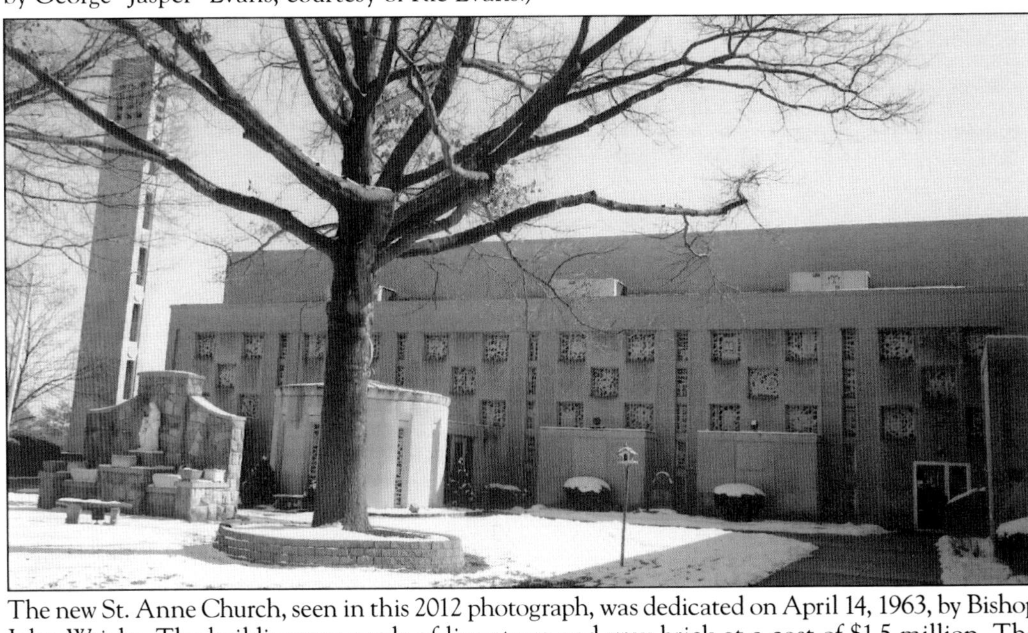

The new St. Anne Church, seen in this 2012 photograph, was dedicated on April 14, 1963, by Bishop John Wright. The building was made of limestone and gray brick at a cost of $1.5 million. The circular structure behind the tree was built for baptisms. (Photograph by Charles LeClaire.)

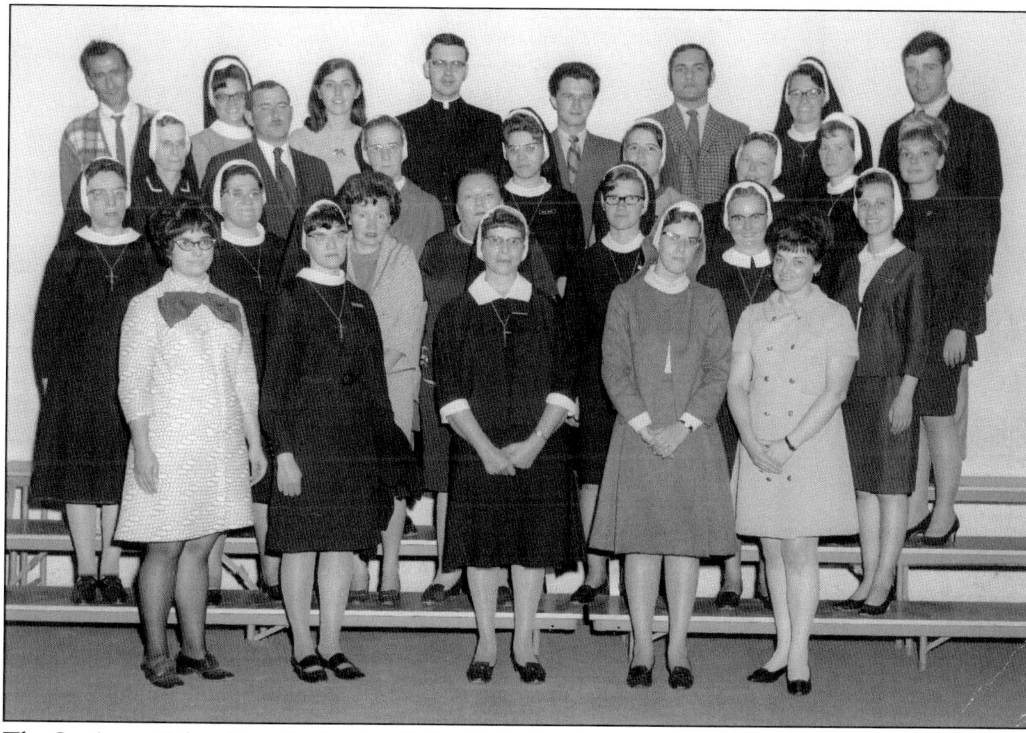

The St. Anne School faculty for the 1969–1970 school year is pictured here. Note the abundance of nuns who taught in the classroom. That is no longer the case; by the 2000s, laypeople comprised the entire school faculty. One of the nuns, Sister John Ann, later became the principal at Butler Catholic School. (Photograph courtesy of St. Anne School.)

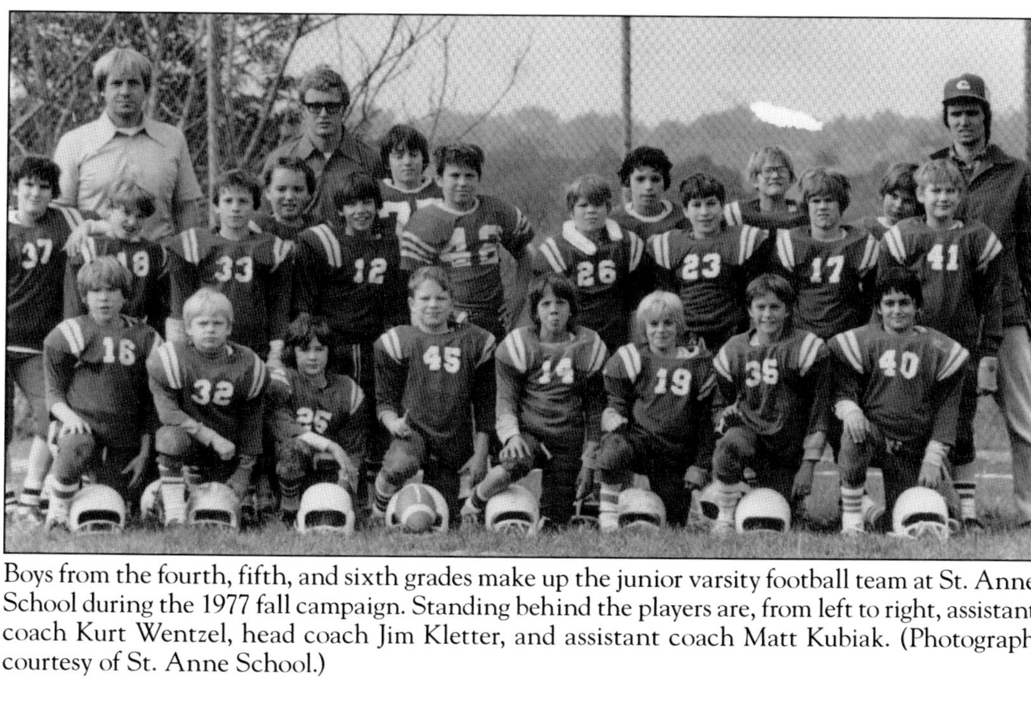

Boys from the fourth, fifth, and sixth grades make up the junior varsity football team at St. Anne School during the 1977 fall campaign. Standing behind the players are, from left to right, assistant coach Kurt Wentzel, head coach Jim Kletter, and assistant coach Matt Kubiak. (Photograph courtesy of St. Anne School.)

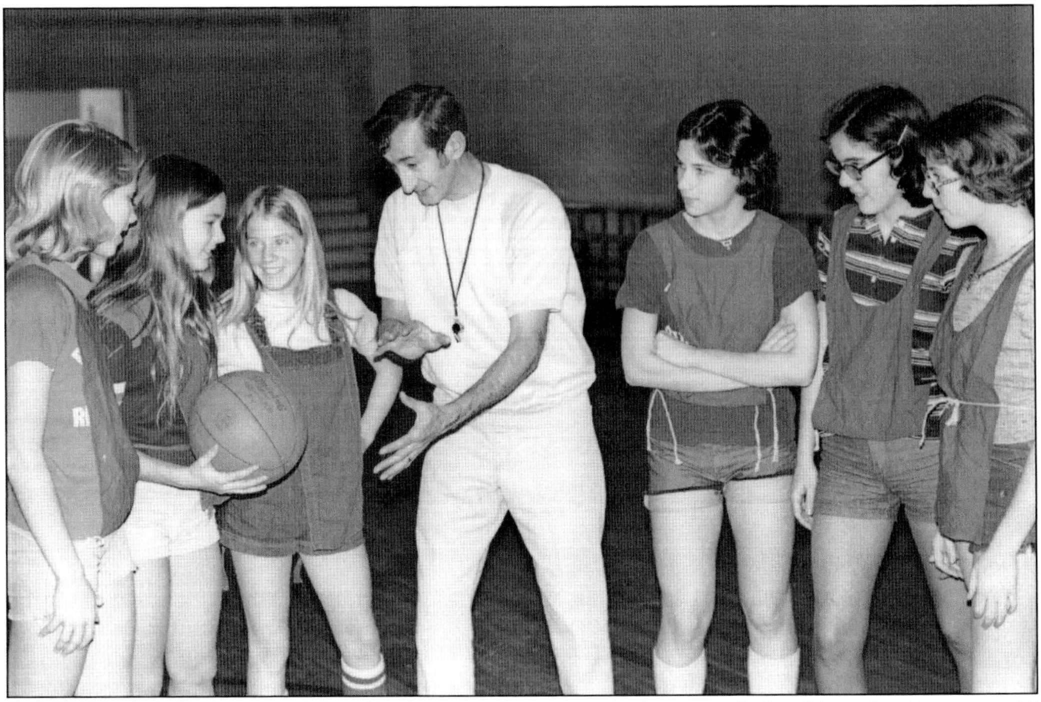

"You can call me Mister Q!" Castle Shannon youngsters who attended public schools were told about the popular gym teacher at St. Anne School, Joe Quaquarucci, even if they never did get to see him in person. Here, Mister Q explains the finer points of basketball to this 1970s class in the St. Anne gymnasium. (Photograph courtesy of St. Anne School.)

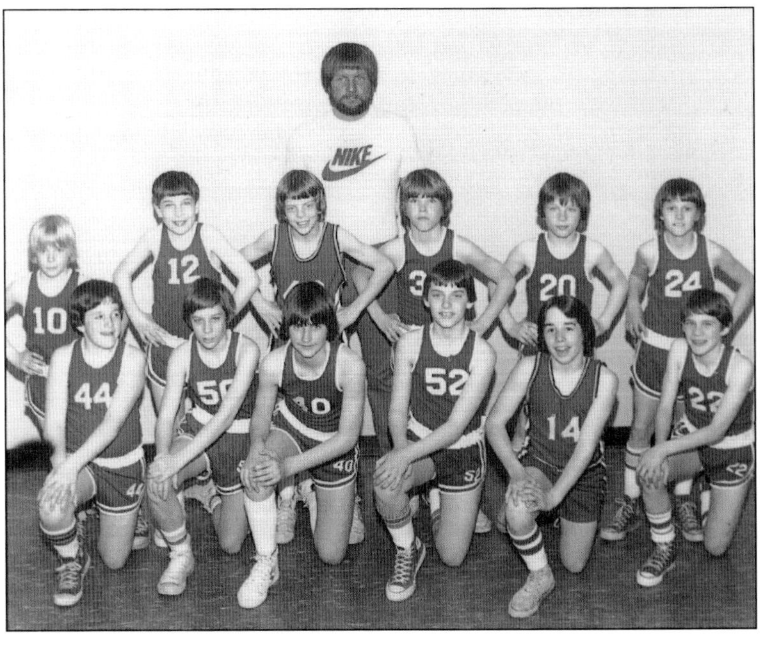

Coach Kurt Wentzel is shown here with the 1977–1978 St. Anne boys' junior varsity basketball team. The players are, from left to right, (first row) Tim Hillebrand, Daniel Baumgart, John Hokaj, James Dieterle, Jeffrey Wank, and Brian Klisavage; (second row) Kevin Schram, Mark Welch, Dave Swisher, Matthew Williams, Matthew Banbury, and Clint Lange. (Photograph courtesy of St. Anne School.)

Father Eugene Harkins poses with some girls who have just made their first communion at the old St. Anne Church. The little boy had to wait a couple more years. Father Harkins was a priest in the Catholic diocese for 55 years and pastor at St. Anne for 19 years. He died in 1981 at the age of 85. (Photograph courtesy of St. Anne Church.)

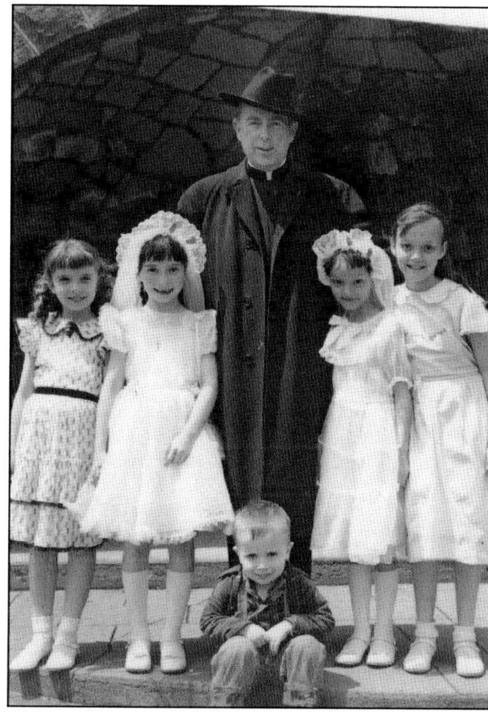

Father Eugene Harkins (in back, center) stands with the first communion class at the new St. Anne Church, May 11, 1963. Students from St. Anne School, as well as other children of the parish who were students in the school's Confirmation of Christian Doctrine (CCD) program, comprise the class. (Photograph courtesy of St. Anne School.)

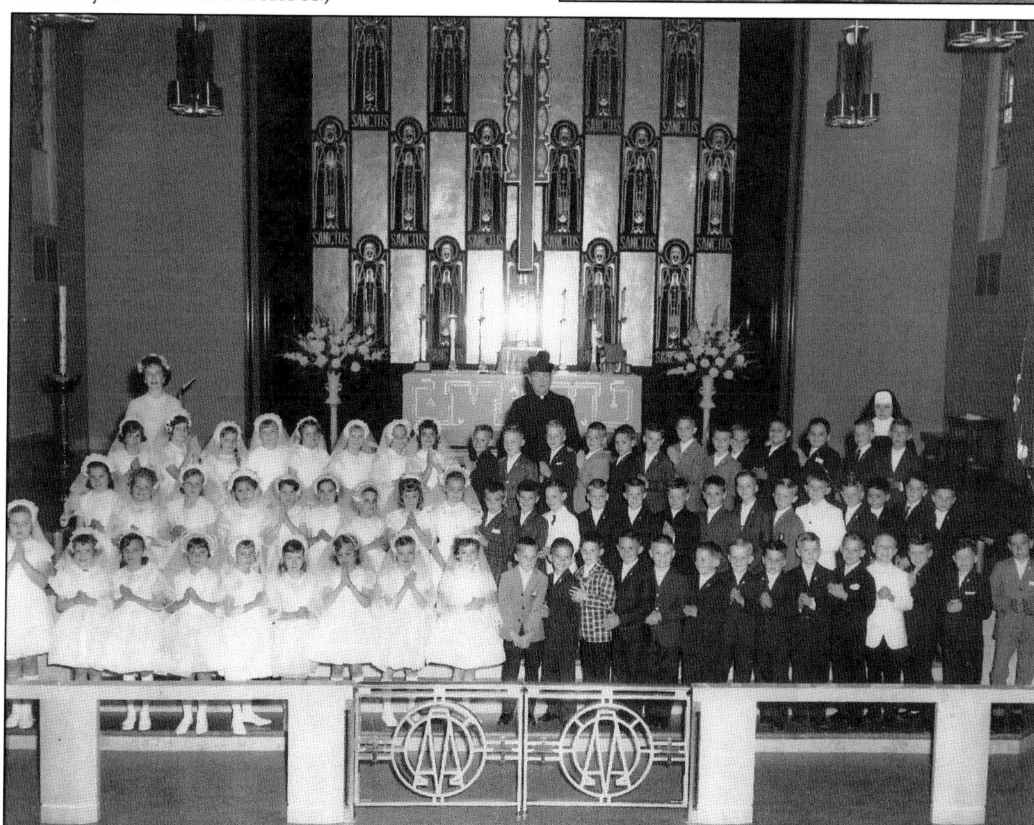

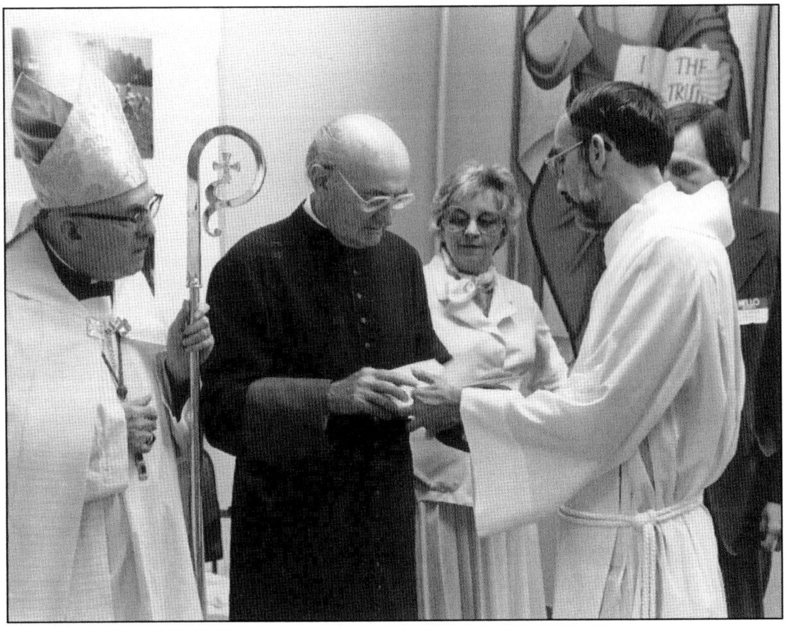

Msgr. Charles Rice (center) receives instruction from Fr. John Garvey (right) as Pittsburgh Diocese bishop Vincent Leonard (left) observes. The occasion was the rededication of an addition to St. Anne School on September 10, 1978. (Photograph courtesy of St. Anne School).

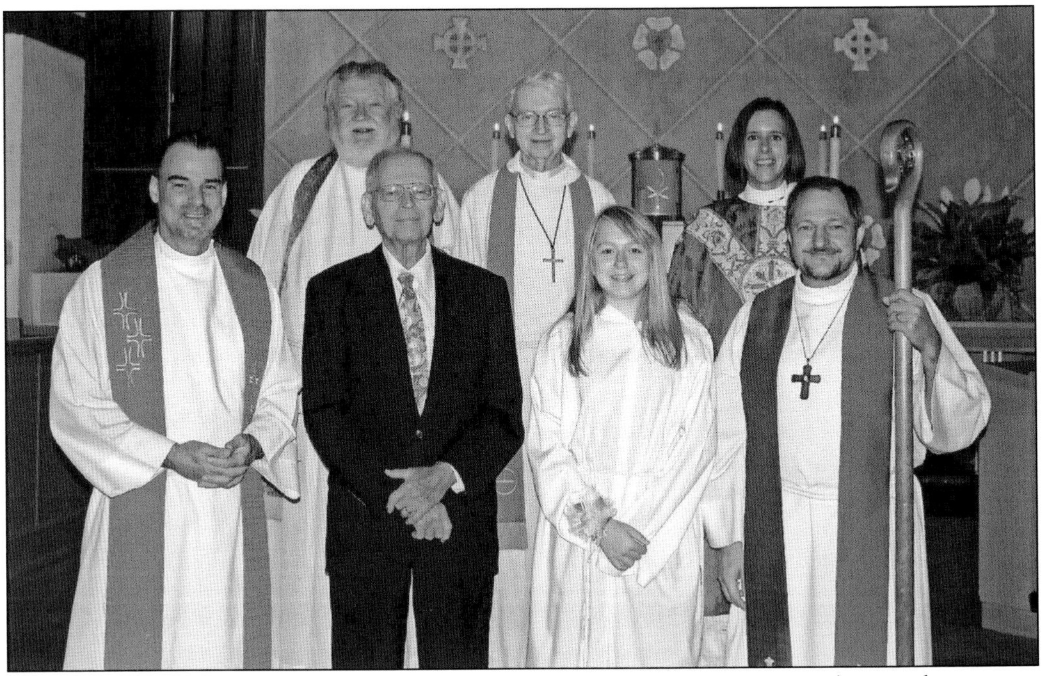

Emmanuel Evangelical Lutheran Church celebrated its 125th anniversary with a worship service and dinner on September 12, 2010. Shown attending are, from left to right, (first row) the Reverend Larry Kemp (pastor, 2001–present), Wilford Hogle (member), Kaylin Crawford (confirmand), and the Reverend Kurt Kusserow (bishop, Southwestern Pennsylvania Synod of the Evangelical Lutheran Church in America); (second row) the Reverend James Wente (pastor, 1979–1989), the Reverend James Graeser (son of the congregation), and the Reverend Sarah Lee-Faulkner (assistant to the bishop). (Photograph by Joyce Lynn Johnson, courtesy of Emmanuel Evangelical Lutheran Church.)

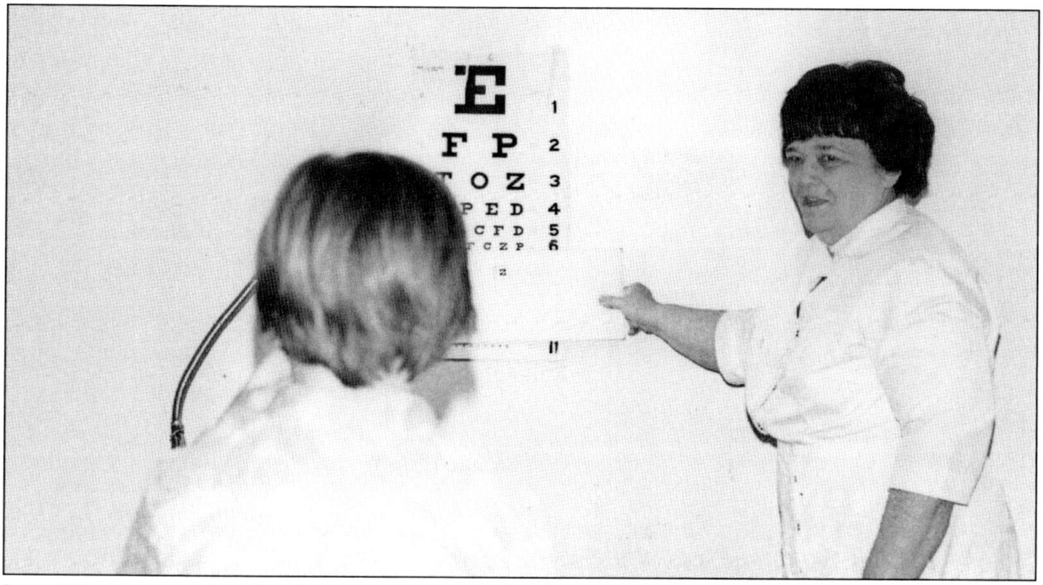

Jane O'Brien was a familiar figure to many Castle Shannon schoolchildren in the 1960s. She lived on Frank Street, about an equal distance from both St. Anne School and Vernridge Elementary School, and would travel from her home to either school. Here, she administers an eye test to a St. Anne student. (Photograph courtesy of St. Anne School.)

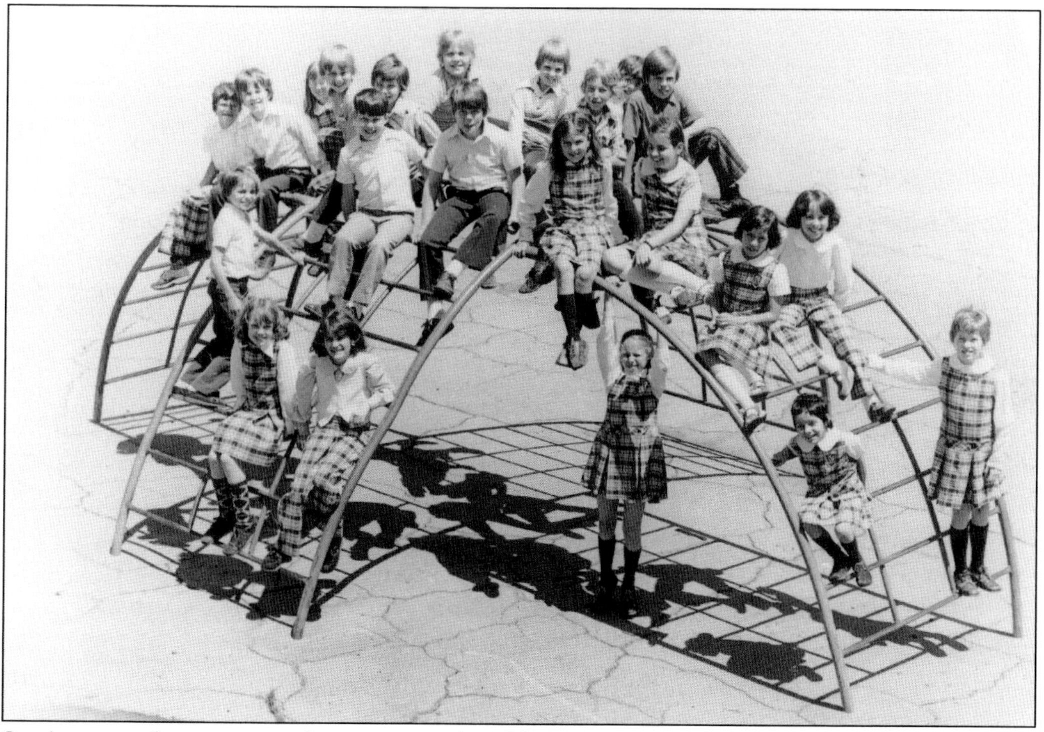

St. Anne students are monkeying around and hamming it up for the camera in this undated photograph. Although the girls appear in uniform, wearing plaid dresses, note the young lady at lower left, wearing plaid slacks. White shirts were the uniform of the day for St. Anne boys. (Photograph courtesy of St. Anne School.)

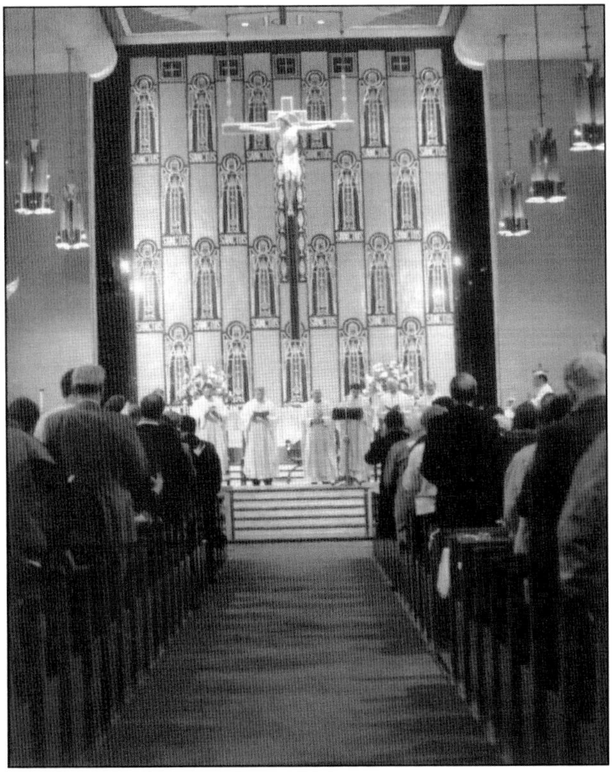

The interior of St. Anne Church is seen in this photograph. Fr. Donald Breier, who was at St. Anne from 1986 to 2004, is conducting the mass. St. Anne used to have as many as five Sunday masses. Currently, there are three morning masses and an early Sunday evening service, plus a Saturday mass in late afternoon or early evening, depending on the season. (Photograph courtesy of St. Anne Church.)

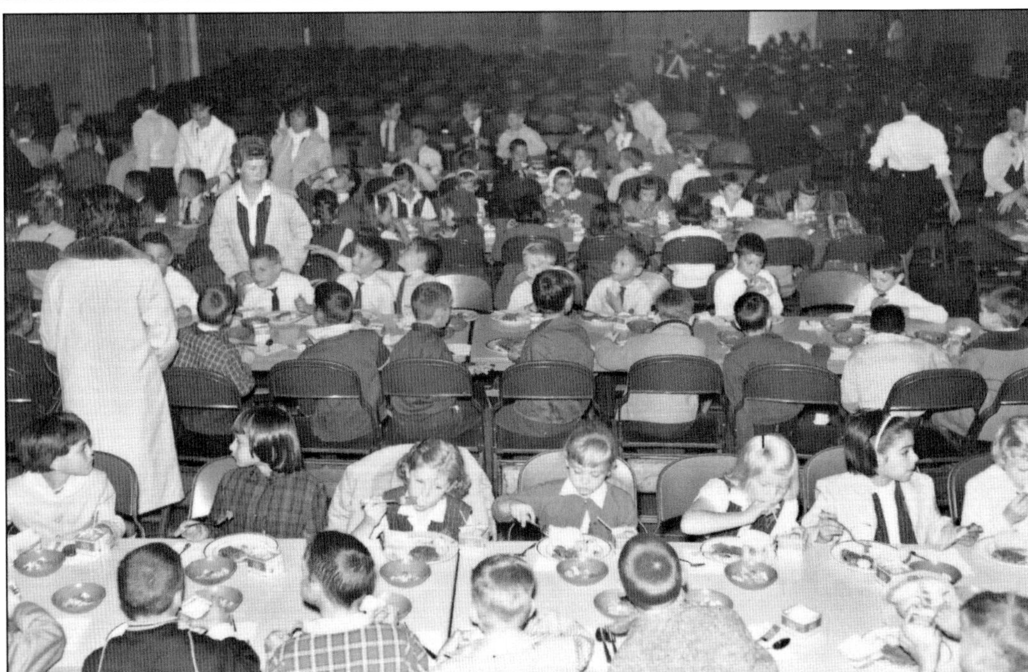

St. Anne students are seen eating their lunches in the multipurpose gymnasium of the new school in an undated photograph. In the upper right portion of the photograph, a boy is wearing a safety patrol belt. (Photograph courtesy of St. Anne Church.)

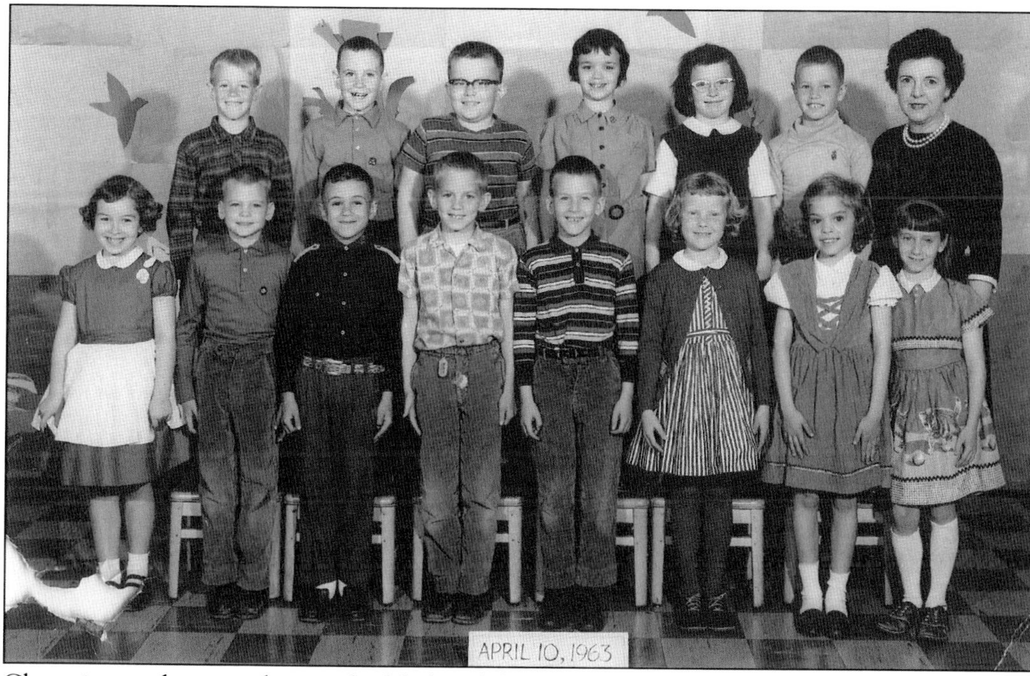

Class picture day was always a highlight of the school year for Vernridge Elementary School students. This photograph shows Mrs. Sanner's second-grade class on April 10, 1963. (Photograph courtesy of Sciullo family.)

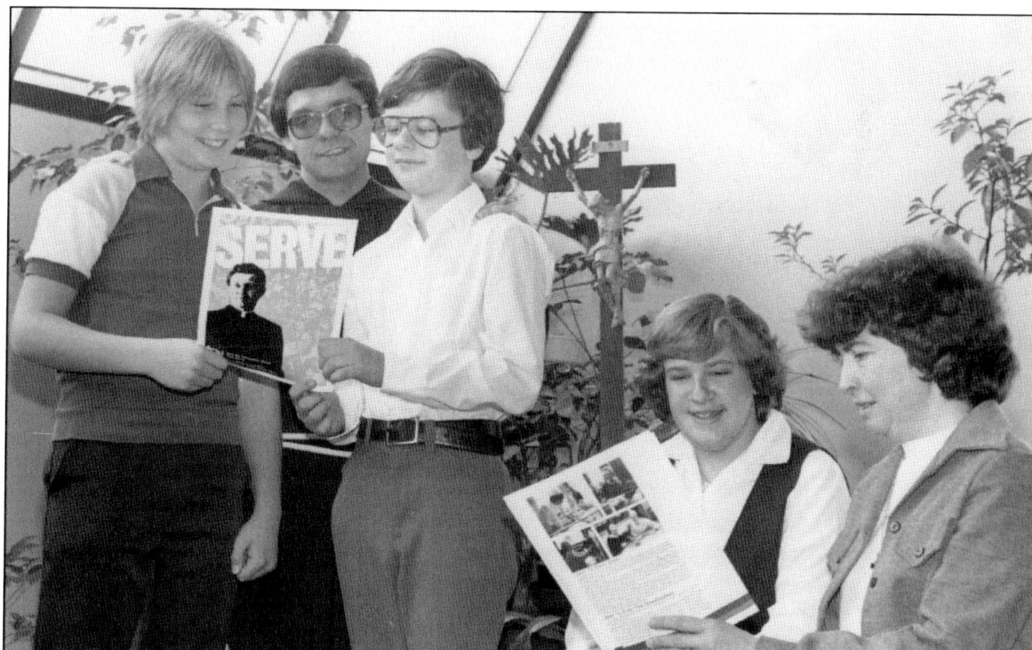

Students at St. Anne School were asked to consider a career in the Catholic Church. This 1980 photograph shows a group of students with literature on the subject. Many students would serve at the altar or in the church choir early weekday mornings before heading to school. (Photograph courtesy of St. Anne School.)

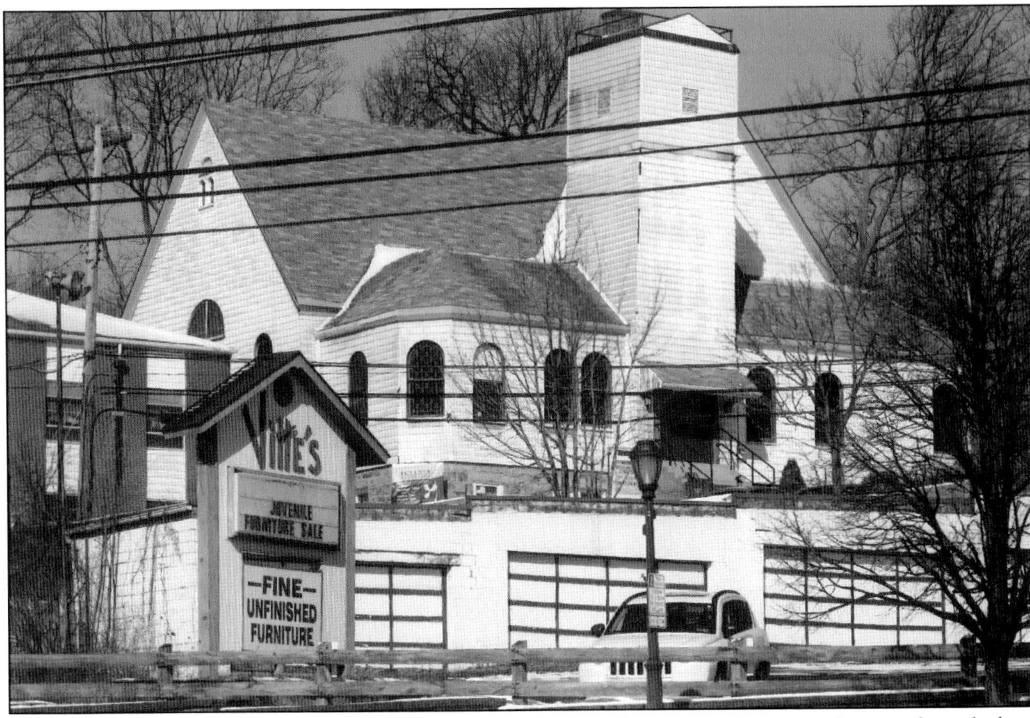

The United Methodist church, seen behind Vitte's in this 2012 photograph, was founded on December 9, 1888, as the Methodist Protestant church. It sits next to the Myrtle Elementary School grounds. (Photograph by Charles LeClaire.)

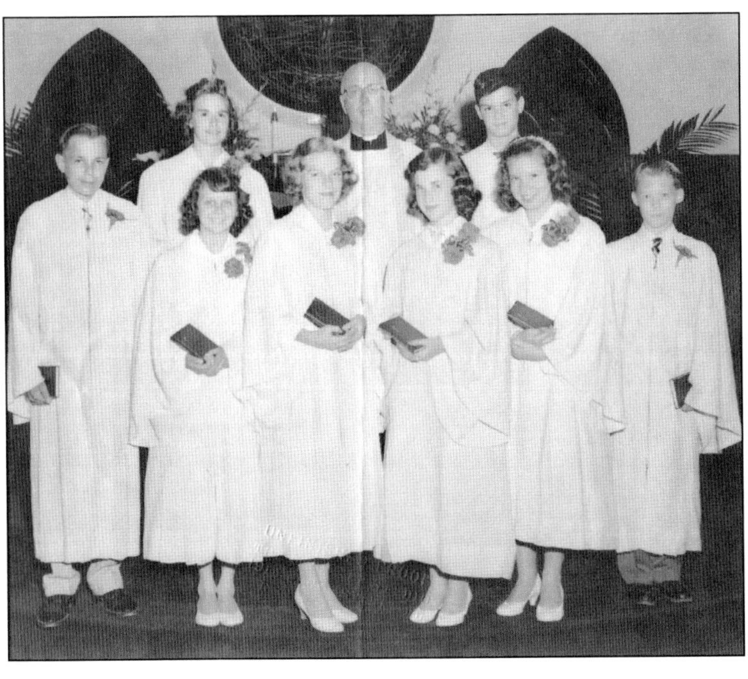

This photograph shows a Confirmation Day from the late 1950s at Emmanuel Evangelical Lutheran Church on Pine Avenue. The ceremony was held in the old sanctuary on the property. The Reverend Oscar Smith (second row, center) performed the service. (Photograph courtesy of Emmanuel Evangelical Lutheran Church.)

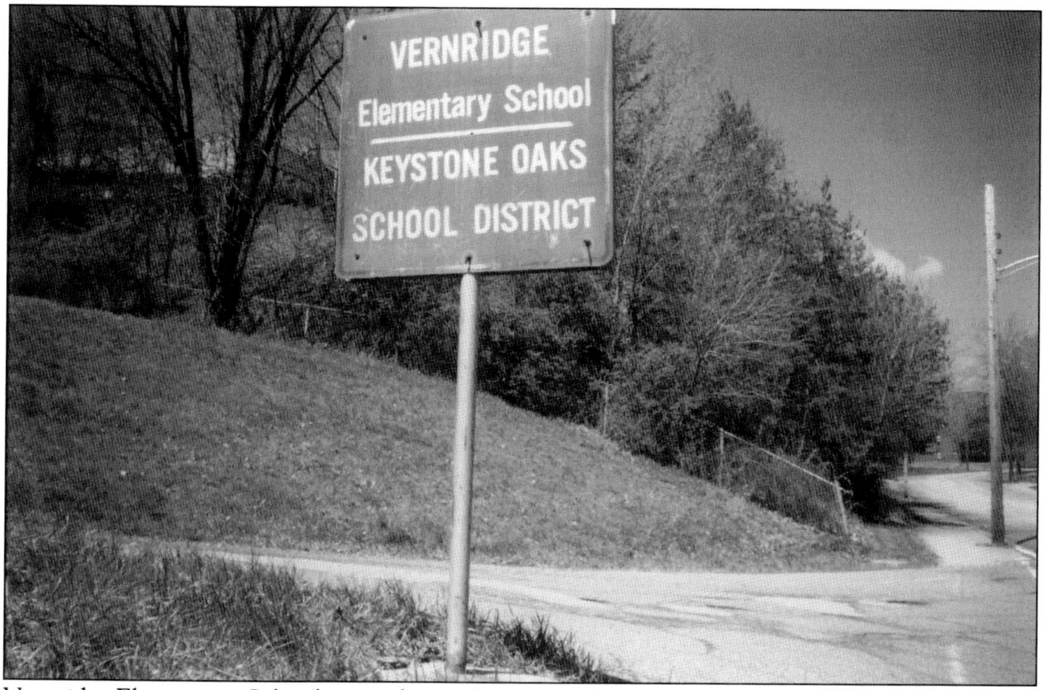

Vernridge Elementary School opened in 1952 as part of the Castle Shannon School District, and was located next to what would become the grounds for the new St. Anne Church. Vernridge, the last school built by the Castle Shannon School District, was torn down in the late 1990s, and was replaced by residential condominiums. (Photograph courtesy of Mary Scabilloni.)

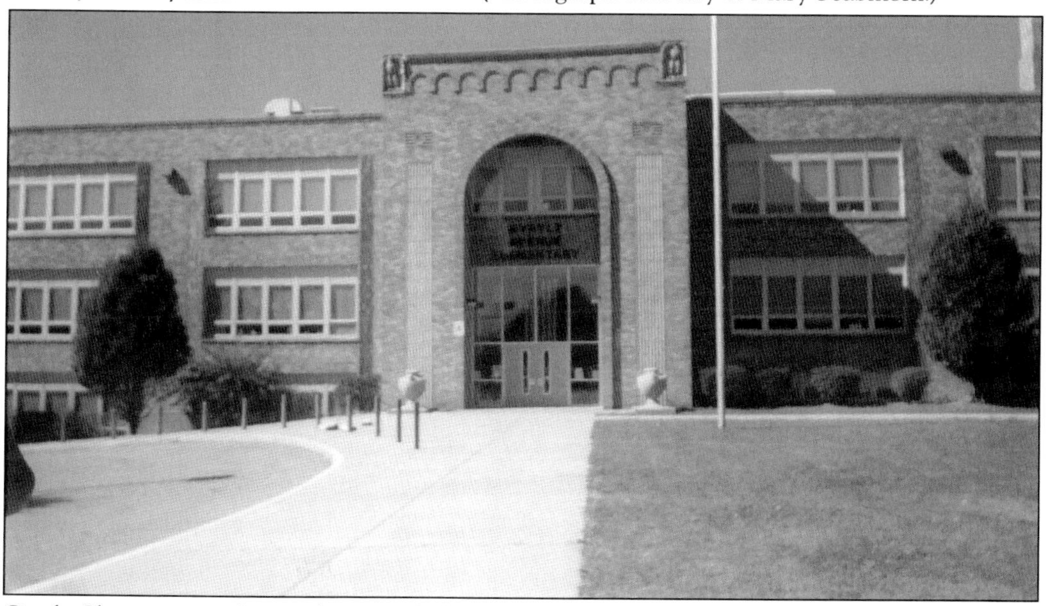

Castle Shannon residents who attended Myrtle School before the 1990s might not recognize it now. The school underwent an extensive renovation in 1995, and the interior looks much different than it did in its earlier years. The playground area behind the school was removed, and a new set of recess equipment was installed alongside the building toward the Methodist church. (Photograph courtesy of Mary Scabilloni.)

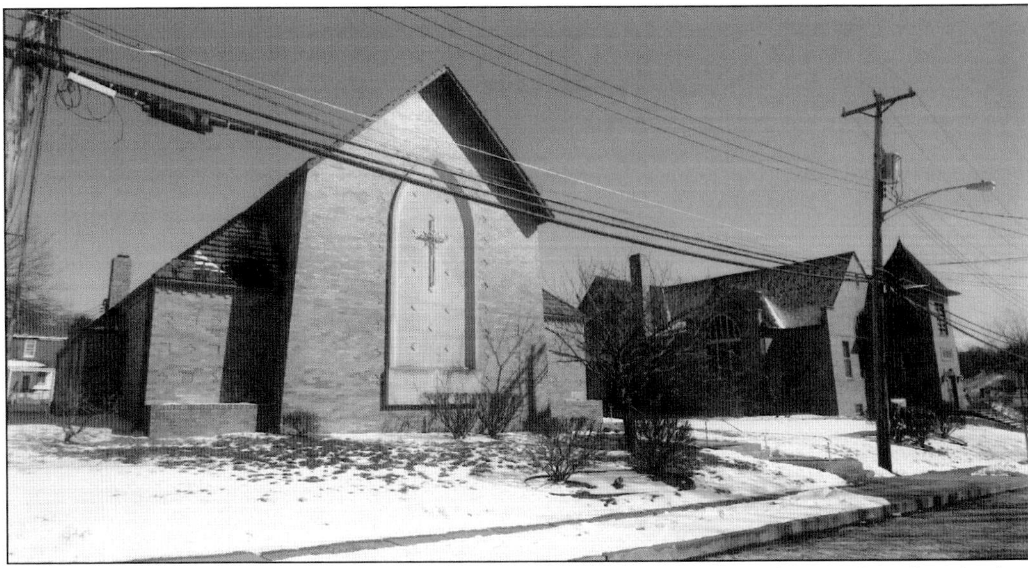

A 2012 photograph shows the entire history of the Evangelical Lutheran church, which is situated in one of Castle Shannon's oldest residential neighborhoods. The old church building on the right, Emmanuel's Evangelical Lutheran Church, was dedicated in 1913; the newer sanctuary at left, Emmanuel Evangelical Lutheran Church, was dedicated in 1960. (Photograph by Charles LeClaire.)

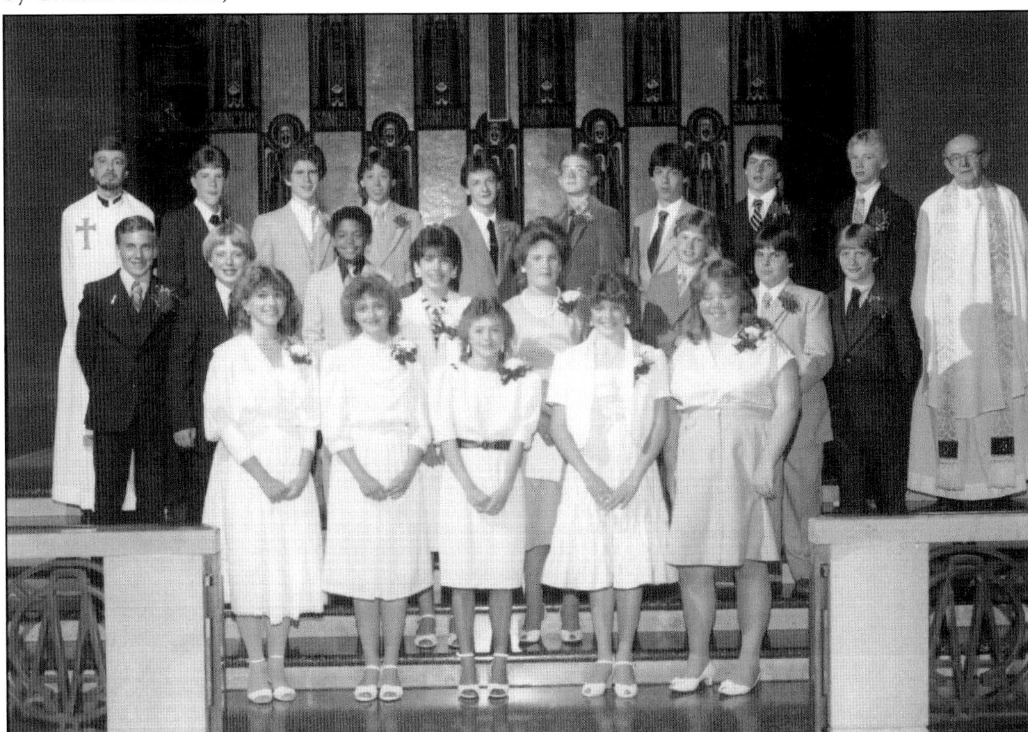

By the mid-1980s, enrollment had been dropping steadily at schools, and Castle Shannon was no exception. This 1984 confirmation class at St. Anne provides visual documentation. Monsignor Rice is in the third row, far right. (Photograph courtesy of St. Anne School.)

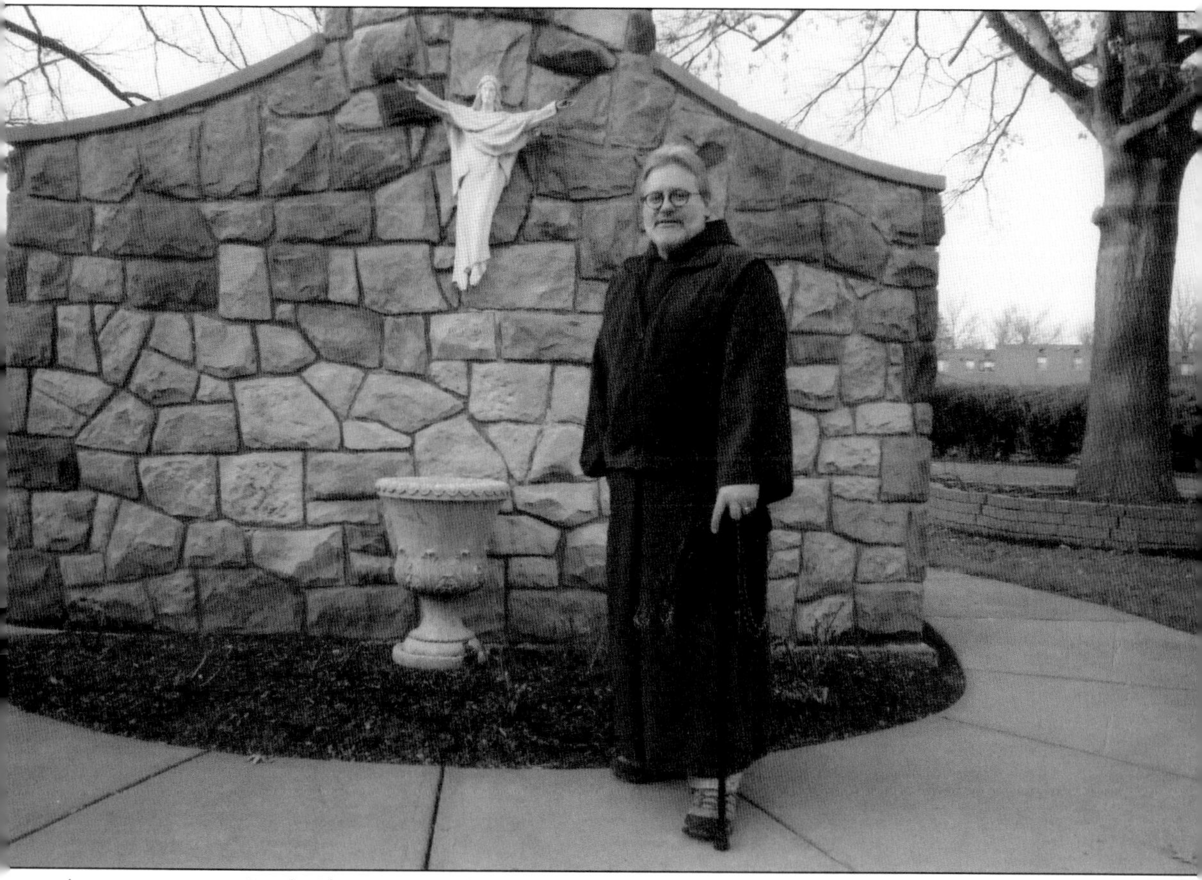

As a teenager in Castle Shannon, Michael Greb loved baseball. But when he realized he probably was not going to replace Roberto Clemente as the Pittsburgh Pirates' next great right fielder, his career path took him in a much different direction. The 1976 graduate of Keystone Oaks High School, who also attended St. Anne School, became Father Greb when he was ordained in 1989 by Bishop Donald Wuerl. Father Greb recalled his roots when asked to consider his influences during a 2012 interview. "I do realize that so many of the values of faith and family, care for people and good citizenship were born in Castle Shannon," he said. "I have always been proud of my hometown and the people. Our parish of St. Anne's will always be where I came to love my Catholic faith and where I discovered my pathway of service and religious life." (Photograph by Sam Sciullo Jr.)

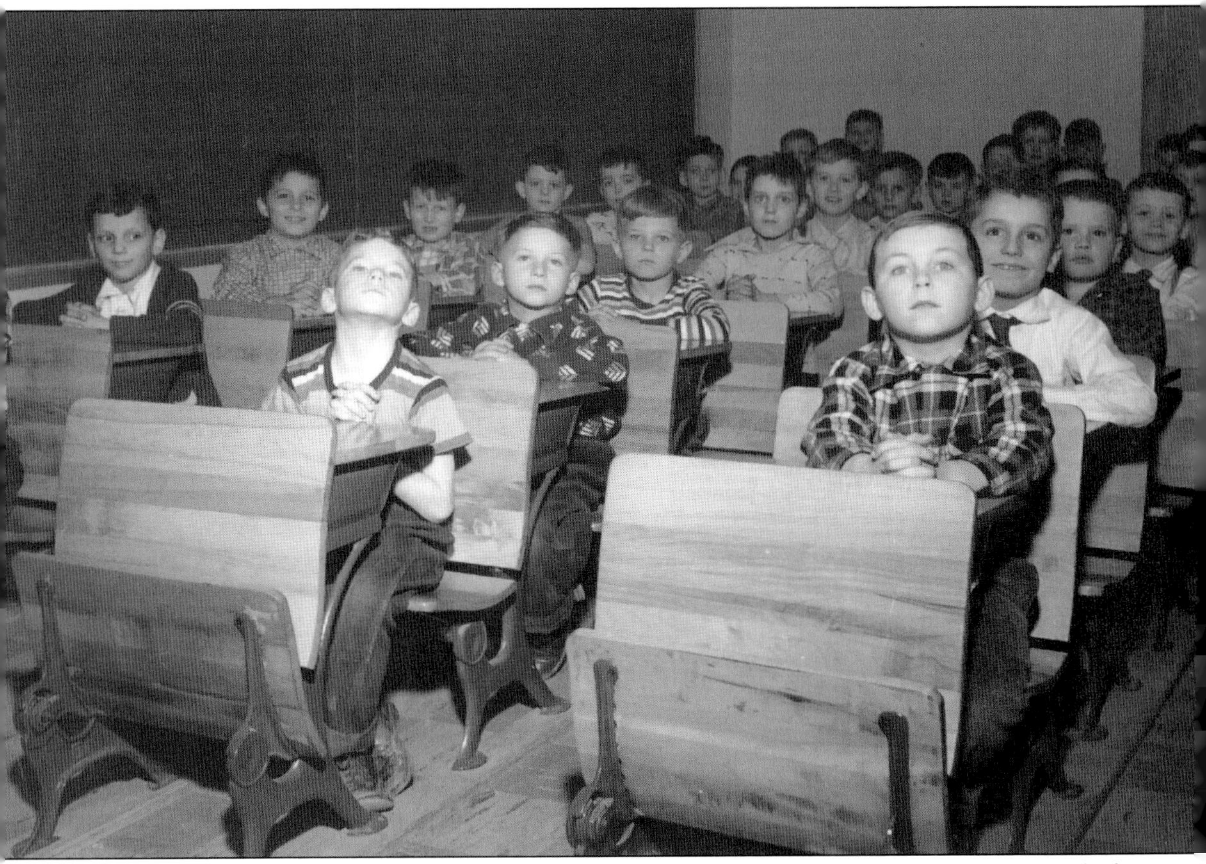

This 1950s photograph shows a classroom of St. Anne students, hands clasped prayer-style for the camera. There were no uniforms then. Note the seriousness of the boys in the foreground and the relaxed casualness of a few on the far left. The desks are one-piece oldsters, not unlike the cramped cars of a roller coaster. (Photograph courtesy of St. Anne School.)

Five

Recreation

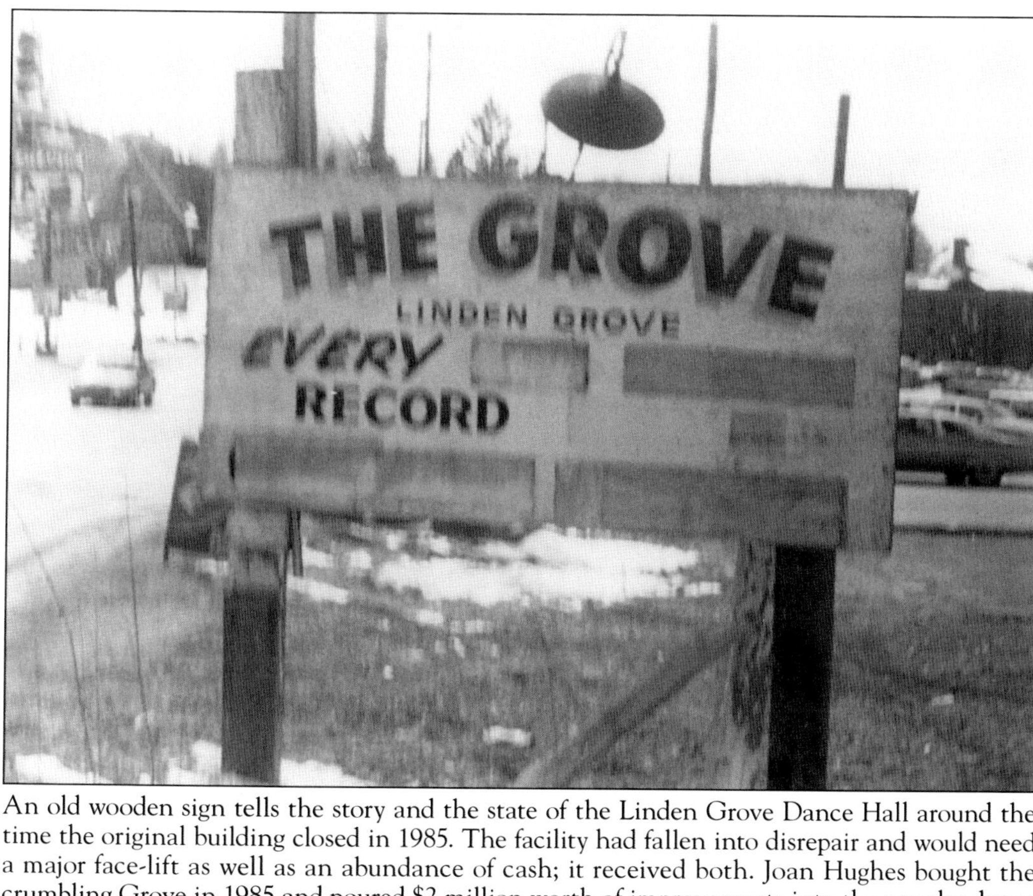

An old wooden sign tells the story and the state of the Linden Grove Dance Hall around the time the original building closed in 1985. The facility had fallen into disrepair and would need a major face-lift as well as an abundance of cash; it received both. Joan Hughes bought the crumbling Grove in 1985 and poured $2 million worth of improvements into the popular dance hall, helping to spark a revitalization for one of Castle Shannon's most endearing nightspots. (Photograph courtesy of Mary Scabilloni.)

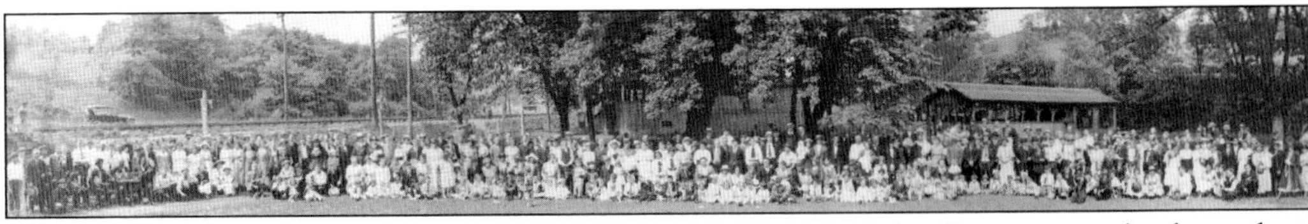

At its inception, Linden Grove was intended as a picnic spot for Germans and other ethnic groups—a place to congregate on a warm afternoon. Musicians would stroll through the grounds entertaining the crowd. Other parts of Castle Shannon also drew crowds for parties and picnics during the first part of the 20th century, including Sleepy Hollow, Adams Grove (the area near the old St. Francis Academy School), and the area along the top of Hamilton Road that eventually became Hamilton Park. (Photograph by George "Jasper" Evans, courtesy of Ric Evans.)

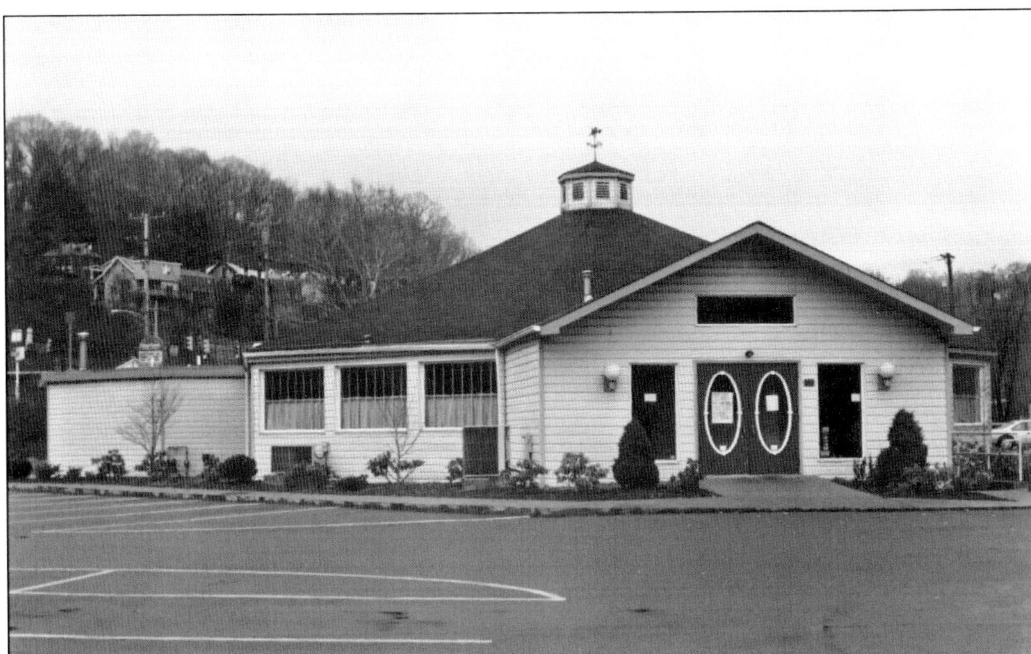

Linden Grove is shown as it appears today. A new entrance is the major change to the original octagonal design. People from Pittsburgh would flock to the Grove via trolleys to dance, mix, and mingle. In its heyday, Perry Como, the Ames Brothers, and Patti Page were just a few of the big-name acts who performed live at Linden Grove. The Grove adapted to the times, too—accommodating the big band sounds at mid-century and disco during the 1970s. (Photograph courtesy of Jean O'Malley.)

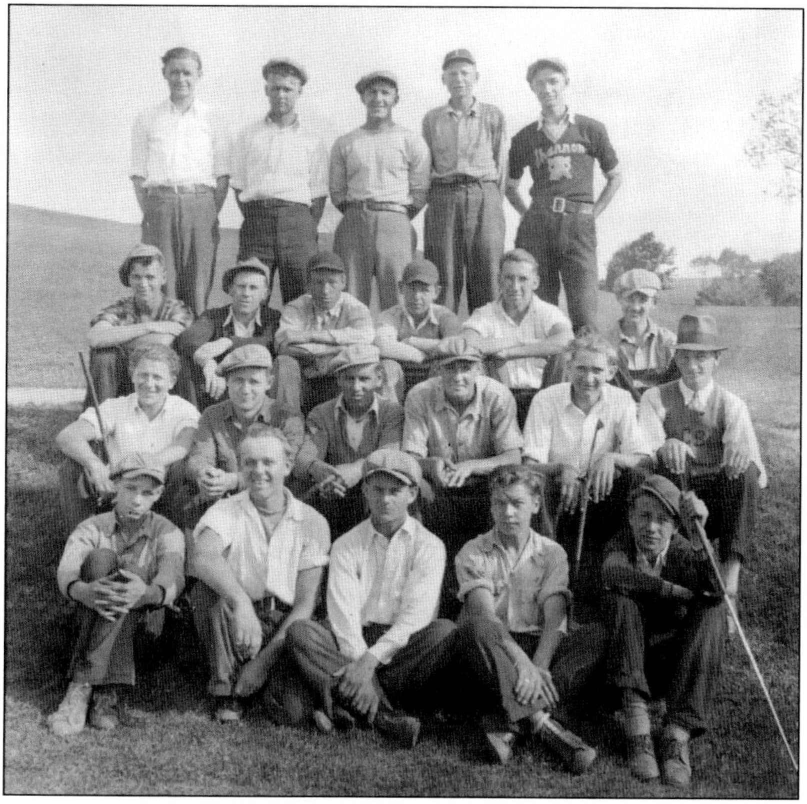

This 1934 image shows a group of caddies who worked at the Castle Shannon Golf Club. The club was known by that name from 1907 to 1946, when Stevenson-Williams Real Estate bought the property and sold it to Mt. Lebanon. In second row, note the caddie master at far right. (Photograph by George "Jasper" Evans, courtesy of Ric Evans.)

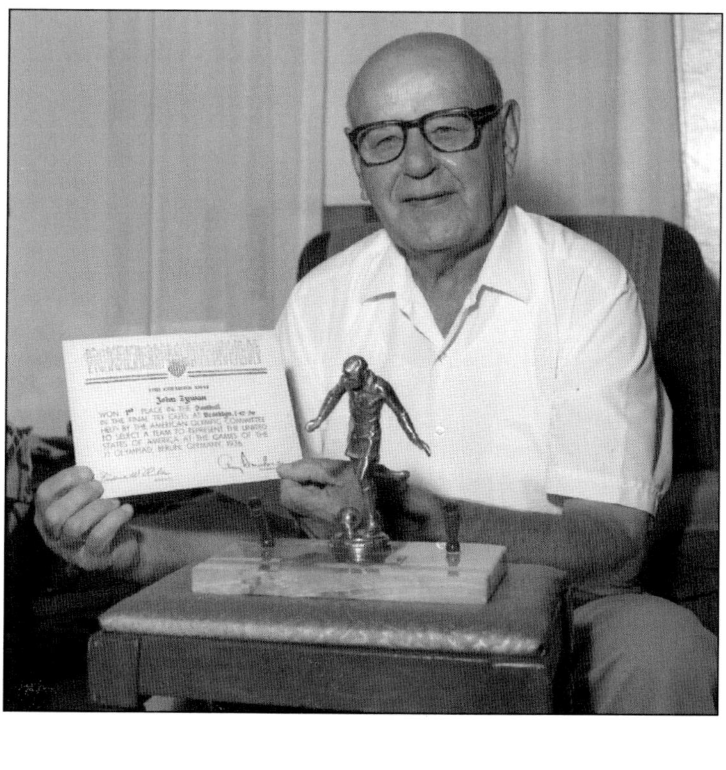

Castle Shannon's own John "Zip" Zywan represented the United States in the 1936 Olympics in Berlin, Germany. An outstanding soccer player, Zywan received a commendation from the Castle Shannon Borough Council that same year for his contributions to the sport, his country, and his hometown. In this photograph, Zywan displays a certificate of achievement for finishing in first place in a soccer tryout in Brooklyn, New York, held to select the Olympic team. (Photograph by George "Jasper" Evans, courtesy of Ric Evans.)

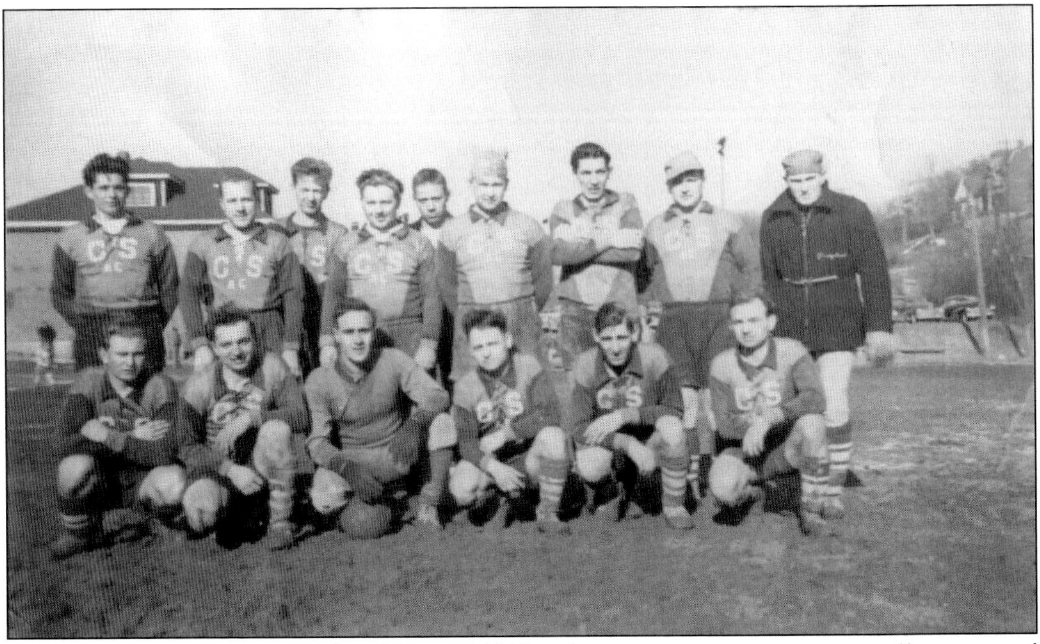

Unlike other communities in the 1930s and 1940s, whose soccer teams were generally sponsored by ethnic cultural clubs, Castle Shannon's squads usually had commercial sponsorship. Soccer was big in this area; many of the players were sons of immigrants who had been drawn to Castle Shannon by its mining opportunities. Castle Shannon won the West Penn Cup in 1947 and was a national runner-up in 1936. This is a team photograph from 1952. The teams also competed in the Keystone League, a statewide organization. The W.W. Riehl Soccer Club won the National Amateur Cup in 1935. (Photograph by George "Jasper" Evans, courtesy of Ric Evans.)

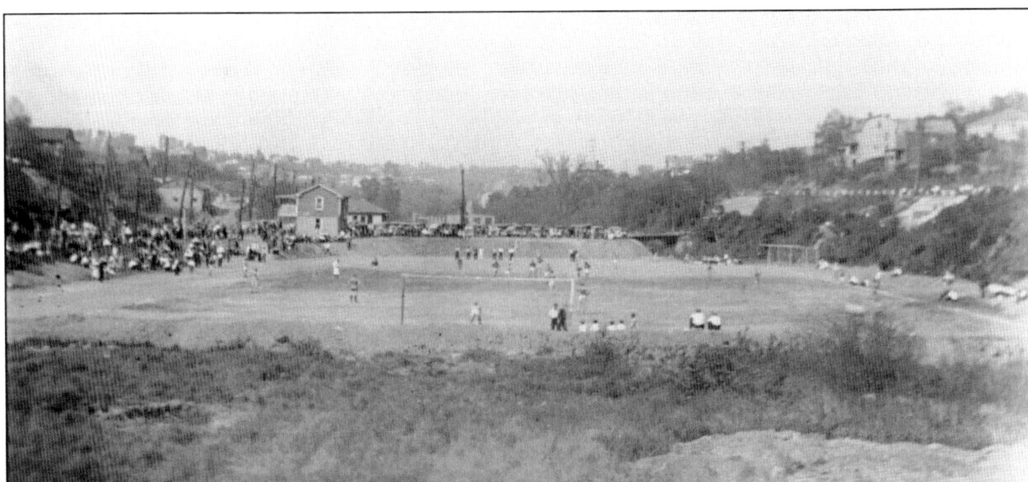

This photograph shows action from a soccer game in the area of Cretestone, located below Route 88 in Castle Shannon. Games also were played in a field that would later become the site of Bob Smith Ford for many years, then Kenny Ross Ford, closer to the road. Castle Shannon teams also played games at the Allegheny County Fairgrounds. (Photograph by George "Jasper" Evans, courtesy of Ric Evans.)

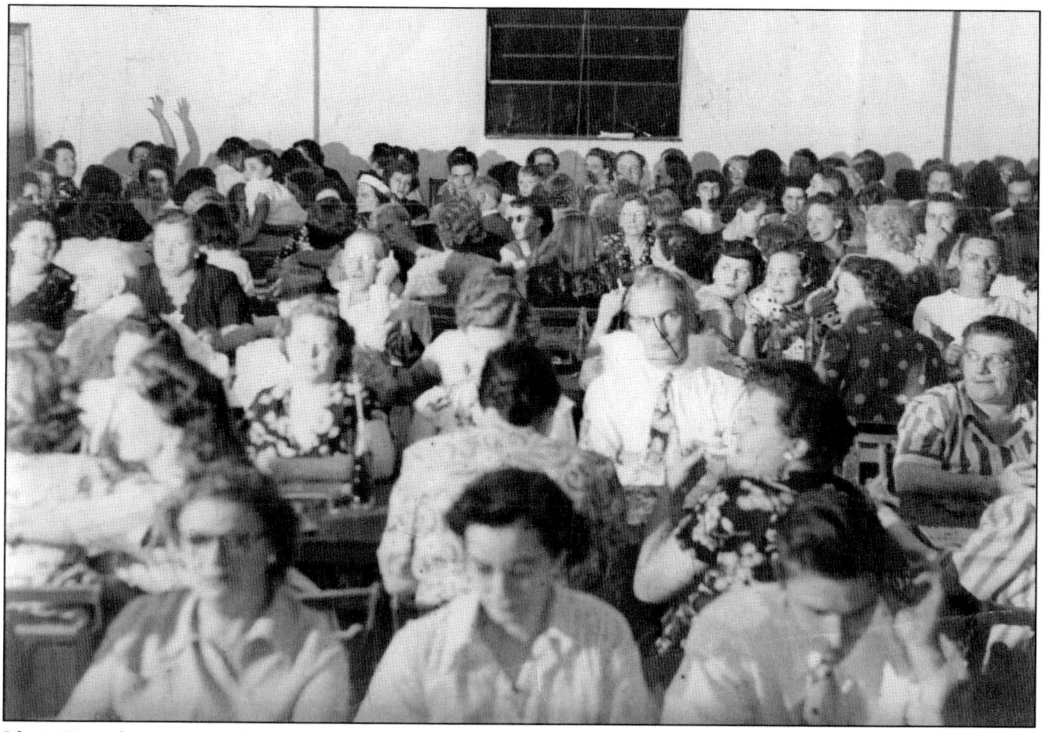

If it's Tuesday, it must be Bingo Night in Castle Shannon. For decades, residents of all ages have penciled in Tuesday nights on their calendars to play bingo for the benefit of the Castle Shannon Volunteer Fire Department—and maybe themselves. This gathering during the 1940s takes place at the old fire hall on Park Avenue. Note the raised winning hand in the upper left of the photograph. (Photograph courtesy of Castle Shannon Volunteer Fire Department.)

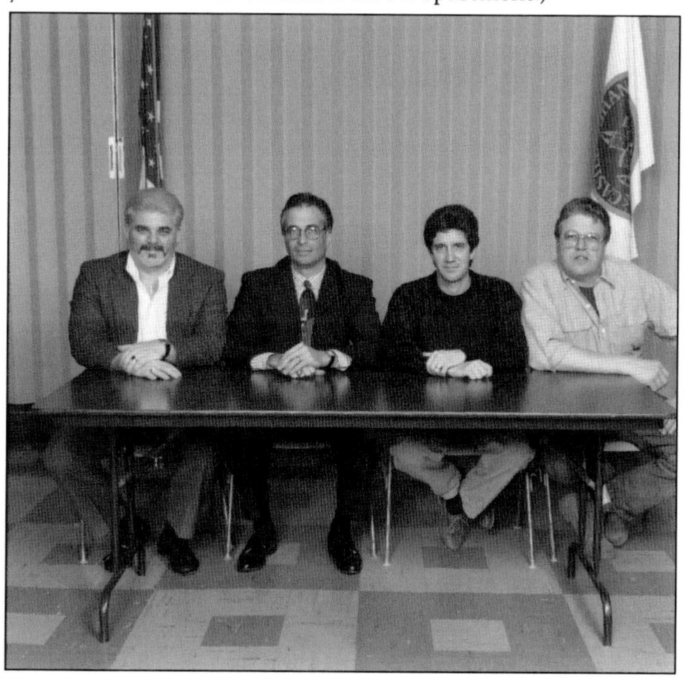

Castle Shannon has provided a rich array of activities for its youngsters. Staff members of Castle Shannon Youth Activities (CSYA) shown in this mid-1990s photograph are, from left to right, trustee Gary Petrucci, president Nicholas Fortunato, trustee Joseph Lawler, and treasurer Tom Miller. (Photograph courtesy of Jean O'Malley.)

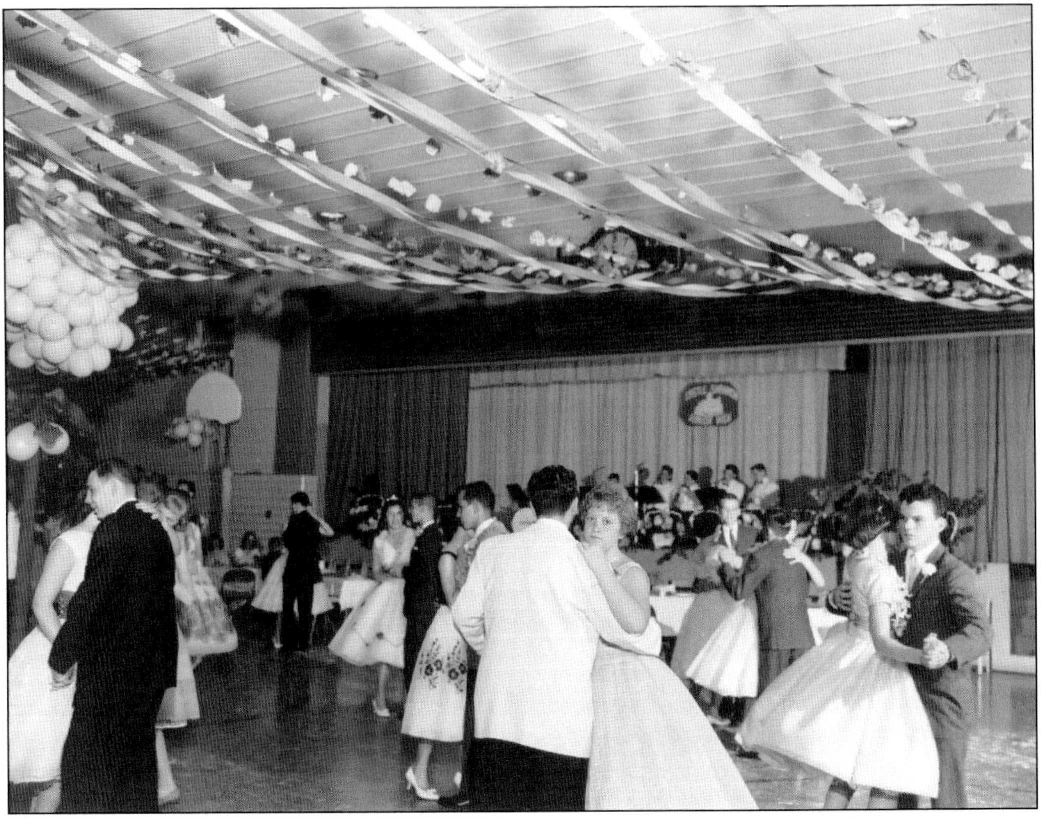

This early-1960s prom night is in the gymnasium at Castle Shannon Junior High School, which later became an elementary school. Before the formation of the Keystone Oaks School District in 1965, Castle Shannon Junior High School (Myrtle Avenue School) was composed of seventh-, eighth-, and ninth-graders. The school has maintained a fine gymnasium over the years, including a regulation-size basketball court and a stage (in background of photograph) for drama productions. School council meetings and public hearings were also held on the stage, with seats arranged on the gym floor. (Photograph by George "Jasper" Evans, courtesy of Ric Evans.)

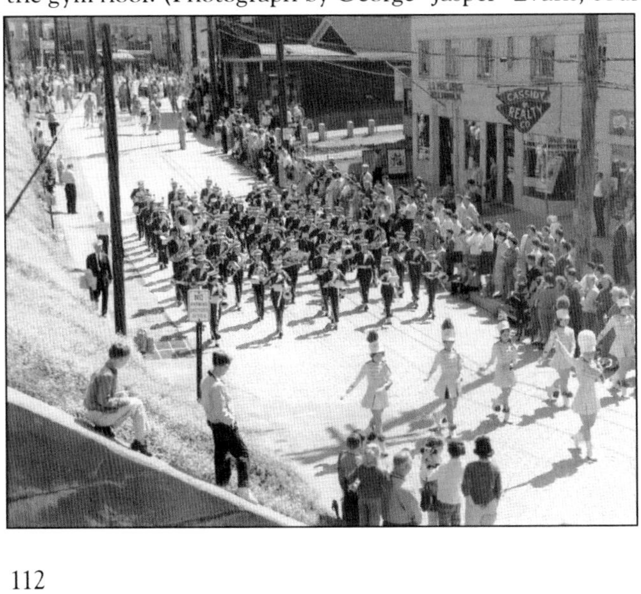

The annual Memorial Day parade is a festive event in Castle Shannon, and the parade route has not changed too much since its inception. For this 1960s march, participants would have assembled around the borough building in mid-morning, marched to Baldwin Street and up that residential road before making the sharp turn up Vernridge School Road, then gathering in St. Anne Cemetery for a military ceremony to honor the nation's war dead. (Photograph by George "Jasper" Evans, courtesy of Ric Evans.)

This is an action shot from a 1968 Little League baseball game for nine-year-olds at the old borough building field. There were several leagues for boys in those days, nine being the youngest age group. The boys would then graduate to play in leagues at Myrtle Avenue Field and also at Highland, with competition restricted to same-age groups. In later years, T-ball became the youngest age level in Castle Shannon Youth Activities baseball. The girls' softball league, which played its games at Vernridge, did not have age-specific leagues; girls of different ages competed together. (Photograph courtesy of Sam Sciullo Jr.)

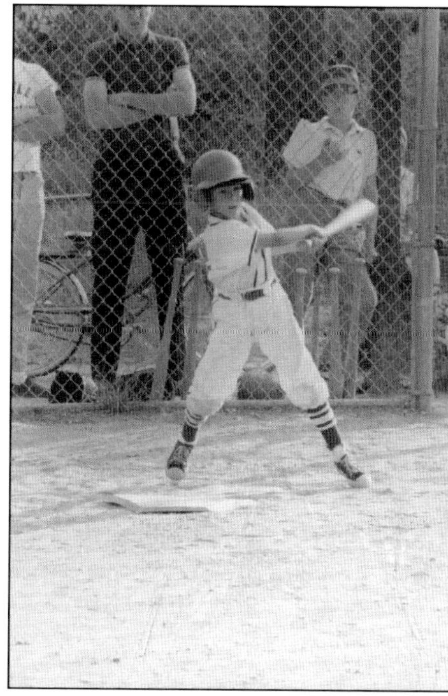

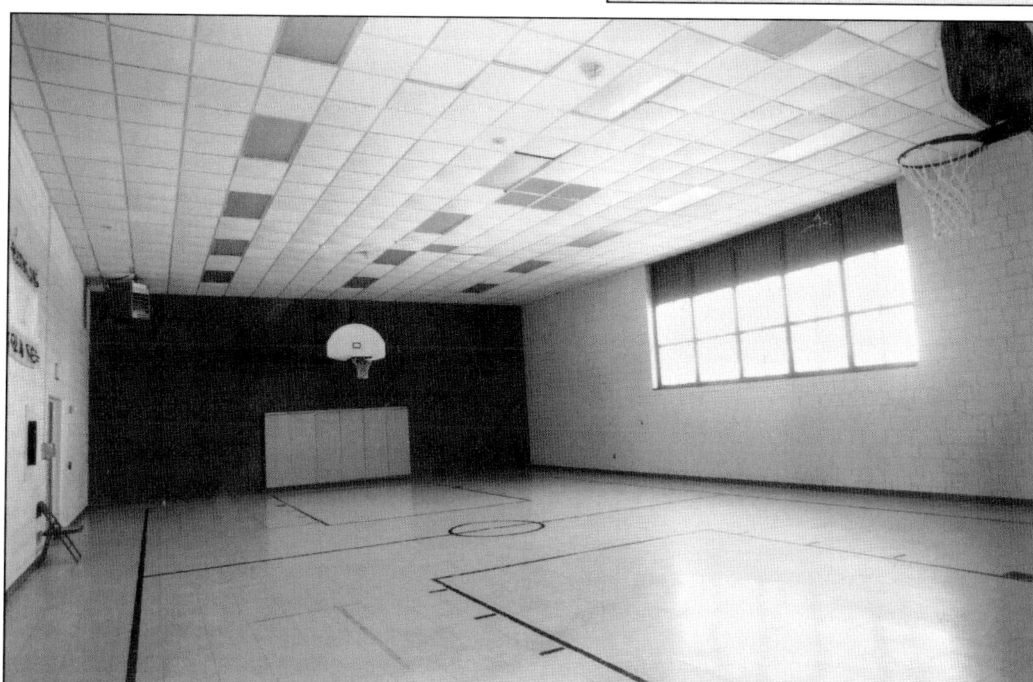

Many Castle Shannon students learned to play competitive basketball and dodgeball and to straddle a pommel horse inside the Highland Elementary School gymnasium. The gym originally featured baskets that were only eight feet high, making it easier for smaller children to shoot, but in later years the rims were raised to the regulation 10 feet. This photograph shows how the gym appears as part of the borough's Municipal Center complex. It is available to groups and parties on a rental basis. (Photograph by Charles LeClaire.)

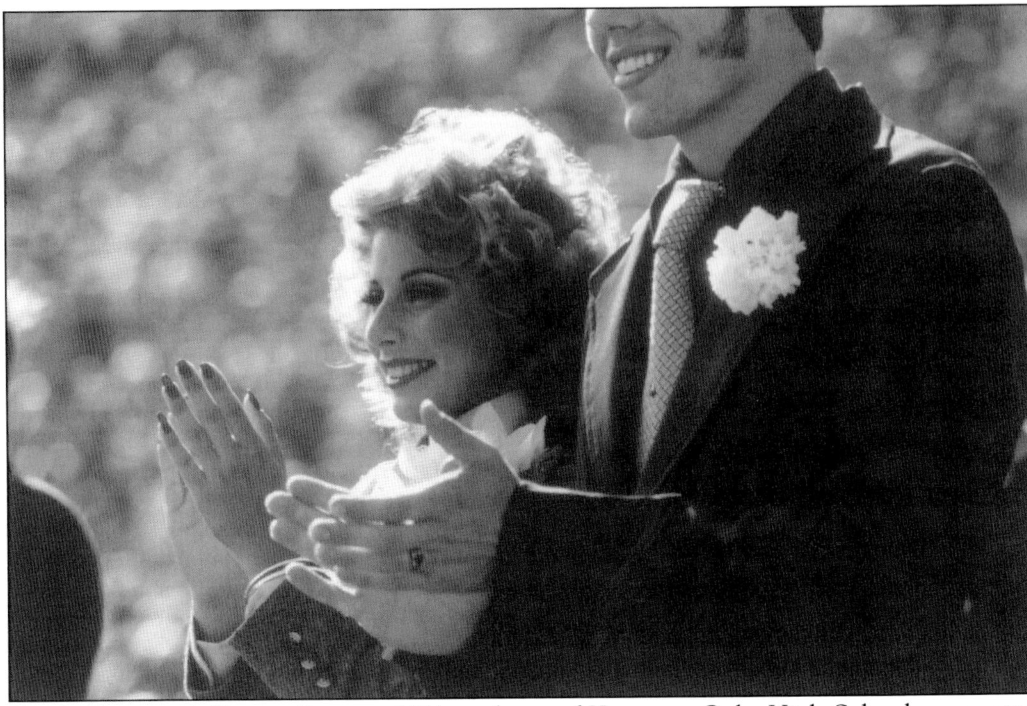

Castle Shannon's Donna Farey, a 1974 graduate of Keystone Oaks High School, was voted homecoming queen at the University of Pittsburgh. This photograph shows Donna during halftime ceremonies on the field of the Pitt-Navy game at Pitt Stadium on October 15, 1977. She later married Tony Liska, and the couple still resides in Castle Shannon. (Photograph courtesy of Tony Liska.)

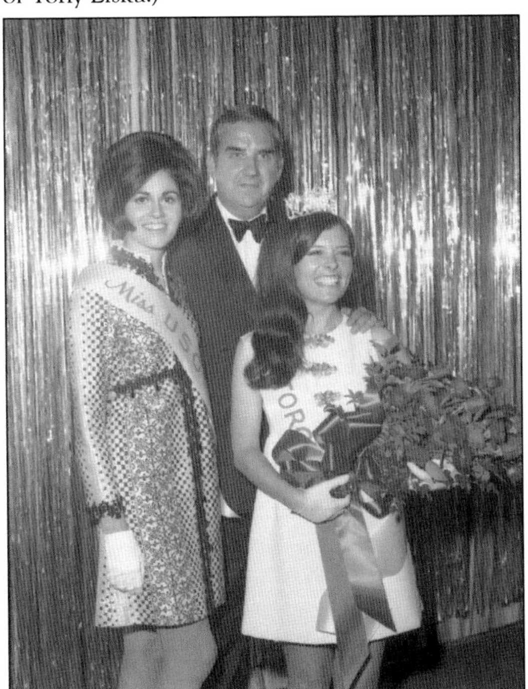

Longtime Castle Shannon councilman and later mayor George "Jasper" Evans lived a full and versatile life. Many of his fine photographs appear in this book. In addition to taking pictures at the Miss Castle Shannon Pageant, staged in 1969, he also shot photographs for the Miss Torch Pageants in Pittsburgh. This picture from the 1960s includes master of ceremonies Ed McMahon, a veteran actor and television personality best known for his work on *The Tonight Show* with Johnny Carson. (Photograph by George "Jasper" Evans, courtesy of Ric Evans.)

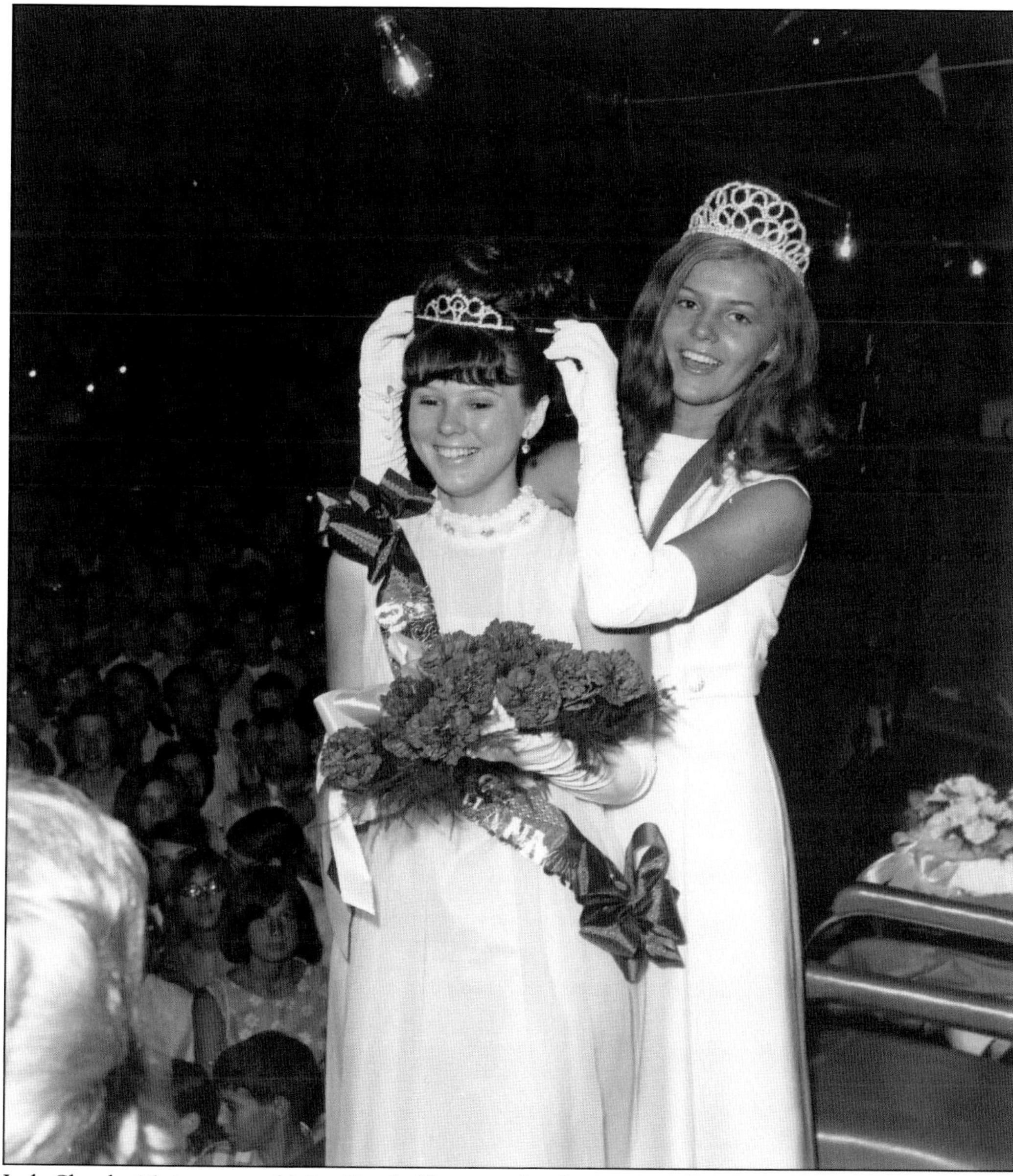

Judy Shock, 16, is crowned Miss Castle Shannon by the reigning Miss Teenage America, Melissa Babish, during the 1969 Miss Castle Shannon Pageant. The event, which was held on the upper level of the borough's Municipal Building, was part of a series of special shows and activities to celebrate the borough's 50th anniversary in 1969. The master of ceremonies for the pageant was WTAE-TV personality Paul Shannon. He was familiar to a generation of Pittsburgh-area children for his popular variety-style after-school show, which featured Three Stooges film shorts. Judy Shock still resides in the area and works for the Mt. Lebanon School District. As of 2012, she was the president of the Castle Shannon Volunteer Fire Department's Ladies Auxiliary, and her mother, Bobbi Shock, served as first vice president. Judy's father, Bill Shock, is a veteran member of the fire department. Carnival-goers will remember his many years of service, with his familiar pipe tucked in the corner of his mouth, calling the "Over and Under" game. (Photograph by George "Jasper" Evans.)

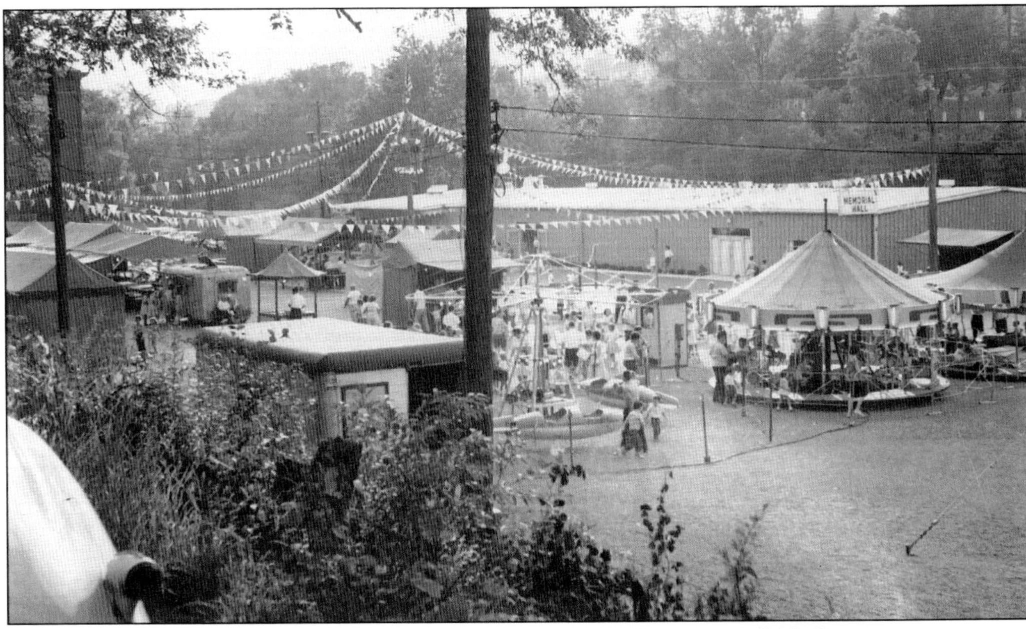

A mention of the last week of July to anyone from Castle Shannon will likely prompt a response about the annual Castle Shannon Volunteer Fire Department Carnival. The carnival format has not changed much over the years: lots of games of chance, roulette wheels, stuffed animals, popcorn, cotton candy, and bingo inside Memorial Hall. Taken from Route 88, the above photograph shows the carnival grounds in 1963. Memorial Hall is in the background. Below is a scene from the 1962 carnival, which shows a Ferris wheel to the left of the grounds. It was later moved to the opposite side, where the trucks are located in this photograph. Hamilton School, in the background, was nearing its final years by this time and was used as a business center by the firemen during carnival week. The firemen used an upstairs classroom as a counting room each night. The carnival traditionally runs for six evenings, Monday through Saturday. (Both photographs courtesy of Castle Shannon Volunteer Fire Department.)

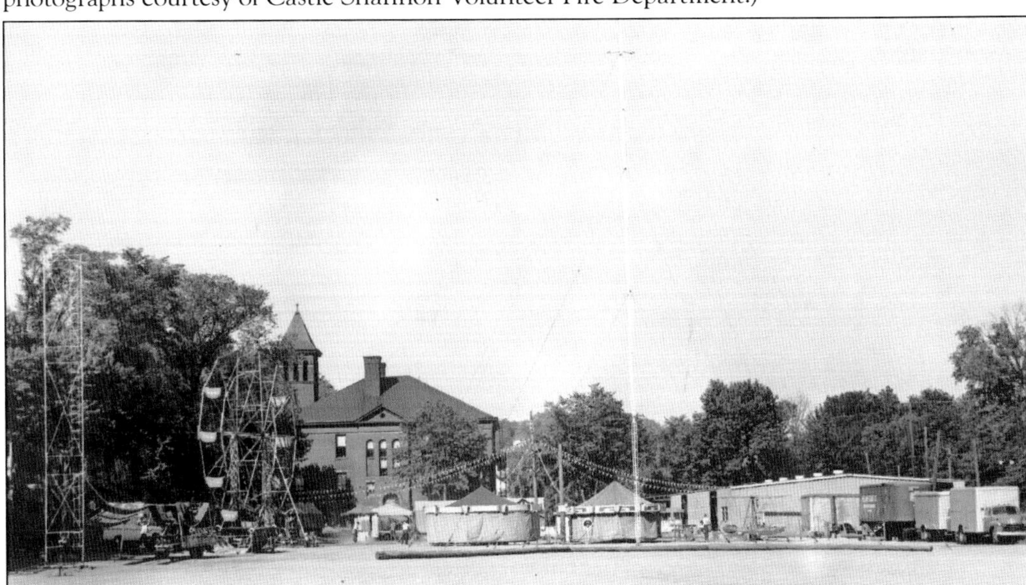

The Castle Shannon Volunteer Fire Department Carnival has always featured entertainment, including that shown in the two photographs. During the 1960s, a high-wire act thrills the crowds (below). Throughout the 1970s, skydivers were brought in, and carnival-goers could participate in the event. During setup for the carnival, a large checkerboard-type box was drawn in an area adjacent to the parking lot and carnival grounds. A number was assigned to each box. Tickets were then sold with the corresponding numbers. If any of the three skydivers landed on the box matching a customer's ticket, he or she would win a cash prize. The weather sometimes threw the contest off the mark, however. On one particularly windy night in the mid-1970s, heavy wind blew all three skydivers into the residential area of Castle Shannon above Route 88. There were no winners, and angry customers demanded their money back. (Right photograph by George "Jasper" Evans, courtesy of Ric Evans; below photograph courtesy of Castle Shannon Volunteer Fire Department.)

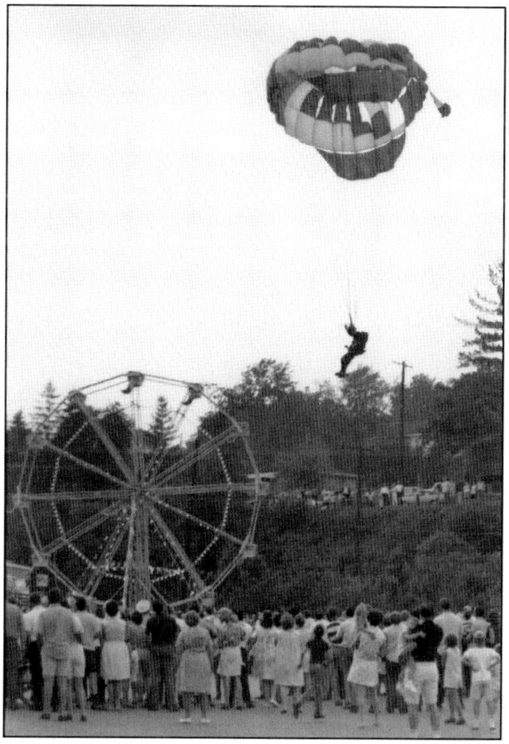

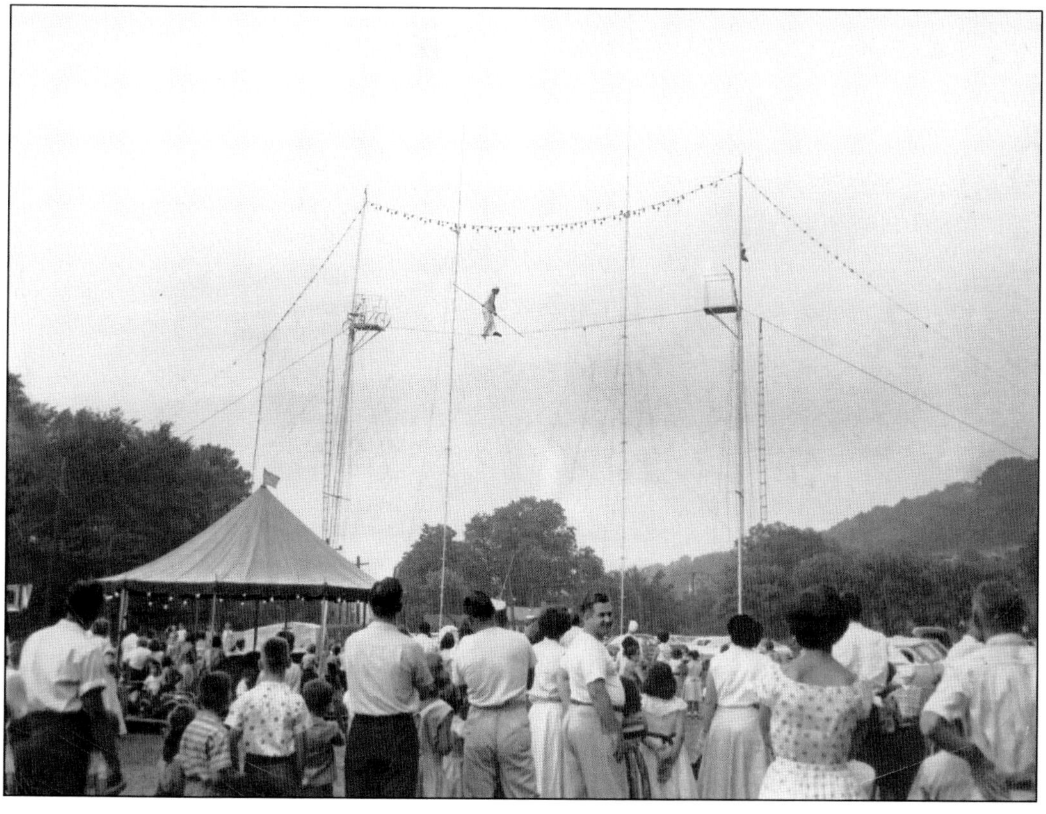

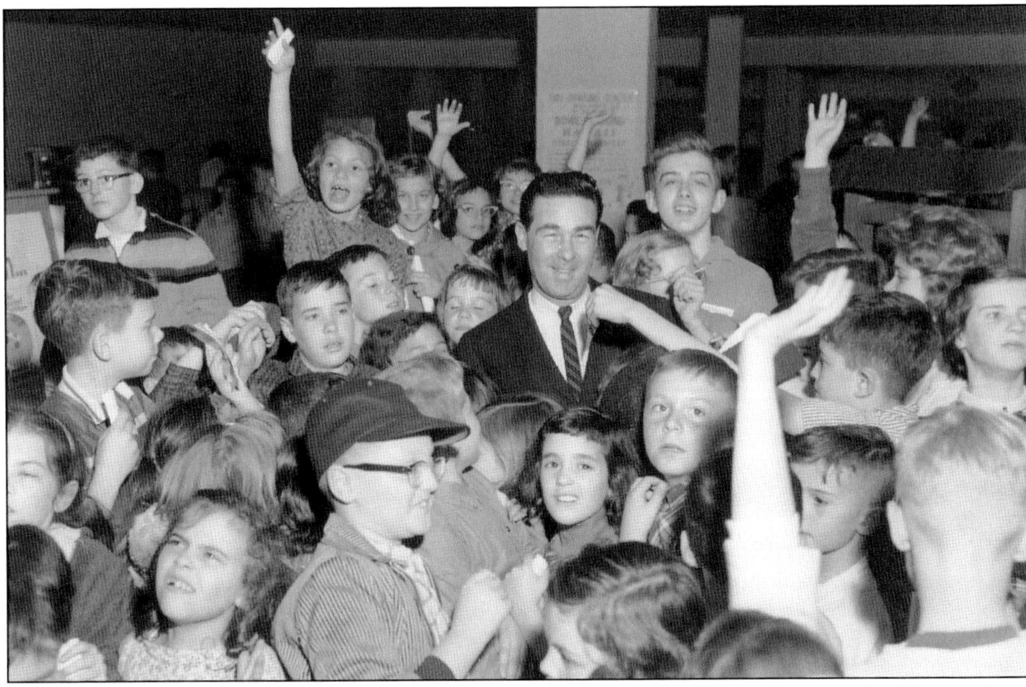

WTAE Channel 4 television personality Paul Shannon was a hero to young people. This undated photograph shows a delighted Shannon surrounded by Castle Shannon kids. Shannon's daily variety show typically involved visits from Boy Scouts, Girl Scouts, Cub Scouts, and Brownies who made up the studio audience. (Photograph by George "Jasper" Evans, courtesy of Ric Evans.)

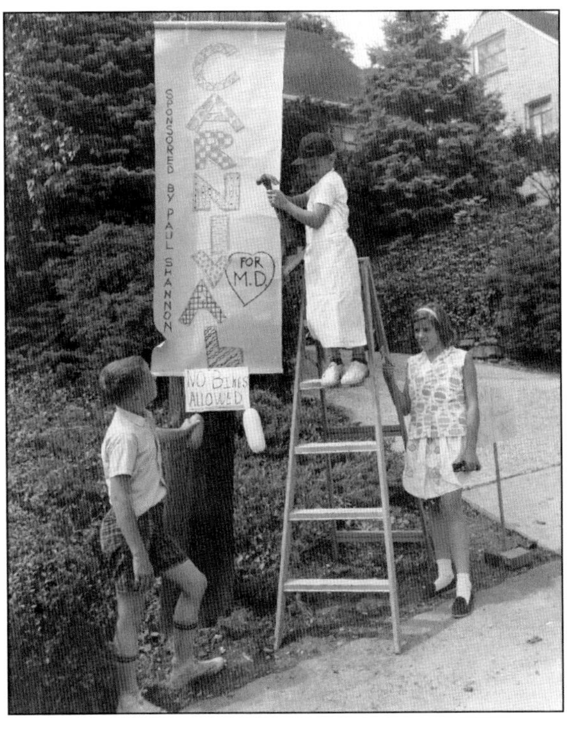

Paul Shannon's *Adventure Time* television show acted as a forum for research into muscular dystrophy. This photograph from the 1960s shows a trio of Castle Shannon children preparing to host their very own backyard carnival to raise funds to fight the disease. During the show, Shannon would invite viewers to mail in for a carnival kit, which included instructions and suggestions about how to put on an event for a good cause and have a whole lot of fun at the same time. (Photograph by George "Jasper" Evans, courtesy of Ric Evans.)

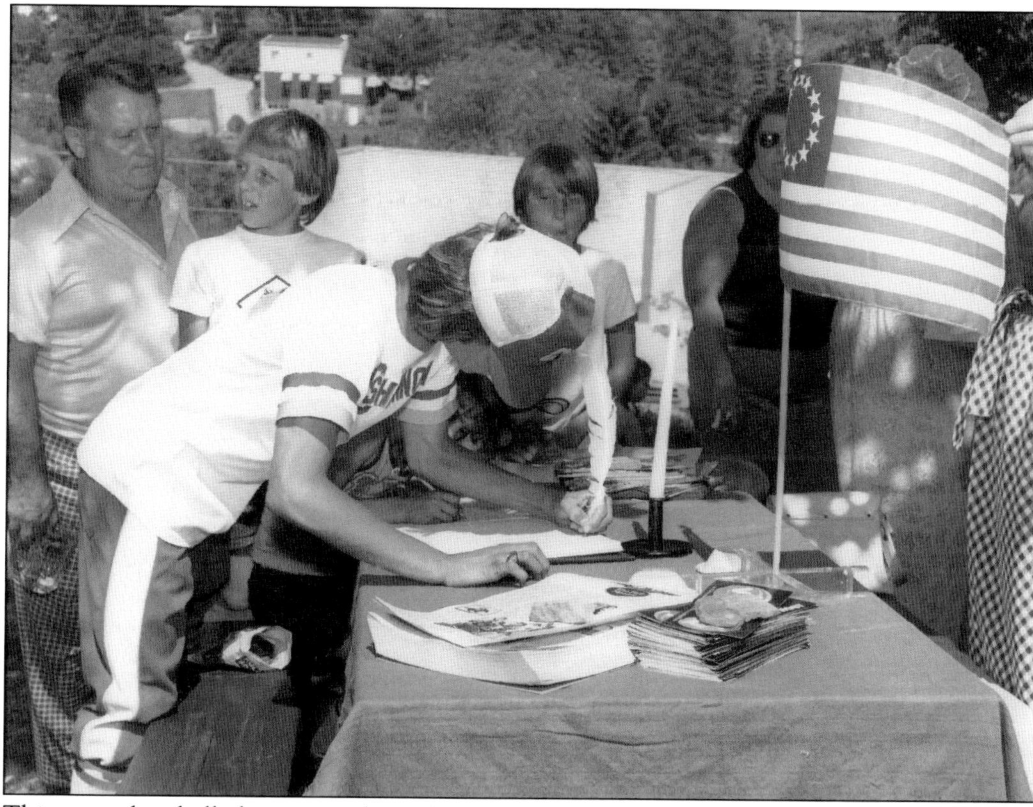

This young baseball player, a product of Castle Shannon Youth Activities, puts his name on the dotted line at this mid-1980s Community Day event at Hamilton Park. Traditionally held at the park on Memorial Day weekend, Community Day features a number of activities for people of all ages and is usually highlighted by an evening fireworks show. (Photograph by George "Jasper" Evans, courtesy of Paul Dudjak.)

Tucked away beneath the old Castle Shannon Volunteer Fire Department headquarters on Park Avenue was a marvelous little recreational hideaway. This 1961 photograph shows the eight-lane duckpin bowling alley that was, in some ways, one of Castle Shannon's better-kept secrets. Because it did not have automatic pinsetters, local youngsters with quick, dexterous hands and flexible backs were hired to set pins throughout the evening. (Photograph courtesy of Castle Shannon Volunteer Fire Department.)

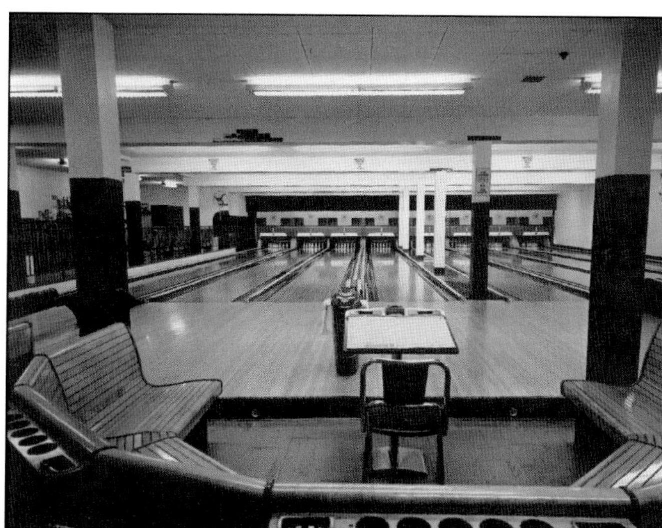

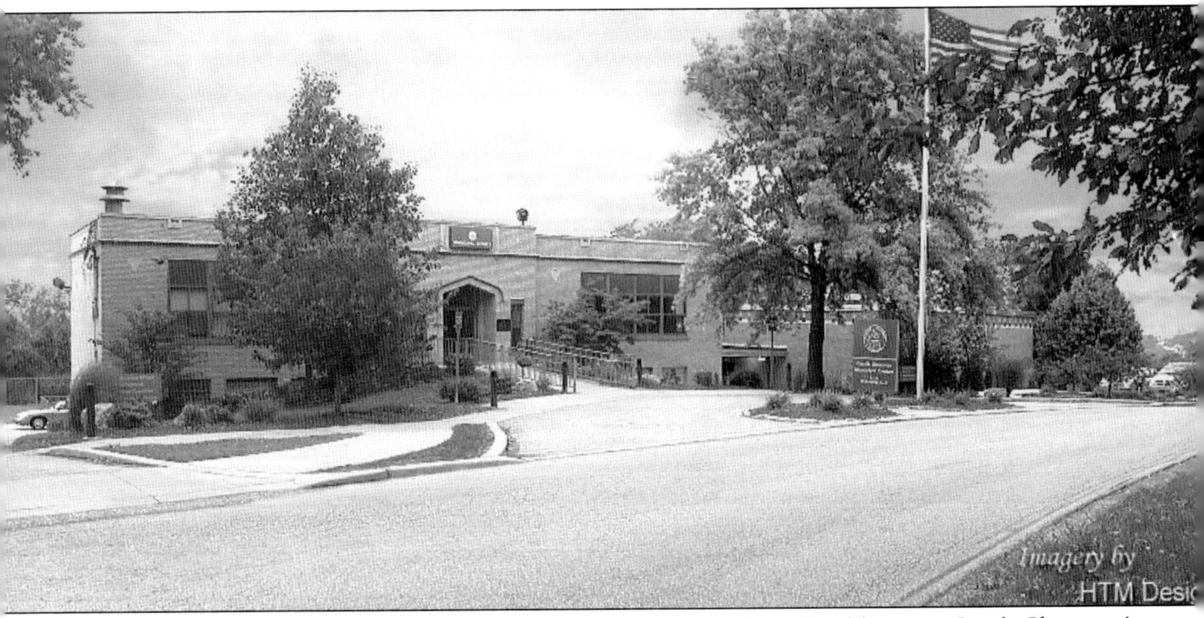

The municipal building high atop Castle Shannon was not the only addition to Castle Shannon's upper reaches. The former Highland School baseball field also received a complete makeover, providing an excellent venue for Castle Shannon Youth Activities games. The complex includes a separate batting cage and an electronic scoreboard, along with dugouts and new bleachers. (Photograph courtesy of Mike Warhold.)

Six

21st Century

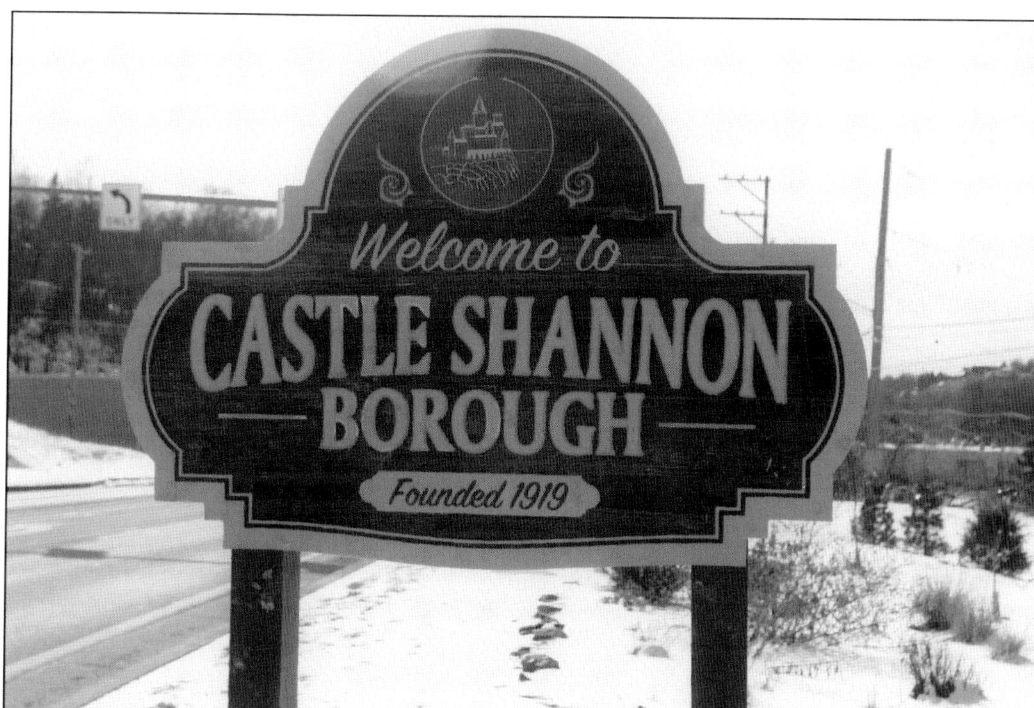

Among the most recent of the many Welcome to Castle Shannon Borough signs that are posted at entrances around town, this one appears along Route 88 just before Killarney Drive. In this area, many of the streets defer to Castle Shannon's Irish heritage. Just up the road and to the left, not pictured, is Calabria's Italian restaurant. (Photograph by Charles LeClaire.)

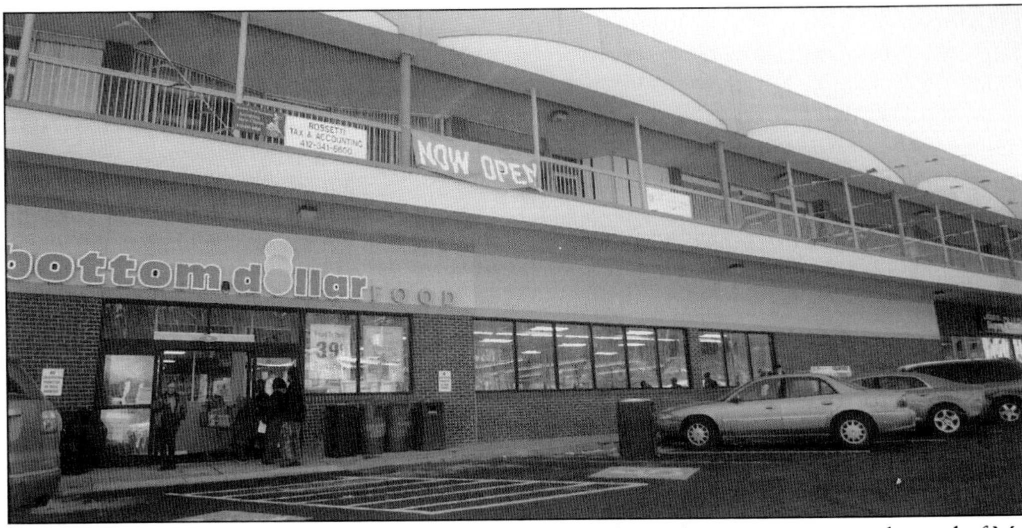

When Foodland grocery store abandoned the Lebanon Shops shopping center at the end of May 2010, it left a substantial void in the neighborhood. Bottom Dollar, another grocery chain, moved into Foodland's former spot in February 2012. Foodland had been at the Lebanon Shops since Kroger grocery store left the same spot following the devastating fire in January 1977. (Photograph by Charles LeClaire.)

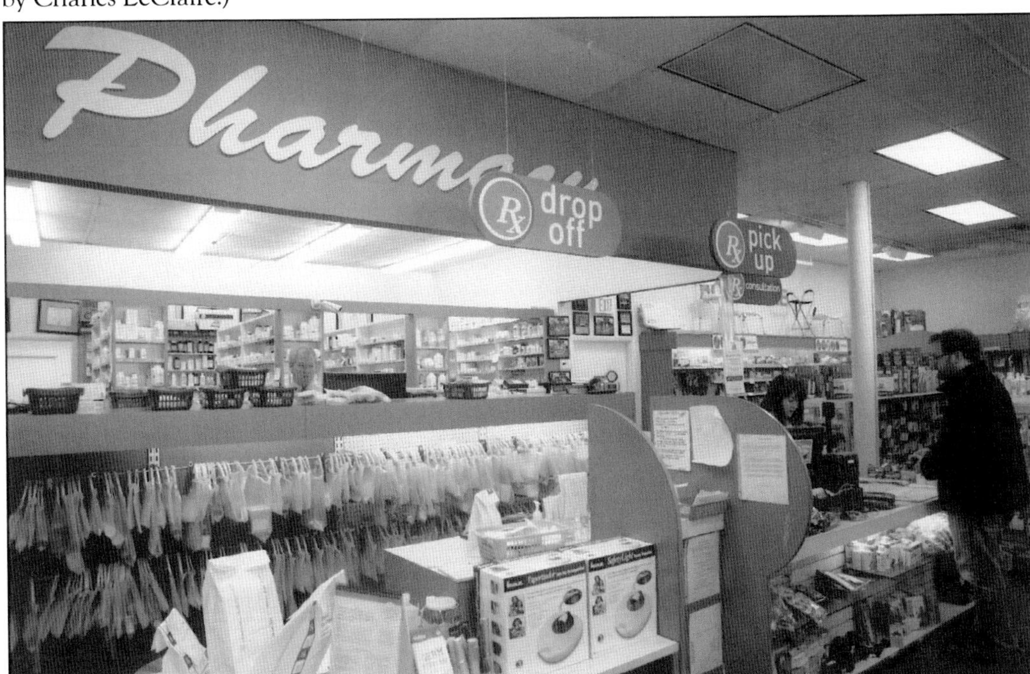

This photograph shows the familiar Drop Off and Pick Up counter at Lebanon Shops Pharmacy inside the Lebanon Shops center. Originally a Thrift Drugs Pharmacy, the current drugstore has been owned and operated by pharmacist brothers Tom and Bill Riley since 1983. Each is a graduate of Duquesne University. The store also supplies many over-the-counter health and beauty products and has an extensive magazine and paperback book selection. (Photograph by Charles LeClaire.)

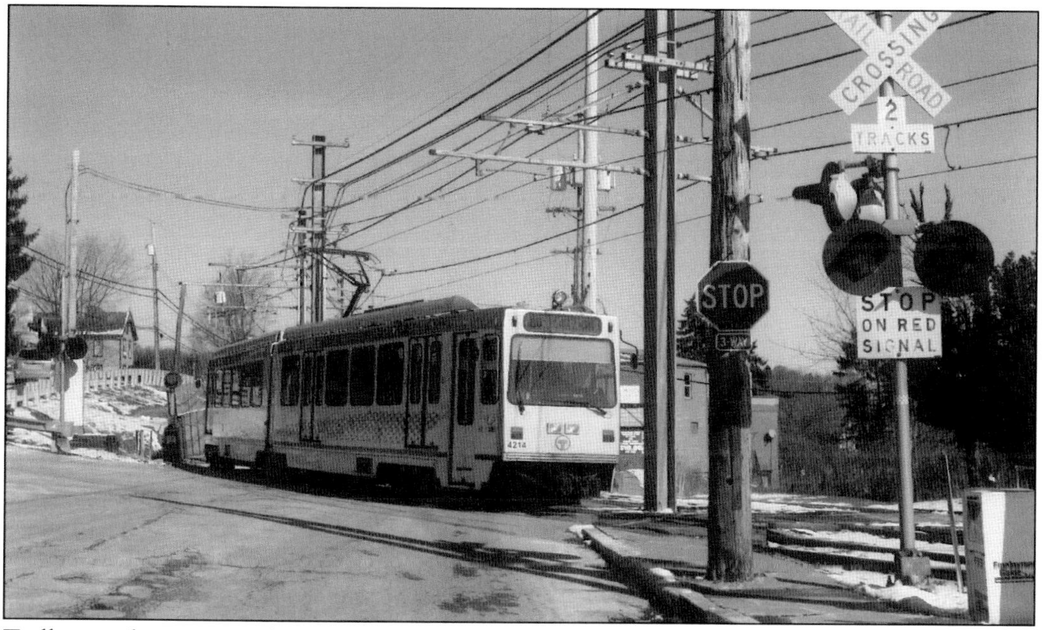

Trolley cars have come a long way in Castle Shannon. This modern "two-in-one" version, similar to a big-city subway train, approaches the Martin Villa stop, with St. Anne School only a short distance away. Trolley cars no longer travel aboveground through the streets of downtown Pittsburgh, but are still quite visible in the South Hills suburbs. (Photograph by Charles LeClaire.)

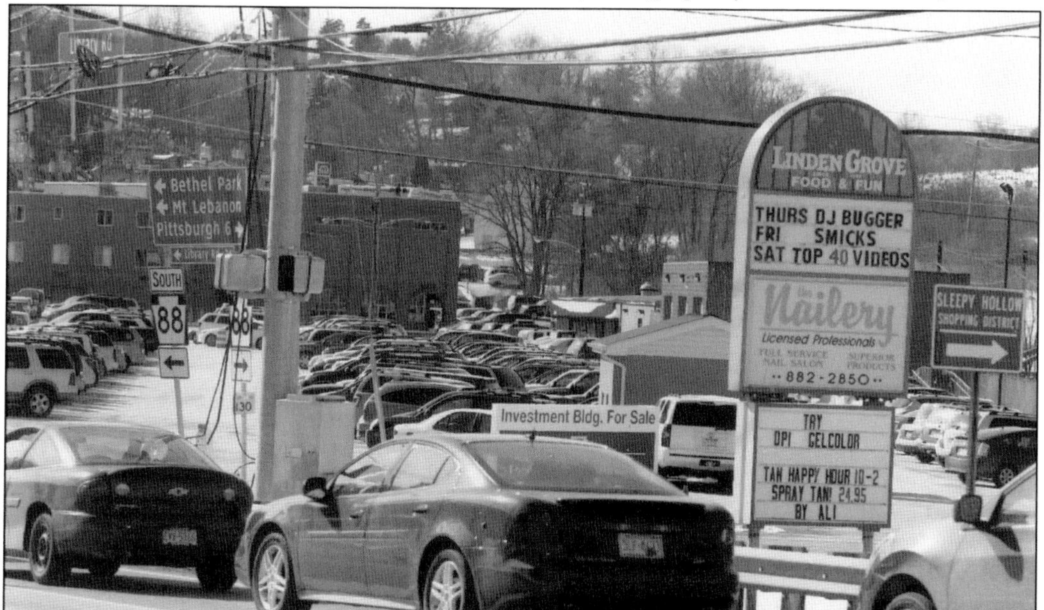

Traffic flows along Route 88 into the heart of the Castle Shannon business district. The marquee for Linden Grove advertises upcoming musical attractions. Street signage indicates that the city of Pittsburgh lies six miles in the opposite direction; neighboring towns Bethel Park and Mt. Lebanon adjoin the borough. The Castle Shannon Volunteer Fire Department building is in the background. (Photograph by Charles LeClaire.)

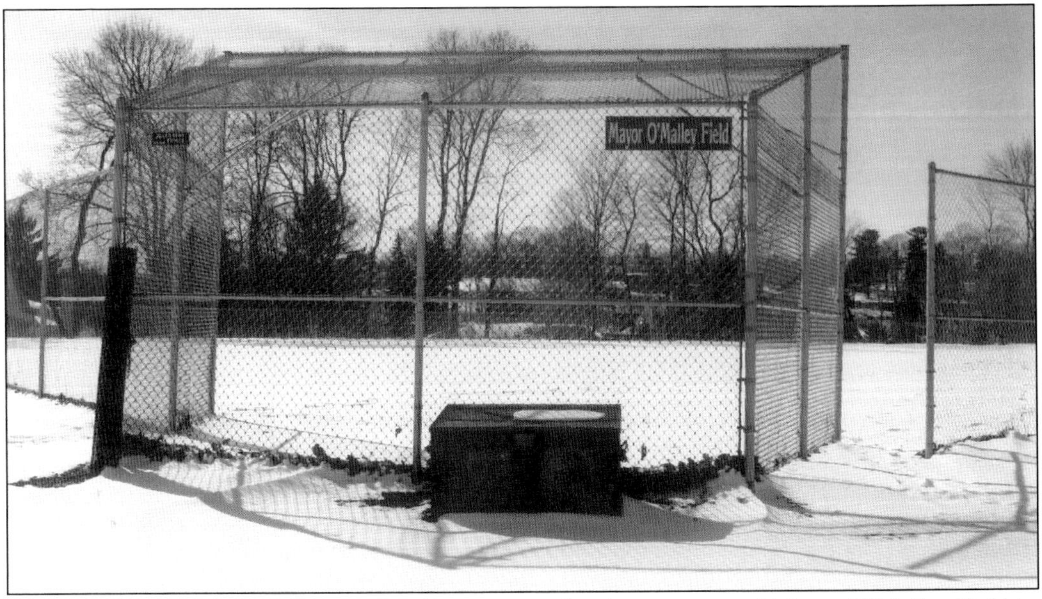

The baseball field at Myrtle Avenue Elementary School was renamed Mayor O'Malley Field in 2001 in honor of Castle Shannon's late mayor, Tom O'Malley. O'Malley, who died in 2000, was long active in Castle Shannon youth activities. He coached and was commissioner of the girls' softball league during the 1960s and 1970s. He also helped institute the antidrug DARE program in Castle Shannon elementary schools. O'Malley was Castle Shannon's mayor from 1986 until failing health forced him to step down in January 2000. He and his wife, Jean, a Castle Shannon councilwoman, had five children. (Photograph by Charles LeClaire.)

This photograph shows an interior view of the Castle Shannon Community Library in February 2012. Dedicated in 1966, the library features books, magazines, newspapers, and DVDs covering a wide variety of topics. A reading program for children is offered, and the library's lower level features a large meeting area and kitchen. It is also used as one of several polling places for elections. (Photograph by Charles LeClaire.)

When the Castle Shannon school system merged with Dormont and Green Tree in 1965, a contest was held for students to come up with a name for the new school district. One creative youngster took the *key* from the high school in Dormont, the *stone* from the castle in Castle Shannon, and the *oaks* from the tree in Green Tree, and created the new name, *Keystone Oaks School District*. Interestingly, none of the three towns adjoins the others. This banner hangs in front of Myrtle Elementary School in Castle Shannon. (Photograph by Charles LeClaire.)

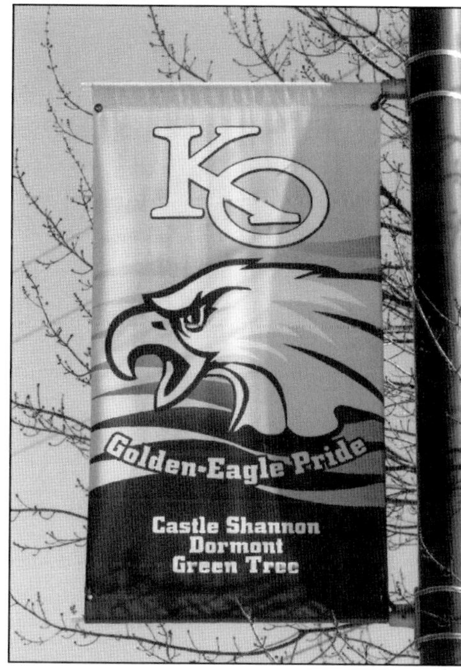

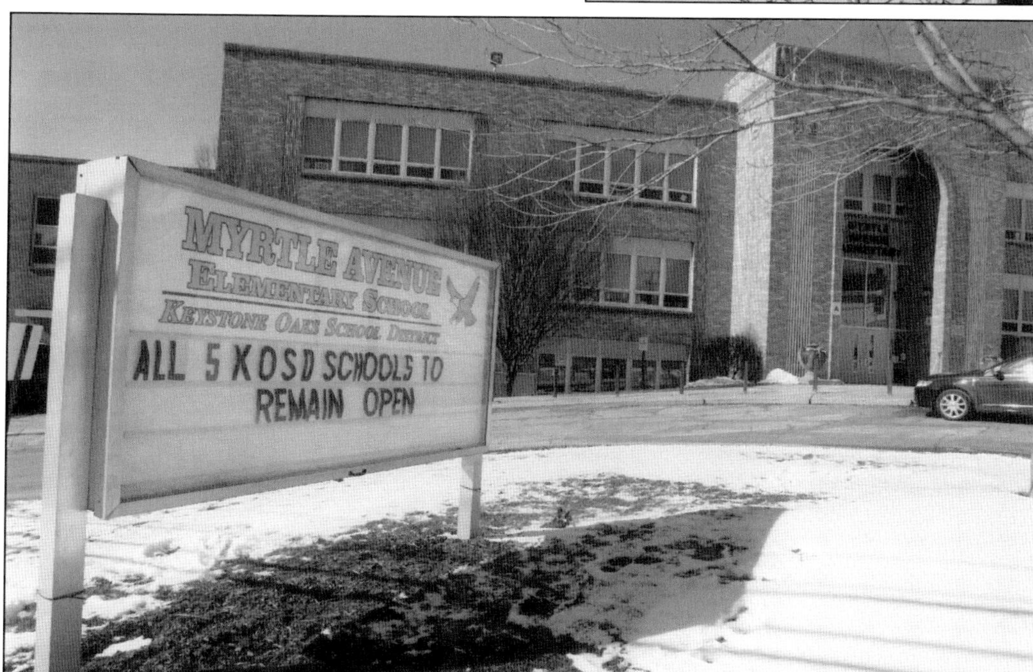

The marquee in front of Myrtle Elementary School in February 2012 announces that all five Keystone Oaks School District schools will remain open. In December 2011, the new Keystone Oaks School Board voted to overturn a decision by the previous board that would have closed Myrtle School and Aiken School in Green Tree. Such a decision would have left Castle Shannon without a single public school. Hamilton, Vernridge, and Highland schools had been eliminated in the past. (Photograph by Charles LeClaire.)

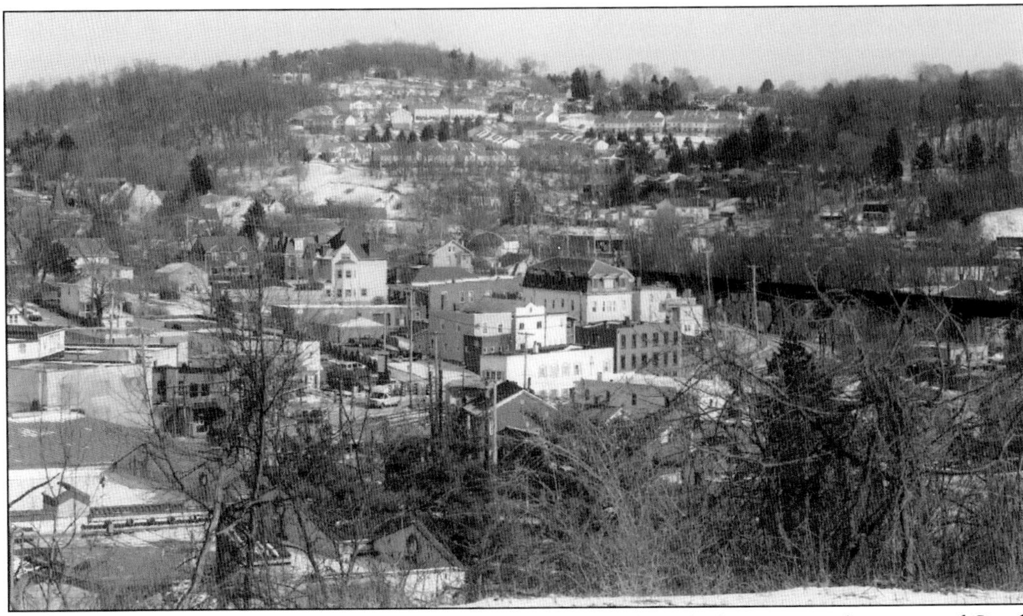

This February 2012 panorama, taken from the author's backyard, shows a good portion of Castle Shannon's Willow Avenue business district directly below. A few of the buildings have been in Castle Shannon for more than 100 years. Townhouses began appearing more frequently throughout the 1980s and 1990s. Castle Shannon's Municipal Center can be discerned through some trees near the top of the photograph on the left side. (Photograph by Charles LeClaire.)

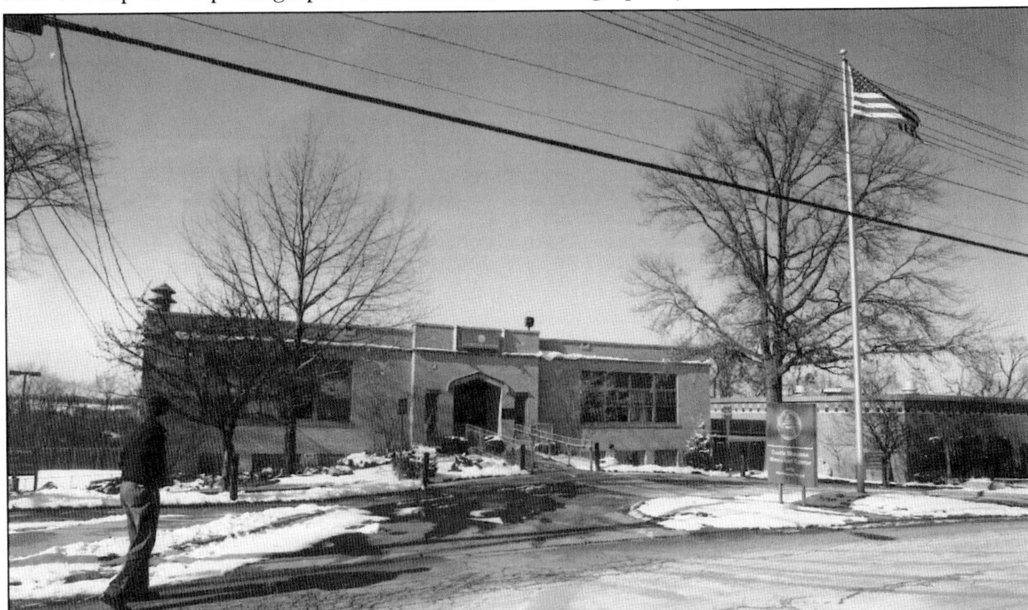

Highland Elementary School closed its doors following the 1983–1984 school year. The Keystone Oaks School District sold Highland to Castle Shannon for $1 in July 1984 with the understanding that the building would be converted for municipal purposes, and Castle Shannon began using the structure as its new municipal center on May 6, 1995. It now houses all of the offices that had been in the old borough building on Willow Avenue. (Photograph by Charles LeClaire.)

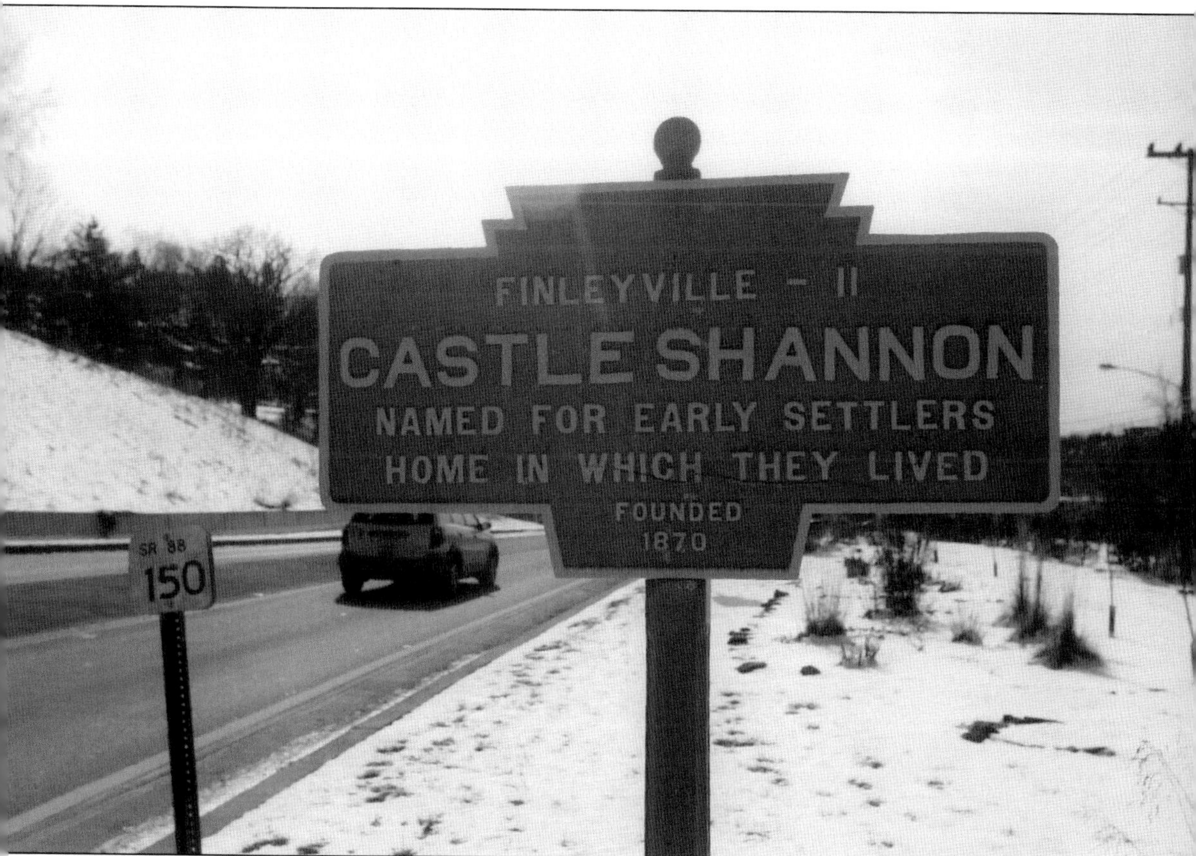

Just yards away from a Welcome to Castle Shannon Borough sign, this sign features the Pennsylvania "Keystone State" design. Castle Shannon has come a long way since changing its name from Shanahan to Shannon. The streets are paved instead of dirt, Route 88 is more heavily populated with businesses on both sides of the road, and the borough has a large, expansive recreational area called Hamilton Park. Finleyville, a town 11 miles south of Castle Shannon, features a swimming pool called Mineral Beach, a facility frequented by many Castle Shannon residents over the years. And before Finleyville, along the winding stretch of Route 88, is South Park. That town once had two swimming pools on Corrigan Drive, and now has only one, known simply as the Wave Pool. Castle Shannon has many attractions, but the borough has never had a public swimming pool. During the 1960s, bus transportation was provided twice a week from the borough building to South Park for residents looking for an afternoon of sun and fun. Still, no neighboring community can boast of a meeting place like Linden Grove, which is open and bustling year-round. (Photograph by Charles LeClaire.)

DISCOVER THOUSANDS OF LOCAL HISTORY BOOKS FEATURING MILLIONS OF VINTAGE IMAGES

Arcadia Publishing, the leading local history publisher in the United States, is committed to making history accessible and meaningful through publishing books that celebrate and preserve the heritage of America's people and places.

Find more books like this at
www.arcadiapublishing.com

Search for your hometown history, your old stomping grounds, and even your favorite sports team.

Consistent with our mission to preserve history on a local level, this book was printed in South Carolina on American-made paper and manufactured entirely in the United States. Products carrying the accredited Forest Stewardship Council (FSC) label are printed on 100 percent FSC-certified paper.

MADE IN THE USA